ARISTOTLE'S ONTOLOGY OF CHANGE

SERIES EDITOR

John Russon

REREADING ANCIENT PHILOSOPHY

ARISTOTLE'S ONTOLOGY OF CHANGE

MARK SENTESY

NORTHWESTERN UNIVERSITY PRESS • EVANSTON, ILLINOIS

Northwestern University Press
www.nupress.northwestern.edu

This title is licensed under the Creative Commons Attribution-NonCommercial 4.0 International License (CC BY-NC). Read the license at https://creativecommons.org/licenses/by-nc/4.0/legalcode.

This book is freely available in an open access edition thanks to TOME (Toward an Open Monograph Ecosystem)—a collaboration of the Association of American Universities, the Association of University Presses, and the Association of Research Libraries—and the generous support of the Pennsylvania State University. Learn more at the TOME website, available at openmonographs.org.

DOI: 10.21985/n2-rfhb-1f34

Copyright © 2020 by Northwestern University Press.
Published 2020. All rights reserved.

10 9 8 7 6 5 4 3 2 1

Library of Congress Cataloging-in-Publication Data

Names: Sentesy, Mark, author.
Title: Aristotle's ontology of change / Mark Sentesy.
Other titles: Rereading ancient philosophy.
Description: Evanston, Illinois : Northwestern University Press, 2020. | Series: Rereading ancient philosophy | Includes bibliographical references and index.
Identifiers: LCCN 2020000111 | ISBN 9780810141889 (paperback) | ISBN 9780810141896 (cloth) | ISBN 9780810141902 (ebook)
Subjects: LCSH: Aristotle. | Ontology. | Change.
Classification: LCC B491.O5 S46 2020 | DDC 111—dc23
LC record available at https://lccn.loc.gov/2020000111

To Oscar, Amelie, and Sophia, for changing everything

CONTENTS

Acknowledgments — ix

Introduction — 3

Chapter 1. Change and the Many Senses of Being in *Physics* I — 17

Chapter 2. The Demonstration of Change in *Physics* III.1–2 — 39

Chapter 3. *Energeia, Entelecheia*, and the Completeness of Change — 63

Chapter 4. The Being of Potency — 81

Chapter 5. The Ontology of Epigenesis — 109

Chapter 6. *Genesis* and the Internal Structure of Sources in *Metaphysics* IX.8 — 135

Conclusion — 161

Notes — 165

Bibliography — 197

Index — 211

ACKNOWLEDGMENTS

The project exists because of Rudolf Bernet, who led me to this subject and set the highest standard for meaningful philosophical work; Bill Wians, in whose richly challenging seminars I began to find my way; and John Sallis, whose vital, careful questions encouraged me to follow the arguments to their source. Christopher Moore, Uygar Abaci, Brady Bowman, Eric Sanday, and Bill Wians offered valuable guidance that I used to rewrite the book. Several colleagues read the manuscript after that: Will Britt and Jon Burmeister, who in addition have thoroughly shaped my understanding of philosophy; Josh Wretzel, who gave honest, thorough comments; and John Gordon, who dotted a lot of *i*'s. This book would not be what it is without them. They have done well; the remaining flaws in the book are mine. Finally, my gratitude for Maureen is unmeasurable. In her continuous care, Oscar, Ami, and Sophie thrive, even when writing pulls me away. This book is also their work.

ARISTOTLE'S ONTOLOGY OF CHANGE

INTRODUCTION

This book examines what change is, and what it contributes to ontology in the work of Aristotle. Before turning to the claims of this book, let me describe the task in general terms.

Ontology is the account (*logos*) of being (*on*).[1] For most of the history of philosophy it went by the name "metaphysics," a word derived from the title that editors gave to Aristotle's book on being, which comes with or after (*meta*) the study of nature (*phusis*). Ontology investigates the fundamental philosophical question: what is being? To offer an ontology is to lay out in speech what is and what is not. But an ontology is not merely an inventory of what is: it must articulate the principles and patterns by which the different parts or aspects of what *is* differ, identify with each other, and organize in relationships. Ontology, then, studies the basis for everything else: it is an inquiry into the basic structures of thought, knowledge, and action. In this respect ontology can have both an enabling and a limiting role: it can both expand and restrict what we think is real, possible, and necessary, and how beings and their relationships fit together or separate off from one another.

But the basics of what and how being *is* are not necessarily clear at the start, and even if its principles must in some sense be inescapable, we still might not know or be able to articulate them. This is why ontology is necessary: it is the discipline by which we know and articulate being, and part of it is devoted to the discovery of the principles of being.[2]

Ontology studies all things insofar as they are, which is why it takes a position on the being or non-being of change. This book investigates two parts of ontology: the part of ontology that studies the being of change and its concepts, and the part that discovers and develops the principles of being. It examines the ontology of change with the secondary goal of discerning what this leads us to discover about ontological principles. Broadly put, the latter question is: what does change tell us about being? Or, more precisely, what are the ontological consequences of change? The consequences of change for being depend, clearly, on what the being of change is. But no matter what we say it is, if change is to exist, some things must be true of being. For example, we must either say change has a different sort of being than objects do, in which case it makes being more diverse in kind, or we must say that the being of change is the same as everything else, in which case change will

3

constrain what we think being must be, since then being cannot be defined as something unchanging.

There would be merit in offering an independent answer to the questions of the being of change and its consequences for ontology, but it is more valuable, at least at first, to understand how the greatest thinkers grappled with them.

Aristotle may be the only thinker to have provided a noncircular definition of change.[3] His work represents one of the most serious and sustained analyses of change in the Western tradition. It is also an exemplar of what we can discover about being through the study of change. This is in part because its effects on his ontology are quite clear because of the contrast between his and his predecessors' accounts of change and being: Parmenides and his successors rejected the existence of change, and it fell to Aristotle to establish its existence on philosophical grounds and establish it as a subject of positive philosophical inquiry. But the analysis of change led him either to develop or transform concepts in ways that became fundamental to ontology in general for two millennia. These concepts include, as I shall argue, material, form, potency, activity, fulfillment, and source. Aristotle, then, seems to be the best candidate to answer our two core questions: What sort of being does change have? And, for change to exist, what must being be like?

This book approaches Aristotle as someone who has grappled with problems of general interest to ontology, namely, the being of change and the meaning of change for being. This has an important advantage: it presents Aristotle's argument as confronting permanent problems that ontology still faces. His contribution can thereby become more than just an item of historical curiosity. This is how Aristotle himself approaches his predecessors, inviting us to interpret his work as innovating within a common intellectual inheritance.

My primary method for pursuing this task is to examine the form and content of Aristotle's arguments, paying particular attention to how and why he frames them the way he does, and examining what we can learn about his core concepts through what they accomplish in the course of the argument. This method helps to resist the tendency to present Aristotle as a dogmatist. To communicate the coherence and complexity of Aristotle's work, it is easier to present it as a doctrine that refers to itself, a set of beliefs that makes sense on its own terms. I think this approach does a disservice to Aristotle, whose primary philosophical strategy is to start with and stay alert to unsolved problems (*Met.* III.1 995a24–b4). So my goal is to analyze his banner arguments concerning the ontology of change in order to highlight how important, effective, questionable, and audacious they are. Therefore I aim to present these arguments closely enough to exhibit their structure and turning points, but also at a scale that exhibits their stakes and meaning.[4]

There are many issues I have had to refrain from elaborating in order to make the case clear. The aim of this book is not to work out in detail Aristotle's relationships with his predecessors, or to follow the reception of his arguments in the history of philosophy, or to relate his account to contemporary ontology. Although this book seeks to give a charitable account of why Aristotle makes the arguments he does, its aim is not to defend them against every alternative. It concentrates on Aristotle's discussion of change insofar as change *is*, that is, on its ontology, rather than on its physical, psychological, biological, or ethical aspects. This book is, therefore, not a presentation of his theory of science. It is not limited to an examination of the kinds of changes, or the properties of beings insofar as they change. The aim here is not to give a systematic account of how change fits in with Aristotle's other distinctive ontological commitments; for example, the theory of definition and individual form, whether there are activities without potency, the nature of the unmoved mover, or the material of heavenly bodies. There is, of course, merit in pursuing each of these goals, and all of these tasks have been performed with exceptional rigor and creativity by other scholars.[5] I do not make it my purpose to do so here, *except insofar as Aristotle's ontology of change itself requires it.*

Synopsis

Aristotle's work suggests that two things must be true about an ontology that includes change: first, that being is many in aspect. For change to exist, there must be several ways of being the same thing: on the one hand, it must be different to be an underlying material or form, and on the other hand, subjects and predicates must constitute a different sort of being than do potencies and activities. Second, ontology must distinguish between a thing's being a source of change (e.g., potency) and the accomplishment (*telos*) toward which that thing is oriented (e.g., activity), and thereby provide a teleology.

Twice in the *Physics* Aristotle argues that, to understand change, it is necessary to distinguish between ways of being. In both instances, he does so in order to establish that change admits of being—that is, that it exists or is real. The first two chapters of this book examine how the structure of change motivates and shapes the claim that being is multiple.

Chapter 1 examines *Physics* I. There, Aristotle argues that sources are ontologically multiple, but to substantiate this claim, he gives an analysis of coming to be (*genesis*), claiming that his predecessors' arguments for monism were based on a mistaken analysis of change. Their argument against the existence of change was that it is ontologically self-contradictory: change is the coming-to-be of something that was not (e.g., this rabbit, or its white color), but since nothing can come from non-being, and what already is in being cannot come to be what it already is, change must be impossible; it mixes being and non-being. In arguing against the existence of *change*, Aristotle says, they generalized all difference by conflating it with non-being: hence, they said, all that *is* must be the same. To reject this view, Aristotle separates being from non-being by making distinctions between particular aspects of change. Distinguishing the three elements of all change (form, material, privation) allows Aristotle to demonstrate that change is not contradictory, because we can now say that a particular form (e.g., a rabbit) in fact comes to be out of what *is* (e.g., nutrients), and that its predecessor *only happens not to be* that form. Aristotle's restitution of the being of change depends, then, on making categorical being multiple in these three aspects; being must be multiple because the existence of change requires it. But, crucially, this argument neither defines *what* change is nor shows *that* change is: distinguishing between "white" "rabbit" and "not-white" yields the elements involved in change, not change itself. A different sense of being is required for that. This argument, then, simply clears the way for Aristotle's definition of and argument for change, which I turn to next.

Chapter 2 examines *Physics* III.1–2. The standout arguments of this chapter are, first, that to define change a sharp distinction is necessary between what I call the categorical and energetic senses of being; second, that the potent being (*to dunamei on*) is an independent being that remains itself even when it is actively at work; and third, that the definition of change doubles as a demonstration of its existence. The demonstration works as follows: the same being may be both a categorical object insofar as it bears properties (e.g., a colored rabbit), and an energetic being insofar as it is capable of action (e.g., a rabbit being visible). But once the distinction between these ways of being is established, it is clear that there are real, concrete, recognizable, dynamic subjects of change (e.g., construction materials, marathon runners, rabbits). Being subjects of change (potent beings) means that what they are involves change, that what makes them what they are is change, which makes change their complete being (*entelecheia*, often translated as "actuality"). The evidence of one reveals the other.

Chapters 1–2, then, make the case that the analysis of change includes an argument that being is multiple. Being is distinguished into incidental, categorical, and energetic senses, and the latter two each includes three subordinate ways of being. The ontology of change, in addition, requires Aristotle to develop three of his core ontological concepts: first, potency (*dunamis*), to name the definite beings that are subjects of change; second, complete being (*entelecheia*), to name that on which such changeable beings depend, namely, change, and third, activity (*energeia*). For this reason, chapters 3–6 are devoted to the analysis of these terms.

Chapters 3 and 4 examine separately each term that appears in the definition of change, since these are among the greatest contributions that change makes to ontology. They are the concepts of potency (*dunamis*), the accomplishment of being-complete (*entelecheia*, often rendered as "actuality"), and being-at-work or activity (*energeia*, often rendered as "actuality").[6] These, again, are terms that Aristotle either formulated or thoroughly revised in order to accommodate the existence of change within ontology. In my argument, activity and complete being have different meanings, while potency is the aspect of a being that originates and determines the pathway of activity. Chapter 3 examines being-at-work and being-complete. I undertake a philological and then semantic analysis of both these terms, with particular attention to their meanings in the demonstration of the existence of movement. In chapter 3, the study of *entelecheia*, in particular, constitutes the greater part of the intellectual effort. This is because its meaning in the definition of change requires us to directly oppose the prevailing scholarly view of the concept, namely that *entelecheia*, understood as actuality, is in some sense incompatible with change. Yet Aristotle emphasizes that change is an *entelecheia* of a certain kind. Thus, a primary concern in the latter part of the chapter is to restore *entelecheia*'s relationship to change. I distinguish the ways that change and potency are incomplete from the ways they can be complete: a potency and its activity are incomplete insofar as they require other things, but change is the concrete activity of those things when they are together, that is, the single completion of their several capacities.

Chapter 4 examines potency (*dunamis*), its being, its claim to be a sense of being, and how it helps to describe the process of completion. Sources like potency set to work when conditions are right. What distinguishes potency is that it requires others in order to set to work, and that it is able to accomplish opposite things, but only one at a time: its whole range of effects can never be active simultaneously. But it is when an individual's potency is complete, that is, when it has become disposed to act immediately when its other is present, that it is most obviously a sense of being: when someone's capacity to play the violin is complete, we call that person a violinist. There are two ways of describing such a process of completion: the first is that completing an ability removes the ability to fail, that is, the opposite of its goal, while the second is that completing an ability preserves, and in fact reveals, the ability that was already there.

Change contributes to ontology the idea that being is or has a source (*archē*, also translated as "principle"). But this analysis shows that to be a source is also to be an accomplishment (*telos*). Aristotle's ontology of sources and their accomplishment develops most directly through analyses of natural generation (*genesis*) (chap. 5) and the temporality and being of sources (chap. 6).

Having shown in chapter 4 that beings-in-potency are in a certain way independent beings, chapter 5 works out the basis for this claim, namely, that to be an individual being (*ousia*) is to be a source. Aristotle's description of how potencies and natures come to be shows that the being a source (*archē*) is the basis for his claim that what has them *is*. Aristotle distinguishes sharply between the process of generation and its result: the thing that is coming to be does not have its nature, he says, until it is complete (*teleia*). He makes this distinction in an attempt to take seriously the idea that change in fact occurs, that beings genuinely appear which are not reducible to their parts. Generated beings *are* in a robust sense, once they have themselves come to be sources of change. Yet, while there are strict requirements for what counts as a being, Aristotle places few ontological requirements on the process leading up to their arrival in being: they can be generated by nature, by artifice, or by accident. This is a strong but metaphysically minimal account of epigenesis.

Chapter 6 examines *Metaphysics* IX.8, in which Aristotle argues that activity is primary in being because it is a source of generation in an even more decisive way than potency. To make this argument, Aristotle analyzes the new way of being a source that I examined in chapter 5, namely, being a completion or accomplishment (*telos*). The source of the concept of accomplishment in this argument is the concept of *genesis*. What is distinctive about change is not that it is incomplete, but that it is a way of being-complete, an active accomplishment (*entelecheia*), as it is defined. Fully understanding the change-related sense of potency and activity leads naturally to Aristotle's reinterpretation of material and form in energetic terms, as source and accomplishment. It is, therefore, through the analysis of generation that Aristotle places sourcehood and accomplishment at the heart of ontology.

Being in Many Ways

The claim that being is many is the distinguishing feature of Aristotle's ontology. The problem of change, I contend, provides an important argument for this position and a basis for distinguishing between ways of being. It will be useful to give an overview of how, for Aristotle, being is manifold, since I shall be dealing with parts of this view throughout the book.

Being, Aristotle claims, *is* straightaway in one of four different ways: incidental-essential, categorical, dynamic-energetic, and alethic.[7]

(1) Beings either come along with others incidentally (*sumbebēkos*), or are related to them through their own being essentially (*kath' auto*): being short is incidental to being a doctor, while, by contrast, someone is a doctor precisely through being a healer. Thus, being in this sense consists both of incidental and essential being.

(2) Being has a categorical structure through which features belong to things. It is different to be a property, for example, 1 kg, green, or 10 m away, than it is to be the underlying being that has them, for example, this parrot. Yet this form (predicate) and its material (subject) are in a way one thing. The primary concept of categorical being is the individual being (*ousia*).

(3) Being is an active achievement, for example, running, thinking, or maintaining a particular shape; and a capacity or potential is the being's disposition to do this, for example, someone capable of doing geometry is a geometer. I shall call this dynamic or energetic being, after its concepts, activity (*energeia*) and potency (*dunamis*). Aristotle never gives a single name to this sort of being, and always lists both terms. This is important, and a central part of my argument is that potency and activity cannot be reduced to one another, but are different in kind.

(4) To be is to be true and not to be is to be false; for example, for someone to be a geometer is for this to be true of her, while not to be a geometer is for this not to be true of her. This is being true or alethic being, after the word *aletheia*.

There are several things to note about these four greatest senses of being. First of all, each is a distinctive way of being as such.[8] Each is being without qualification, for "being, spoken of *simply*, is meant in more than one way" (*Met.* VI.2 1026a33).[9] Moreover, when addressing an individual being, each sense of being accounts for its being as a whole in a particular respect: being 1 kg accounts for the whole being, insofar as it has weight; a marathon runner (i.e., a being-in-potency) is a being considered as a whole, insofar as her body structure, metabolism, training, planning, social relationships (e.g., support networks, membership in the event of the race), perseverance, and goals make her ready to run a marathon.

Second, Aristotle describes the four different ways of being as *different in kind:* they do not share an underlying being or class, and they are irreducible to one another (*Met.* V.28 1024b10–17).[10] As Wieland argues, "Aristotle recognizes a plurality of systems of principles, which lie unconnected side by side, and cannot be reduced in their turn to a common higher principle."[11] They are four distinct pillars of ontology. This is to say that each is sufficient to describe a way of being entirely: only the being of activity accounts for a being insofar as it is active; no other way of being describes or explains how things are true.

This is important to note because it is commonly thought that Aristotle's ontology reduces ultimately to the concept of *ousia*. Aristotle appears to say this at *Metaphysics* VII.1 1028b3–8, but in the context of that passage, *ousia* is primary *among the ways of attributing or predicating being*, that is, among the categories (*Met.* VII.1 1028a33–b3).[12] *Ousia is only ever called the primary sense of being with reference to the categorical sense of being* (*Met.* V.7, V.8, VI.2 1026a33–b2, VII.1 1028a10–20, VII.3 1028b22–1029a35).[13] *Ousia* is never called primary in reference to the other three fundamental senses of being. More tellingly, Aristotle explicitly distinguishes the discussion of *ousia* and its primacy from the discussion of energetic being:

> What concerns being of the primary sort, toward which all the other ways of *attributing* being [*hai allai katēgoriai tou ontos*] are traced back, has been discussed, namely what concerns primary being [*ousia*] . . . but since being is spoken of in one way by way of what or of what sort or how much something is [i.e., the categories], but in another way in virtue of potency and being-complete [*entelecheia*], and of a doing-something [*ergon*], let us make distinctions also about potency and being-complete. (*Met.* IX.1 1045b27–35)[14]

Here, having completed the discussion of categorical being and the primacy of being (*ousia*), Aristotle leaves priority in *ousia* behind, and turns away from it to a new subject, namely dynamic and energetic being.

The mistaken idea that categorical being (*ousia*) is the primary sense of all being stems from the fact that each of the four principal sorts of being is subdivided into further ways of being: the *Categories* divides the categorical sense of being into quality, quantity, relation, position, primary and secondary being, and so on, which are related to each other through the core concepts of the underlying material subject and the form or predicated attribute. The primary concept in categorical being is primary being (*ousia*), since all properties are said to be *of* the *ousia*, while it is something definite that is not said of anything else (*Met.* V.8 1017b23–26). For its part, dynamic and energetic being is divided into potency, activity, and being-complete (*entelecheia*). Having several manifolds on the table means that when Aristotle says something about the many senses of being, we are apt to misconstrue which set of senses he means. Priority itself has many senses (*Met.* V.11), so that different ways of being have their own pivotal concepts and structures of priority: the primary concept in energetic being is sourcehood (*archē*).[15]

Third, when Aristotle says that being *as such* is many, he means that there are many *aspects* of being, not that there are many individual beings (though that is true as well). Each thing *is* in each of the four primary ways; any particular being can be grasped in all of the four senses of being. Its being is overdetermined: a single being or phenomenon admits of multiple determinate ways of being.

Heidegger summarizes Aristotle's position this way:

> This sentence, *to on legetai pollachōs* [being is said in many ways], is a constant refrain in Aristotle. But it is not just a formula. Rather, in this short sentence, Aristotle formulates the wholly fundamental and new position that he worked out in philosophy in relation to all of his predecessors, including Plato; not in the sense of a system but in the sense of a task.[16]

Heidegger argues that Aristotle never completed the task of working out a comprehensive view of the multiplicity of being. Indeed, Aristotle does not deduce the senses of being, and nowhere presents the basic senses of being as a single integrated system.[17] Even in the cases where he establishes a relationship between the four senses of being, these relationships are promises (*Met.* VIII.6 1045b18–24), analogies (e.g., *Met.* IX.6 1048b8–9), or conclusions (*Met.* IX.8 1050b2), rather than starting points for a single overarching system of being. They remain, as he said, four irreducible ways that being *is*.

Terminology

Each sense of being has a cluster of terms appropriate to it. When Aristotle lists the ways that categorical being is many, he often gives several categories, such as quality, quantity, place, "the what" of something (i.e., its essence or secondary *ousia*), and "some *this.*" Implicit in this list is a distinction between predicates and the underlying thing in which they are said to be. The structure that relates the many categorical beings to one another, then, is made up of several concepts: material (*hulē*) and the underlying thing (*hupokeimenon*), form (*eidos*) and shape (*morphē*), being (*ousia*), the composite (*sunholon* or *suntheton*), and the particular *this* (*tode ti*).[18] The terms that make up the energetic sense of being are potency (*dunamis*), being-at-work (*energeia*), and being-complete (*entelecheia*), along with its key term "completion" (*telos*), and source (*archē*). The terms of categorical being are discussed in chapters 1, 5, and 6, while the terms of energetic being are examined throughout the book.

Aristotle's repertoire of change words is different than ours, and there are some features of his usage that need clarification. Perhaps the most general of his words for change is *metabolē*, "turning over from/to," which he describes as follows: "every change [*metabolē*] is from something to something (as the name [*metabolē*] makes clear, for 'after' [*meta-*] something else shows that there is one thing before and another after)" (*Phys.* V.1 225a1–3).[19] The word *metabolē* thus covers all changes, including *kinēsis* and *genesis*, but it has a specific structure: changes are between contraries and have an underlying subject (*hupokeimenon*) or being (*ousia*) (*Met.* VIII.1 1042a33–b2). In terms of the work Aristotle does with the concepts, *kinēsis* and *genesis* are much more important than *metabolē*, and I shall concentrate on those.

The word "alteration," *alloiōsis*, means to become other and *thereby* to cease to be what one was. It is based on the word *allo*, "other," "something besides."[20] Thus the verb *allassō* means to alternate, turn into something other, or interchange. It is closely related to the term *existasthai*, related to the word "exist," which in Greek literally means to stand outside, to put out of place, and *thereby* to alter utterly. If being elsewhere means being something else, a thing's place determines what it is. This is an ecological concept, that is, an account of the dwelling-place, *oikos*. Aristotle uses "alteration" to describe qualitative change, or, more precisely, changes in what sort a thing is. But in his most important philosophical engagement with the concept, in *Soul* II.5 417b2–418a4, he rejects the idea that becoming-other is the paradigm of change. Instead, he uses the relationship between potency and being-complete (*entelecheia*) to argue that changes make things into what they already, in a certain respect, are. I shall translate *alloiōsis* as "alteration," or, where necessary, "change," and append the Greek term.

The word *kinēsis*, "movement," too, has a general and a specific sense. In *Physics* III.1–3, the definition of *kinēsis* covers all changes, of every type: "the being-complete of what is in-potency, as such, is movement [*kinēsis*]: of the alterable, as alterable, it is alteration, of what can grow and its opposite, what can shrink . . . it is growth and shrinkage, of the generable and destructible it is generation and passing away, and of the movable in place it is change of place," and similarly of even more particular types, such as learning, healing, rolling, leaping, and ripening (*Phys.* III.1 201a11–16, my trans.). But in *Physics* V.1–2 Aristotle introduces a much narrower use of the word, namely motion in place (*kata topon*), in contradistinction to change in quality, quantity, and being (*ousia*).²¹ I shall normally translate *kinēsis* as "change."

The verb *kineō* is always transitive: one thing always moves another. Its middle voice is never used in philosophical writing, so self-movement is always described as one part moving another, which is a central thesis of *Physics* VIII.4–5.²² Mourelatos argues that, at least until Parmenides, *kinēsis* meant egress, that is, setting forth, moving away from one's place, and thereby from oneself.²³ But Aristotle turns this concept on its head: *kinēsis*, as change of place, is the sort of movement in which the moving thing most obviously remains what it is. *Kinēsis* indicates changes that have a persisting subject, for example, a rabbit turning white, a runner running. Thus, while he uses *metabolē* to emphasize the difference between what came before and what is now, *kinēsis* emphasizes the continuity: the mobile (*kinoumenon*) stays what it is while it moves.

The third and most important word for change, for our purposes in this book, is *genesis*, "coming-to-be," "generation," or "origin." Parmenides denies the existence of all kinds of change through an analysis of *genesis*.²⁴ It is also the first sense of change that Aristotle seeks to save in his defense of the possibility of change in *Physics* I.7–9. The concept is particularly fraught because it emphasizes the appearance of something different, the arrival of *a new subject of predicates*, for example, the birth of a child, or the change of grapes into wine. *Genesis* thus provides Aristotle with a core phenomenon to analyze.

Genesis becomes a particularly important investigative tool for Aristotle.²⁵ For example, he takes it to be the meta-structure of changes (both *kinēseis* and *metabolais*): first, whenever he describes change categorically, as a form coming to be in an underlying material (e.g., *Met.* VIII.5 1044b21–29), he uses the concept of *genesis* worked out in *Physics* I.7–9, namely that each type of change can be described as the coming-to-be of a form, for example, a tree, or a specific size, color, or location. Since the form could be anything, *genesis* is flexible enough to cover all types of change, much as "becoming" covers all types of change in English. Second, Aristotle describes potency as *generating* either the change itself, its product or outcome, or activities that have no further product (*Met.* IX.8 1050a24–31). The analysis of *genesis*, then, gives it an even wider range than *kinēsis* or *metabolē*: although it is one of the kinds of *metabolē*, it is the ontological structure of all changes. In different contexts, I shall translate *genesis* as "becoming," "coming-to-be," or "change," and will append the transliterated word wherever there might be ambiguity. *Metabolē* and *genesis* are both used directly to argue for ontological structures proper to change, but *kinēsis* is not: the ontological import of *kinēsis* is worked out through the concepts of *dunamis*, *energeia*, and *entelecheia*.²⁶

Elements, causes, and sources are distinct and not interchangeable, even when they point to the same numerical being. The word *archē* means "source," "origin," or "beginning," but also "principle," which carries the appropriate connotation of something that orders or organizes what it initiates. A source originates change, coming-to-be, being, or knowing (*Met.* V.1 1012b34–1013a23). *Archē* is used loosely to mean anything that is first, but it is associated primarily with generation and change, and thereby, I shall argue, with being. I shall mostly render it as "source" to highlight its relationship with change. A cause (*aitia*), on the other hand, is a discrete, already constituted object bearing properties, named insofar as it is responsible for a being or event (*Met.* V.2). For its part, an element ("letter," *stoicheion*) is a differentiated constituent part or being that admits of combination with other parts or beings (*Met.* V.3).[27]

Finally, I shall not render *ousia* as "substance," the word most often used in translations and secondary scholarship, because that is not a translation of *ousia* but of *hupokeimenon*. Scholars continue to use the word "substance" in an attempt to maintain continuity with earlier scholarship and the Latin tradition of commentary. But this means, for example, that when *ousia* is translated as "primary substance," as it frequently is, both words refer to features of the concept, while neither translates the word. This dissolves the word into some of the most difficult arguments in the history of philosophy, making it difficult for readers to understand. So I shall render *ousia* as "being" and append or simply use the transliterated word itself. When continuity is particularly important, I shall use the translation "primary being," a recognizable hybrid.

A Note on Activity and Change

There is an important point of relationship between change-analysis and being-analysis: while attributes of change may have no relevance to the study of being, the analysis of the being of change is part of ontology. In other words, since ontology studies being insofar as *it is*, it must study change insofar as *it is* (if it can be shown to be at all), and it must study its consequences for being. Thereby, change can contribute to our understanding of being. For Aristotle, the study of change and coming-to-be shows a distinctive aspect of what it is to be a source (*Met.* III.2 996a9–13), and thereby shows being to be multiple. The knowledge of sources is the goal of first philosophy, that is, ontology (*Met.* I.1 981b26–982a7, IV.2 1003b15–19, VI.1 1025b3–4). To understand how sources contribute to the account of being, it is necessary, then, to interpret this account of change and its sources.

But the interpretation of Aristotle's work on the relationship between change and being has long orbited around "the Passage" (*Met.* IX.6 1048b18–35), in which a contrast is drawn between *kinēsis* and *energeia*. This distinction became the subject of particularly intense discussion through Ryle, Vendler, and Ackrill's analysis in the 1950s and 1960s.[28] The Passage appeared to confirm the idea that Aristotle was, at bottom, a Platonist about change, which meant that the analysis of change would contribute little or nothing of importance to ontology.[29]

But the Passage should not be the centerpiece of an account of change or being in Aristotle. In a 2008 article, Myles Burnyeat showed, through examination of the manuscript evidence as well as philosophical analysis, that the passage which drew this distinction was copied in error. All of the Passage's appearances in the manuscripts could be traced back to a single relatively unreliable source, in which it is error-ridden and crossed out. Based on the unparalleled textual corruption of the passage, Burnyeat suggested that it was likely an elucidation written in the margins of the text, which was later mistakenly incorporated into it. Moreover, Burnyeat added, the arguments in the rest of Aristotle's corpus show no indication of the distinction, and often explicitly conflict with it.[30] Therefore, he argued, the passage should be secluded, saying: "Present-day scholarship should stop citing the Passage as a source of standard Aristotelian doctrine. It is a freak performance."[31]

In other words, the Passage is at the very least not from *Metaphysics* IX, where it is printed, and there is a fair chance that Aristotle did not write it. Having proposed this, however, Burnyeat backtracks, suggesting that the Passage likely was by Aristotle, asking: "who else would have such thoughts?"[32] But there were others, notably Theophrastus, who wrote on such issues, and made such distinctions.[33] Still, no matter what its authenticity, the upshot is that *the Passage should not be pivotal for our understanding of Aristotle's account of change or being*. Now, it does not matter to my argument whether the Passage has been secluded or not, since the philosophical insight it is purported to offer, namely an account of how change (*kinēsis*) is incomplete, is more clearly put elsewhere. Prominent among these other passages is *NE* X.4 1174a13–b23, where Aristotle either qualifies or resists the claim in the Passage that change (*kinēsis*) is incomplete by arguing that it is incomplete in its parts, but complete as a whole (see "Wholes and Parts of Changes" in chap. 3). More importantly than this, however, is that the Passage testifies to the fact that Aristotle uses change to develop his ontology. It is to the exploration of how and why he does this that we now turn.

CHAPTER 1

Change and the Many Senses of Being in *Physics* I

This chapter examines the first part of Aristotle's argument that change *is*. The first part occurs in *Physics* I.7–9, and the second in *Physics* III.1–2. Chapters 1 and 2 of this book will be devoted to discussing these two parts of the argument, respectively. Parmenides led his Eleatic colleagues in arguing that change cannot be, since in any change something must emerge from or enter into non-being. Aristotle accepts their premises, but rejects their conclusion. He argues, first, that the phenomenon of change establishes that being itself has multiple senses: form, its privation, and what underlies them. Therefore, he shows, change always comes from and enters into *what is* (form and the underlying thing), so that *what is not* (the privation) is incidental to the description of change. What gets Aristotle through the Parmenidean impasse, then, is his argument that both change and being are composite.

Aristotle's accomplishment in this argument is not only to make way for the existence of change. He sets up his analysis of change first of all as the answer to the question of how many being is; the structure of change is the basis for the claim that being is multiple. This reveals Aristotle's own understanding of the argument's importance.

In this chapter I first examine the framework of this argument and the general plan of Aristotle's argument that change, in fact, *is*. Then I take Aristotle's insight into what makes change appear self-contradictory and reconstruct it in reverse order, starting with its outcome: the idea that being is general rather than particular. Aristotle's analysis of change reveals, instead, that the structure of changing beings consists in a *particular* predicated form (or its privation), and a *particular* underlying subject. This means the analysis of change reveals the structure of being (*ousia*) insofar as a unique being is a bearer of predicates: the ontological structure of changing beings just is the structure of categorical being.

This chapter closes by addressing the other most likely explanation for Aristotle's claim that being is multiple, namely, the structure of speech (*logos*). But the case for a linguistic or logical (*logikos*) ground for multiplicity,

17

I will show, depends on categorical concepts drawn from Aristotle's analysis of change, notably the underlying material, and the particularity or individuality of primary being (*ousia*). Yet the problem of change remains, since it is not possible to define change using these categorical concepts: it can only be defined using the dynamic-energetic sense of being.

The Lines of Argument in *Physics* I

Aristotle's argument for change requires being to be multiple. One of the principal pieces of evidence for this claim is in how Aristotle frames the key questions of *Physics* I.7–9. Specifically, he uses his analysis of the description of change to answer the question of how many being is. By framing the analysis of change in this way, Aristotle indicates its ontological consequences.

Aristotle links the analysis of sources in *Physics* I to the analysis of being. To see why, it will help to start with a broad view. If being has different regions and aspects, there are different disciplines that study them: for example, biology studies beings that live insofar as they are living beings, and physics studies natural beings insofar as they are sources of change and resting, or, more generally, beings that move insofar as they move (*Met.* IV.1 1003a21–31). Each discipline seeks the sources (*archai*), causes (*aitia*), and elements (*stoicheia*) of its subject (*Phys.* I.1 184a15; compare *Met.* I.1 181a24–982a3, VII.17 1041a29). First philosophy is capable of studying all things, because, Aristotle says, it studies beings insofar as they *are*, especially the highest sources or principles (*archai*) of being, for example, god (*Met.* IV.2 1004b1, *Met.* VI.2 1026a18–22, 27–33).

The problem of *Physics* I, Aristotle announces, is figuring out how many sources there are: "There must be either one source or more than one" (*Phys.* I.2 184b15, my trans.).[1] He clarifies: "We are here raising the same question as those who ask how many *beings* there are: they are really inquiring about the primary constituents of things . . . so they too are inquiring into the number of sources and elements" (*Phys.* I.2 184b15–24).[2] The question of ontology is really the question about sources, causes, and elements. To say how many sources or principles there are is to say how many being is. Why is this? To say how many sources there are, we must say *what* beings there are, *what it means for them to be*, and what originates or is responsible for their being. In short, archaeology is ontology. To the extent that any analysis leads to knowledge of the primary sources, causes, and elements, it can contribute to first philosophy.

In this case, Aristotle investigates the puzzle (*aporia*) of *how many sources or elements there are*—the same question as how many beings there are—by analyzing *change*. He begins by working up the debate between his predecessors.[3] But he introduces his own answer by saying: "This is how I tackle it [the *aporia*] myself. I shall be dealing first with coming to be in general" (*Phys.* I.7 189b30–31).[4] Aristotle sets out to answer the question of how many *being* is by examining *coming-to-be* (*genesis*). This, I argue, is not a mistake.[5] Since all change can be described as the coming-to-be of a property (e.g. this wood gains the property of being a *table*), the structure of *genesis* obtains for all change. The reason why the study of *change* can show us the number of *being* is that change reveals sources (*archai*), causes (*aitia*), and elements (*stoicheia*) that are responsible for the being of changing beings.[6]

Aristotle's analysis of coming-to-be provides him with multiple forms of ontological multiplicity. He distinguishes *three* elements: a form, its privation, and the underlying thing. But he notes that in another way, the pair of form and underlying material are the only things that in fact *are*: "From one angle we must say that the sources are two, and from another that they are three" (*Phys.* I.7 190b29–30, my trans.). In yet another way, these are aspects of a *single* being. A single being does not just have several elements, it also admits of being grasped in several different ways. Being does not just have a single type of multiplicity; it is plural in a plurality of ways.

Upon establishing this complex plurality, Aristotle right away argues that this conception of being is the way to undo the ancient impasse (*aporia*) that "nothing comes to be or passes away, because whatever comes to be must do so either out of something which is, or out of something which is not, and neither is possible" (*Phys.* I.8 191a23–30).[7] But what is at stake is simultaneously the possibility of change and fundamental ontology: Aristotle claims explicitly that the argument against coming to be is what led Parmenides and Melissus to "deny a plurality of things altogether, and say that there is nothing but 'what is itself'" (*Phys.* I.8 191a32–34).[8] The reason why Parmenides and his successors make the ontological claim that *being is simple* is that they misunderstand *genesis* (*Phys.* I.8 191b10, b30–35).[9] Since Parmenides's argument against the existence of change was ontological, Aristotle's argument too must be ontological. This means that his analysis of *genesis* revisits the site of the Eleatic argument for monism. What he discovers there leads him to a different outcome about being and about change. Aristotle's explicit claim, then, is that the number of being is determined through the analysis of coming-to-be, both for the ancients and in his own account. The phenomenon of *genesis* shows whether and how being is plural.

Being and Sources

There are several possible objections to reading *Physics* I this way. The most obvious is the idea that physics and metaphysics study different subjects altogether. This leads to the specific claim that "source" in this context means "source of changing things" rather than "source of being."

But this approach abstracts from the content of the argument. Aristotle's engagement with Parmenides shows clearly that in this part of the *Physics*, at least, he is doing ontology. He examines different ways that being could be one, whether parts are reducible to wholes or vice versa, and the thesis that being is one in *logos*, before concluding:

> Things [*ta onta*], however, are many, either in account (as the being of pale is different from the being of a musician, though the same thing may be both: so the one is many), or by division, like the parts of a whole. At this point they got stuck, and began to admit that the one was many. (*Phys.* I.2 185b32–186a2)[10]

This passage would be at home among the later chapters of *Metaphysics* VII. In this debate, Aristotle is clearly making significant arguments about what being is, and what it is like. The specific claim, that the concept of "sources" here is irrelevant to ontology, runs up against the fact that the sources in question are the very ones studied in the core books of the *Metaphysics*, namely underlying material, form, and the privation of form.[11] This is why Ross argues that "the bulk of the *Physics* is what we should call metaphysics."[12] Burnyeat even identifies material and form as the *distinctively metaphysical* solution to merely logical problems.[13] If this is right, then as long as Aristotle is concerned with examining these fundamental being-terms, he is doing ontology. He is doing ontology, for example, when he examines sources of change and generation insofar as they *are*, that is, when he is pursuing what sort of being sources have, how they relate to the being of beings, what is responsible for the being of beings, and how different sources structure what is.

This kind of study is to be distinguished, of course, from the examination in the biological works of what particular properties individual beings or kinds of being happen to have. And if physics is not the study of what it is to be a nature, but instead of being in general merely insofar as it *moves*, devoting itself just to distinguishing kinds of change and their properties, then it will not be relevant to ontology. But in *Physics* I–III.3, Aristotle appears to be studying the being of sources in order to understand what nature is, which makes this an ontological inquiry.

Finally, it is significant that when Aristotle is doing an ontology of sources he most often examines *genesis*. This seems to be because *sources of coming-to-be are sources of being*.

The Two Stages of the Demonstration of Change

I contend that *Physics* I.7–9 and III.1–2 make up a two-part argument for the existence of change. To establish this claim, it will help to start by answering an objection, namely, that Aristotle is *not* interested in showing that change exists. This claim centers on Aristotle's assertion that he does not need to prove the existence of change to those who deny it (*Phys.* I.2 185a1–4; compare *Met.* VI.1 1025b7–14).

When read in context, however, this passage does not in fact set aside the need for a demonstration. The passage says that someone who denies the existence of change is working on a different subject matter than nature, and that we do not need to use that subject to persuade them that change exists. Confronted by someone using symbolic logic to reject the existence of change, we do not need to use symbolic logic to demonstrate its existence. A demonstration will draw on different grounds.

But the being of change must be examined because it is fundamental to the study of nature (*Phys.* III.1 200b12–16). This is why Aristotle follows up his comment about deniers by saying that he will engage them anyway: "But even though they do not speak about nature, they incidentally speak of things that are impasses in the study of nature" (*Phys.* I.2 185a19–21).[14] This is why the argument of *Physics* I is organized to confront and solve the impasse of change in *Physics* I.8.

Now I will outline the two stages of Aristotle's demonstration of change: the first stage demonstrates that change *can* exist by showing how to give a noncontradictory description of changes (the Descriptive Argument, *Phys.* I.7–9), while the second defines change and on this basis provides evidence that it *does* exist (the Definition, *Phys.* III.1–2).

The first stage undertakes the necessary task of finding a way through the impasse about the existence of change. Aristotle's solution is to show that it is possible to describe changes in a precise and noncontradictory way, that is, in a way that does not mix being with non-being.[15] This is not an easy task. For, Aristotle notes, the reason change appears not to be is that it seems to be something indefinite *(aoriston ti)* (*Phys.* III.2 201a24–25). To succeed in showing that change is neither otherness, nor inequality, nor non-being, nor any of the other indefinite principles, as other thinkers had supposed, it is necessary to show how it is possible to describe it in definite terms (*Phys.* III.2 201b23). Change can be described in definite, noncontradictory terms when we distinguish it into three structural elements: form (*eidos*), the underlying material or thing (*hupokeimenon* or *hulē*), and the privation (*sterēsis*) of the form. Again, any change can be described as the coming-to-be-the-case of a categorical property; for example, the coming-to-be of black in a surface.

Aristotle distinguishes the elements of change by developing a typology of ways that we describe changes. Doing so is not just an explanatory task, it is an ontological one. This is because, for Aristotle, being different in definition means being different in being, just as a doctor is different than a patient in *what* each is, that is, in their *being*.[16]

This typology anchors Aristotle's account of being in the experience of change. He outlines his method for working with experience at the opening of the *Physics* (*Phys.* I.1 184a10–184b14). Experience is already rich with principles (*archai*), causes, and elements (compare *Pos. An.* II.19). But our predicament, he claims, is that we start inevitably with things that seem jumbled up or poured together (*ta sugkechumena*). When the principles that distinguish things are confused, misunderstood, or overlooked, our experience will be, too. For experience to yield knowledge, these principles must be discerned *within* experience.[17] The way to knowledge is through distinguishing the principles, causes, and elements in the midst of this confusion. This disentanglement involves distinguishing the many principles of being from one another, and we do this through theoretical discussion. In my view, Aristotle disentangles the elements (in *Phys.* I), causes (in *Phys.* II), and principles (in *Phys.* III) of change within the experience of change, thereby making articulate experience of nature possible.

But this first stage of argument, with which I deal in this chapter, requires a second, with which I shall deal in chapter 2. Although Aristotle opened *Physics* I.8 with the claim that "this is the only way of resolving the difficulty felt by thinkers of earlier times" (*Phys.* I.8 191a23–24),[18] after he provides the resolution, he immediately adds: "this, then, is *one way* of handling the matter; *another* is to point out that the same things may be spoken of either as potent or as at-work" (*Phys.* I.8 191b27–28).[19]

He says this because, while it is necessary to answer the Parmenidean impasse, doing so does not establish the existence of generation and change.[20] No matter how inescapable form, privation, and the underlying material are in the description of change, they do not amount to change. By distinguishing the *elements* of change (form, privation, and the underlying material) in such a way that they are not contradictory, or, put otherwise, by showing how change does not essentially refer to non-being, Aristotle has opened the door to the possibility that change exists, but he clearly has not said what change is. A brown form, its not-brown opposite, and the skin underlying them are just the items involved in an instance of change. Adding them together yields neither the definition of nor the reality of change, just as the set of player positions on a football field constitutes neither the definition of the game nor the reality of football games. It is thus wrong to think, as, for example Graham does, that Aristotle has completely refuted the Eleatics in *Physics* I.[21]

So, since "it belongs to the same act of thinking to make clear both what something is and whether it is" (*Met.* VI.1 1025b18),[22] what is necessary for the demonstration of the existence of change is a definition. The definition of change, and the accompanying demonstration that it can exist, are given in *Physics* III.1, whereupon Aristotle flags his accomplishment, saying that although change is "difficult to see, [it nevertheless] admits of being" (*Phys.* III.2 202a1, my trans.). Aristotle is right to argue that talking about what change is requires a different approach altogether, namely, a different sense of being (*Phys.* III.1 200b28–30, 201a10–12).

The Ancient Impasse

To show something's effect, it is useful first to note how things were beforehand. So we can reconstruct the consequences of change for being by taking the argument against its existence as a baseline, and showing what alterations Aristotle needs to make to ontology to solve the impasse. The argument against change was first formulated by Parmenides, and then refined, notably by Melissus and Zeno, but in *Physics* I, Aristotle does not distinguish them. Instead, he engages the argument in the form in which it had come down to him. It is sufficient for our purposes to take this as the baseline position. Aristotle agrees with what he takes to be the core of the argument against change, and he presents his principal interventions—making non-being specific, distinguishing compatible aspects, and arguing for the existence of underlying material—as corrections to a set of decisions made by his predecessors. Following Aristotle's own approach lets us get precise about the consequences of change by using the ancients' position as a foil.

Aristotle agrees with the ancients, first, in the claim that nothing is a mixture of being and non-being: "there is no violation here of the principle claiming that everything either is or is not" (*Phys.* I.8 191b28).[23] *Change, then, will be neither a synthesis nor a fusion nor a compound of being and non-being.* Second, Aristotle agrees with the claim that what comes to be must come either out of what is or out of what is not (*Phys.* I.8 191b34–35). Third, he agrees that "nothing comes to be simply out of what is not" and that there is no coming-to-be simply out of what is (*Phys.* I.8 191b13, 18–19).[24]

The only remaining path is to qualify the claims that nothing *simply* comes to be directly from nothing at all, or from being considered as a whole. Put otherwise, the strategy is to argue that change is *composite*. By distinguishing between different coinciding elements of changing things, being and non-being cease to be simple or general, and are broken up into specific aspects. If being is specific in the right ways, it will be agile enough to find its way through the gaps in the impasse.

The Problem of Simplicity

In my argument, a key outcome of Aristotle's analysis is his claim that being is specific or particular. We can see most clearly how Aristotle's response to the impasse works by examining the case he makes for this specificity. This argument ties together his account of being's multiplicity and the being of change. First, though, it is necessary to present the problem.

On a typical formulation of Parmenides's argument, if being is one and simple, then change cannot be. In contrast, Aristotle claims that monism *emerges* from the ancients' view of *genesis*: "[It is by] inflating the consequences of this [argument against change] that they deny a plurality of things altogether, and say that there is nothing but "what is itself." They embraced this opinion for the reasons given" (*Phys.* I.8 191b32–33).[25] The rejection of *genesis*, Aristotle says, *leads* to, rather than presupposes, a rejection of the plurality of being. For this to be the case, denying *genesis* must end up denying that particular things are, and asserting that *genesis* occurs must amount to asserting that being is particular.

In claiming that being is particular, Aristotle means particular in aspect. Since particular beings are all both generated and perishable, it seems plausible that denying that *genesis* occurs will *thereby* deny the existence of these particular, numerically different things. But Parmenides's monism does not lead Aristotle to defend a numerical plurality of beings. Aristotle's response is not to demonstrate the sheer number of things, it is to argue for the plurality of *aspects* of beings, for example, that being a wife is a different aspect of a person than being a doctor (*Phys.* I.8 191a34–b11). Aristotle's claim, then, is that the ancients failed to grasp that non-being and being are both limited in *aspect* (*Phys.* I.7 191b8–13). The ancients were at an impasse about change, Aristotle says, because they failed to think "as" or "insofar as" (*hē*) (*Phys.* I.8 191b10). To describe what he means by aspect, Aristotle draws an analogy: a doctor cures someone insofar as he is a doctor, but builds a house as a builder who only incidentally also happens to be a doctor. A man may even cure himself insofar as he is a doctor, but he does not himself convalesce as a doctor: he convalesces as a patient, a living animal who in this case happens also to be a doctor.

Now we can begin from what Aristotle takes to be the *outcome* of Parmenides's argument, namely, the claim that being and non-being are simple, and work backward to see why determinacy matters to Aristotle's argument.

The simplicity of being is less immediately intuitive when we consider *what is*, since we see, or think we see, many beings around us, which inclines us to think of being as specific. But *what is not* seems to be simple; it is much harder to think of non-being as something specific. So let us start with the concept of non-being.

"What is not" for Parmenides is either "something *ouk anuston*, inchoate, unreachable, and unsettled . . . [or] no more than the indefiniteness of empty, unbounded logical space."[26] The inchoate, indefinite, and unbounded silence of non-being seems to imply that it is simple or universal. A thought experiment can help make this clear: after Mariana's death, she precisely is not. Unlike the way she is here or there in a definite way when she exists, "Mariana not being" seems neither to be here nor there; it seems to be everywhere. The negation of her as an individual is not describable as the existence of a particular "not-being of Mariana." After Mariana's death, it cannot be said *of her* (as something that now is not) that she is brown, or tall, or even that she once was. Being-not does not belong to Mariana, since she is not. She no longer has features; her individuality is dissolved in non-being as a whole. Thus, what simply is not seems as though it can have no individuation, and therefore no properties that individuate it. Thus, it seems plausible to say that non-being is always simple or general, because it is indeterminate, infinite, inchoate. If it were possible to transfer the features of non-being to being, it would follow that being, too, is simple, and the simplicity of being would be secured by its implicit opposition to non-being.[27]

The generality of being and non-being makes it impossible to think or describe change. If coming into being is simple or general, or if being has only one sense, the refutation of change follows necessarily.[28] For nothing can come from being, simply (*haplōs*), since there would be no difference between what comes to be and what is, so nothing would have happened. Meanwhile, if something came from what is not, it would have to come from sheer nothingness.

In short, unless *what is* and *what is not* can be made particular, unless we can distinguish particular kinds of being and non-being, then the thinking of change will remain at an impasse. Thus, the impasse about the being of *genesis*, and therefore change, results in a failure to distinguish between particular beings or among particular modes of being. If there is no such diversity, then being will be simply one, and perfectly universal.[29]

The Claim That Being Is Particular
In response, Aristotle searches for a way to show that both being and non-being are determinate. Beginning on Parmenides's territory with an analysis

of speech, at the end of *Physics* I.3 he rejects the idea that being and non-being are simple. He says, first, that nothing forces us to think there is anything that *simply* (*haplōs*) is not; "what is not" (*mē on*) is not simple or general. Second, he argues, to the extent that non-being has meaning at all, it is only as some definite thing that is not. Therefore, he says: "what is not" means "not some particular thing" (*mē on ti*); *the word "not" requires completion*, and implies some other *thing* that gives it meaning.[30] Third, Aristotle extends this account to being as well, asking "who understands by 'what is itself' anything but 'what is an individual something' [*to hoper on ti*]?" (*Phys.* I.3 187a6).[31] In other words, *contra* Parmenides, Aristotle claims that being and non-being are symmetrical in that they are both *determinate*.[32] The claim, then, is that being and non-being are only ever specific, definite terms: not-being is always the not-being of something in particular (e.g., of green, of a child), and being is always this particular sort of being. The meaning of being and non-being, then, get transformed by being limited to a specific aspect.

In this sequence of claims, Aristotle has to push the Greek language, working up general formulae (e.g., *to hoper on ti*) to express *individuality in general*. Elsewhere he uses the phrase "some *this*" (*tode ti*) to express the same concrete particularity, an idea that leads to primary being (*ousia*).

Still, the assertion in *Physics* I.3 that being is specific is not an argument, but a declaration of intent. To undo the Parmenidean impasse, Aristotle will have to disentangle the confused phenomena that led Parmenides to this mistake. Otherwise, it is merely Aristotle's word that being is particular against Parmenides's word that it is not. Aristotle must find a way, then, to show that "what is" and "what is not" *do* have meaning, but in composite expressions. For the specificity of being and non-being to get us through the impasse of change, he must establish that being is specific. He does so by using the description of *genesis* to show that being is composite.

Composite Being

Aristotle's argument that being is composite consists of an intricate analysis of coming-to-be (*genesis*) in *Physics* I.7. First he goes painstakingly through the different ways we speak in ordinary speech of events of coming-to-be, for example, "a student came-to-be educated," "the ignorant became educated," and examining what terms or elements get distinguished in each type of expression (*Phys.* I.7 189a30–190b9). Again, *Aristotle is using "genesis" here to cover all kinds of change*, because each change can be understood as the coming-to-be of a new feature *in* something.

Aristotle then shows that these elements divide into three kinds: (1) the "educated," the form (*eidos*) *that comes to be*, (2) the "uneducated," the opposite or lack (*sterēsis*) *out of which* the form comes to be, and (3) the "man," the underlying material or thing (*hupokeimenon*) staying itself through the change, *the coming-to-be thing*, which loses the *sterēsis* and comes to have the form in it (*Phys.* I.7 190b10–191a7).[33] These can be schematized as follows:

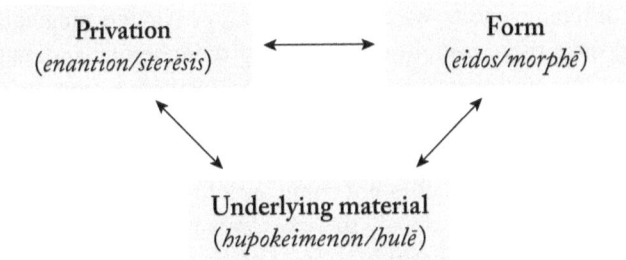

By distinguishing each of these from the others, Aristotle makes them specific. These are, of course, not separate items, but positions in a structure of relations. The material always has a form, and the form always has an opposite.[34] Thus, what counts as each will change depending on the case; for example, a woman (underlying) who comes to know geometry (form), the flesh and bone (underlying) that comes to be a person (form), or the water and earth (underlying) that make up her flesh (form).[35]

Changes occur along the continuity between form and privation, *not* between the underlying material and either the form or the privation. The form is the particular feature, property, or being that comes to be in the course of a change. The privation, meanwhile, derives a pseudo-formal character from the form of which it is the negation (*Phys.* II.1193b19–20). It is, therefore, not itself a property (*Met.* V.12 1019b7–11), but is precisely the non-being of a particular property (*Phys.* I.3 187a4–8).

For its part, the underlying thing is material, and active, a "co-cause with the form of the things that come into being, like a mother . . . which inherently yearns for and stretches out toward it [the form] by its own nature" (*Phys.* I.9 192a15–20).[36] It is not the same as or even similar in kind to the privation, as Aristotle makes clear: "For we say that material and privation are different things, and of these the one is a non-being incidentally, namely the material, while the privation is so in its own right, and the one, the material, is almost, and in a certain respect is, an independent thing [*ousia*], which the other is not at all" (*Phys.* I.9 192a2–7, compare I.7 190a16 and I.8 191a2).[37] It is important to emphasize this point, since due to the complexity of the analysis, some have found it tempting to argue for a special identity between the underlying thing and privation.[38] But as Kelsey showed, Aristotle's innovation is to see the arriving form both as different from, and as an expression of, the positive nature of the underlying thing: since the underlying thing admits of certain forms but not others, the forms it can take on express its character.[39]

It is through this triangular structure that change is liberated from the accusation that it fuses being with non-being. By distinguishing something into these different aspects, we can say that in one way, nothing comes from non-being, since there *was* always something there beforehand, namely, the underlying thing, and that in another way, nothing comes from being either, since the specific thing that came to be was *not* there beforehand (*Phys.* I.8 191b12–19). For example, before a child is born, this exact child did not already exist, but this child does not come out of nothingness, but out of the blood and tissue that were already there beforehand. So if being divides into these aspects, we can say that things come to be out of what incidentally is not, without violating Parmenides's principles (*Phys.* I.8 191a33–b18). For before conception, it is incidental to the blood and tissue that it is not *this* child, even while *this* child precisely *is not*: "to say that something comes to be out of what is not, is to say that it does so out of what is not, *as something which is not*" (*Phys.* I.8 191b8–10).[40]

Distinguishing between these three elements—form, privation, and underlying material or thing—puts us on a path of thought that extricates us from the idea that change cannot be: when we identify a form, we can grasp its opposite, and by doing this we can notice that the form is specific; for example, that the continuum between white and black is different than that between soft and hard. Moreover, in laying out this opposition we notice something else, namely, the underlying thing in which these forms *are*, and we grasp how its being differs from the formal pair.

Distinguishing two senses of being (form and the underlying thing) and showing that non-being is the negation of a specific form (privation) makes being definite. This is how non-being can be incidental both to the change and to being (*Phys.* I.8 191b14–15). The distinction between what is incidental and what is essential is one of Aristotle's four primary senses of being (*Met.* V.7 1017a7–22). The distinction between the underlying thing and the form is the structure of categorical predication, another of these senses of being (*Met.* V.7 1017a22–30). Without making these distinctions, change cannot be at all. The analysis of change leads us to distinguish incidental from essential being, and underlying material from formal predicate.[41]

The purpose of distinguishing these three terms—form, privation, and underlying thing or material—according to Aristotle, is *both* to say how many being is, and to extricate change from the accusation that it depends on non-being. The terms are not applied from elsewhere, they are discovered and marked out completely within the articulation of change, and they refer essentially to change: (a) the look or form (*eidos*) is the pattern of organization that emerges through the process of coming to be, for example, white; (b) the underlying thing is that which comes to be or have that *eidos*, for example, a rabbit; and (c) the privation is that *from out of which* the form comes to be, for example, not-white.[42] Aristotle does not distinguish these terms by an appeal to a preexisting set of terms, not even between material and form. What each is, is differentiated in the event of *genesis*, that is, in the arrival of something new: the underlying thing is what remains, while the privation is what disappears (*Phys.* I.7 190a16, I.8 191a2). Each term presupposes change. Each is a phenomenal element discovered in the articulate experience of change. This means that to distinguish them does not at all give us the definition or essence of change.

Being is composite and therefore specific, therefore change can be. But what makes such composition possible? Aristotle's argument is that it is the nature of the underlying thing, also called the material.

The Underlying Being

Making non-being definite by opposing form and privation does not on its own get us out of the problem of something coming from nothing: if there were only the form and its opposite, then change and generation would still mix being and non-being. It is the underlying thing, then, that makes change and being composite: "this nature, if they had seen it, would have put them right" (*Phys.* I.8 191b34).[43] By showing what structure makes composite being possible, we can understand how Aristotle gets through the impasse.

Aristotle first needs to argue for the existence of the underlying thing, since his predecessors did not distinguish it. The first argument is that in any change, some property ceases to be, another comes to be, and something remains through the change, namely the underlying thing (*Phys.* I.7 190a18–22). The second argument is that the form which comes to be is always said *of* some being (*ousia*), or, put otherwise, "there must be something which is the coming-to-be thing" (*Phys.* I.7 190a31–36).[44] The third argument is that if form and the opposite lack are the only two principles, then change will be impossible, since opposites cannot change or affect each other, so they must change something else, namely the underlying thing (*Phys.* I.7 190b33). For example, if one puts cold butter into a hot pan, it is not the cold that becomes hot, it is the butter.

For the underlying thing to underlie changes is for it to admit of opposites at different times. To do this, it must have a certain structure: at a given stage of change, it must be both a form *and* be something itself, a *this*, which is different than the form (*Phys.* I.7 190b26). Since the underlying material is a conceptual position relative to, that is, underlying the other terms in the structure (e.g., educated and uneducated), clearly it will have its own form (e.g., being a woman), which is different from them.[45] The underlying thing must (a) be something other than the form that comes to be, and (b) be something that takes on different forms, from which it is inseparable. Thus, "the underlying thing, though one in number, is two in form" (*Phys.* I.7 190b23–24).[46] This is a structure Aristotle takes from Parmenides, who, he claims, "set down the causes as being not only one [in the Way of Truth] but in some way two [in the Way of Opinion]" (*Met.* I.3 984b3).[47] But among Aristotle's predecessors, those who argued for underlying material, or held that being was many, missed that *the underlying thing is two, not in number, but in aspect*.[48]

It is this formal, aspectual doubleness of the underlying thing that makes change composite. Being part of a composite requires each part to be distinguished from the others in its determinate character. But there is only a composite at all because the underlying thing is both itself and the form it has. Thus, the underlying thing is what makes it possible for change to be compound and definite, rather than simple and indefinite, as the impasse of the ancients held it to be.

This is clear in the relationship between the underlying thing and non-being. Aristotle takes the underlying thing to change the ontological status of "what is not." Only because of the underlying thing can Aristotle say that, in a way, non-being has being: "in this sense even the not-white is said to 'be' because that to which it is incidental *is*" (*Met.* V.7 1017a18).[49] Non-being will be neither determinate nor incidental to anything unless there is a being with a definite character that does not depend on it, and which can in an indirect way be said to "have" the privation or non-being, namely, the underlying thing. The privation is incidental to something because it is *in* or *said of* an underlying thing *whose being does not refer to it* (*Phys.* I.8 191b7). Non-being can be considered a definite, incidental element only if it is *of* a changing composite.

The most significant accomplishment in this argument, therefore, is not, as Ross holds, the discovery of the opposite privation (*sterēsis*), but the discovery that there is an underlying, remaining thing (*hupokeimenon*) (*Phys.* I.7 190a13).[50] What makes coming-to-be understandable is not privation, but the composite character of coming-to-be, and its composite character is due to the underlying thing.

Thus, the key to disentangling the description of coming-to-be from Parmenides's account of non-being is to exhibit the double character of the underlying being. Doing this makes non-being definite and incidental to change as well. If I am right, Aristotle shows that change is not contradictory by showing that the description of change does not tie being to non-being: instead, change is positive because it, and therefore being, are composite. Its composite character is secured by the existence and nature of the underlying thing. Change establishes the existence of the underlying thing, thereby establishing that being is particular and plural.

Let us turn to the big picture to examine the primary consequences of this view.

The Unruly Number of Being

If my reconstruction of Aristotle's argument is right, then he achieves both of his aims: he extricates change from the contradictions that ensnared it, and he shows how many being is. His final answer to how many aspects of being there are, is this: the sources are in a way one, because the underlying thing is one in number, and the form (*eidos*) is *in* it (*Phys*. I.7 190b23–24); but in another way the sources are two, namely, the underlying material and the form (*Phys*. I.7 190b20), and in still another way, they are three (adding privation, *sterēsis*), "because of the diverse being that belongs to them" (*Phys*. I.7 191a1–2, see 191a16–19).[51]

Being is unstable in number because there are different ways to grasp it. When we seek to grasp beings through their elements, we seem to find three, but in fact there *are* only ever two (the underlying material and some form, either the positive form or its privation, or something in-between), and these are actually only aspects of one thing (the underlying thing) and are distinct only in speech or articulate thought (*logos*). What we grasp changes depending on how we begin to number it.[52]

And yet there is a "best" answer: being is *two*. This is clear from the nature of the terms involved. First, since the opposite privation can be derived by negating the form, it is not an independent term. Second, *since what-is-not is not, it omits itself from the analysis of being*. Third, the privation is an inessential, incidental element of change. Since the non-being of vinegar is by definition something that is *not there* in the wine out of which vinegar comes, the non-being of the vinegar is clearly incidental to what in fact is, and to the changes in the fluid that are really occurring (*Met*. VIII.5 1044b29–1045a6).[53] Therefore, *the description of coming-to-be-something does not have to include non-being in the essence of change at all*. Thus, Aristotle can say that "everything comes to be out of the underlying thing and the form" (*Phys*. I.7 190b20).[54]

If coming-to-be sets out the number of changing being, there will be several consequences for being. First, the fact that form is linked to its opposite and the underlying material means that *form is not simply identified with being*. Second, non-being (*mē on*) has meaning only as a definite not-being, now named privation (*sterēsis*): it is reduced to the not-being *of something*, and tied to that something. By joining it to a particular form, Aristotle cuts non-being into pieces. Third, the underlying material is the cornerstone of this account of being, since it is by differing with the form and privation that change and being can be composite at all. Although the underlying thing is the primary being of which opposite properties can be predicated (*Cat.* 5 4a10–11, 4b3), Aristotle does not directly call it being (*ousia*) most of all (*Phys.* I.7 191a19–20, compare *Met.* VII.3), in part since the underlying thing can, in turn, also be called a form, for example, a human being. Altogether, this establishes that being itself is composite, multiple, plurivocal. Being multiple means that *being is not strictly identical with itself.* Form and material differ from one another without negation being what distinguishes them, since the negation of form is privation. Of course, one can describe the two as not sharing features, but negation is incidental to their differences. Therefore, material and form differ without negation, without the admixture of non-being.

What makes this work is that Aristotle takes being to be multiple in *aspect*. Since the tripartite ontological structure of change articulates one thing, each of its terms will not be a different *thing*, but a different *aspect* of a thing. It is only because being and non-being themselves are specific that it makes sense to claim, as Aristotle does, that whoever argues that being is one must specify in which sense it is one (*Phys.* I.2 185a20–26). This means, in short, that the word "is" only ever articulates a *particular aspect*, which differs necessarily from others: thereby we always grasp being in its *definite* character, and we only grasp some of its aspects. So when Aristotle says he agrees with Parmenides that non-being is not, but that change *is*, what makes his argument consistent is that he has shown that it is possible and necessary to address being *in its particular aspects*. The distinction of a thing into a composite of aspects is underwritten by the underlying thing, the existence of which is secured by change. Thus, it is through the analysis of change that Aristotle establishes the particularity of diverse aspects.

Had he heard it, there is a chance that Parmenides would have been persuaded by this argument, because the hidden premise that makes Parmenides's argument appear to work is that all coming-to-be is coming-to-be-*something particular, out of something general* (non-being). Before any change, the something that comes to be *is not*, and afterward, it *is*. The discrepancy between the general and particular made change appear to tie non-being to being.

Some of Parmenides's successors, such as Empedocles, attempted to allow change to exist while denying that what comes to be *is* in fact *something*: if everything changes, but the things that emerge are not in fact *beings* (i.e., *somethings*), then *being* remains fundamentally unchanged (see "Empedocles and the Being of Individuals" in chap. 5). The hope was that in this way they could allow change to be without incurring any contradiction.

By contrast, Aristotle accepts part of Parmenides's understanding of *change*: all coming-to-be is a coming-to-be of *something*; some particular *thing*, a being, genuinely comes to be. But he uses this account of change to deny the generality of being and non-being that Parmenides discovered. It is *not* the same to say "being" in general and "being-something-particular": being in the primary sense is being-something in particular.[55] So Aristotle takes the claim a step further, concluding from this that all change is *out of something particular* as well, namely the underlying thing. Therefore, he claims that *the being from which* the change comes is *not* the same as the being that emerges. They are different *aspects of being*. Thus, because coming-to-be is always particular and composite in aspect, being's structure is that of a particular aspectual composite.

The Basis for Ontological Multiplicity

I have shown that in *Physics* I the analysis of change is Aristotle's method for determining the number of elements or sources of being, and thereby the number of being. Moreover, for change to be at all, being must be multiple in aspect. The first book of Aristotle's *Physics* offers us a compelling reason for being to be multiple.

There might still be a reason to think, however, that something other than change is the real reason why Aristotle claims that being is multiple. Someone might, for example, think that the multiplicity of being is a framework that Aristotle has already worked out elsewhere, and that he is merely drawing on it in *Physics* I to solve a problem. The question arises, then, what other ground there might be for the claim that being is multiple.

The standard view is that being is multiple because of the structure of speech. The claim is that Aristotle takes being to be multiple because he thinks that the way we speak about being is how being is, in other words, that being and speech are homologous. If so, speech would be the body of evidence for the multiplicity of being. One advantage of this account is that it highlights one of the tropes in Aristotle's formula: being is *said* (*legetai*) in many ways.

One way to argue for this position is to say that Aristotle believes that different sorts of words form the basis for ontology. Since there are many words for being, being is many: each category is made up of words of a certain type, for example, size-words, type-words, position-words. But an acute *disadvantage* of this account is that, of the four primary senses of being (incidental, categorical, energetic, alethic), only categorical being corresponds to different words in this way. What makes something essential or incidental, being-potent or being-active, or being-true and being-false, can be, and usually is, implicit. For example, money-making is incidental to being a doctor, "French speaker" names a person in view *either* of her capacity *or* activity, and "she is an acrobat" is a truth claim, but none of these registers of being is signaled by a distinct word type. But the standard position might still be supported if the basis for ontology was the way words are *used*.

A stronger argument for the position is that Aristotle establishes the form-underlying pair through the analysis of predication in the *Categories* and through the analysis of this categorical structure in *Physics* I.2–3 and *Metaphysics* VII.1–16.[56] These texts have in common that they are analyses of speech and the structure of objects in speech, that is, they are *logikos* arguments.[57]

But these passages also have in common that they appear merely to *presuppose* the distinction between the underlying material and form, and then to work out issues with the different ontological types. For example, when Aristotle claims that being is categorically many in *Physics* I.3, it is merely as a counter-assertion to Parmenides's claim that it is one: "[Parmenides's] false assumption is that things are said to be in only one way, when they are said to be in many" (*Phys.* I.3 186a24–25).[58] Aristotle gives no justification, argument, or reference to support his claim. Form and the underlying thing appear in these passages, but their existence is not justified.

No matter how plausible the arguments from language are, Aristotle does not seem to make them. Moreover, Aristotle's often-repeated caveat, that two things are only separate in speech, along with his argument that the order of words in speech is not the same as the order in being (*Met.* VII.11–12), indicate that there is something other than language involved in our thinking of things.

Furthermore, this argument, that the distinction between the senses of being is derived from language, does not explain why in *Physics* I.7 Aristotle turns to *change* to articulate the number of sources, and thereby the number of being, when he should have proceeded logically (*logikōs*). Besides, if the distinction between the senses of being were derived from an ontology of language, the fact that it happens to solve the impasse about change would be a truly spectacular coincidence, and would fly in the face of that other *logos*-based ontology, namely, the poem of Parmenides.

To more rigorously rebut the claim that language is the basis of ontological multiplicity in Aristotle, I want to argue for a stronger claim, namely, that the very distinction between form and the underlying thing depends on change. I shall try to make this claim plausible by making four points: (i) it is not clear that form and underlying thing can be distinguished on the basis of language alone, because in speech predicate and subject are exchangeable; (ii) change appears to establish the distinction between form and material; (iii) what distinguishes primary being is its singularity, its underlying character, and most of all, its ability to change; and finally, (iv) change establishes the particularity of being which makes a distinction between subject and predicate possible in the first place. I shall take the claims in order.

(i) Based on predication alone, it seems impossible to make a stable distinction between the subject and the predicate. The claim that one of these is prior and the other is secondary is not immediately evident, even from an analysis of the grammar of sentences. For one thing, if we take an inventory of terms, for example, "tree," "green," "moisture," we cannot tell which are subjects and which are predicates by looking at the terms themselves apart from their referents. Moreover, looking at usage does not solve the problem. In many instances of the A is B sentence form, we *just do not say* that B is A; for example, while we *would* say, for instance, that the tree is red, we would not then say that the red is tree. Nevertheless, each term *can* serve as either subject or predicate, for example, we say that this plant is a tree, and also that a tree is a plant. So if in certain contexts we would not switch their roles, nevertheless, in other expressions we do. In sum: the principle that distinguishes subject and predicate is not evident, or at least not straightforwardly evident, either from the terms themselves or from usage itself. This ambiguity of subject and predicate is what enables the formulation of a Platonic "theory of forms," in which the real beings are the predicates rather than the particulars.

(ii) I contend that it is in *Physics* I.7–9 that Aristotle gives his core argument for the distinction between material and form. For one thing, he indicates elsewhere that the *Physics* provides the formal articulation of the concepts of material (*hulē*) and form (*eidos*) (e.g., GC I.317b13, II 329a27, *Met.* XIII 1076a8–9).[59] For another, he claims explicitly that material, like place, only appears to be at all because of change: "If [something] is altered, there is something which is now white but [was] black, and is now hard but formerly [was] soft, which is why we say material is something . . ." (*Phys.* IV.4 211b31–33, my trans.). This quotation could be making either an epistemological claim, that we only *notice* that material is something in examining change, or it could be making an ontological claim, that material only exists for changing things. Either way, without material being evident, we will be unable to distinguish it from form, which means that change is required for us to grasp the fundamental beings; we gain access to hylomorphic ontology through change.

But it is not just our *awareness* of the distinction between material and form that depends on change. Only things that change have material: "Nor is there a matter of everything, but only of such things of which there is coming-to-be and change into each other; but such things as are, or are not, without [such] changing, there is no matter of these" (*Met.* VIII.5 1044b27–29).[60] Fundamentally, to be material is to be what underlies a change.[61] This is what makes material a good candidate for primary being (*ousia*): "it is clear that the material too is primary being [*ousia*], for in all changes between contraries, there is something that underlies the changes" (*Met.* VIII.1 1042a33–35).[62] The distinction between form and underlying material depends, then, on change. Form and material can be distinguished at all because the form is what changes, while the underlying thing is what has it and *also* has its own persisting identity.

(iii) Another feature of categorical predication shows the importance of change, which I can only mention here due to its complexity: the very category of being an underlying thing seems to be distinguished by being the subject of change. Indeed, what distinguishes being (*ousia*) most of all in the *Categories* is that it is the subject of change: "The most distinctive mark of primary being [*ousia*] appears to be that, while remaining numerically one and the same, it is capable of admitting contrary qualities. . . . for it is by itself changing that it does so" (*Cat.* 5 4a10–11, 4b3).[63] Therefore, change is meaningfully involved in being a *this* and in being the thing that underlies properties, two of the criteria for the primary sense of categorical being.[64]

(iv) Finally, all change is necessarily particular. The fact that only particular things can change suggests that the concept of the *this*, which is one of the determinations of primary being, is inseparable from, or at least revealed by, change. I take this to be the force of Aristotle's argument that what changes must *be* (*Met.* IX.3 1047a33–b1). For since change cannot *be* except as something definite, singular, and finite, the subject of change must be a *this* (*tode ti*).[65] This is why it is natural for Aristotle to refer in the *Physics* to "what is at-work and particular" (*ta men energounta kai ta kath' hekaston*) (*Phys.* II.3 195b17–18).[66]

It is not controversial to say that Aristotle explicitly uses change to lead us to ontological concepts in *Physics* I. For change to be, being *must* be multiple. Aristotle claims explicitly that the analysis of change decides how many being is, both for his predecessors and for himself.

I argued that the framework of the argument of *Physics* I is this: Aristotle declared that the question of how many principles (*archai*) there are is the same as the question of how many beings there are. Answering this question requires an account of what being is, and why, that is, an ontology. The ancients, Aristotle argued, declared that being is one and undifferentiated because they rejected the existence of coming-to-be. He gives his own answer to how many beings there are by examining the phenomenon of coming-to-be (*genesis*). For coming-to-be to exist, being and non-being cannot be mixed. For coming-to-be to exist, then, being must be multiple, positive, and definite in aspect. Specifically, it must be such that form and its opposite, privation, are distinguished both from one another and from an underlying material or thing. The underlying thing must possess the special capacity (*dunamis*) to be each of them, while also being different than they are. The underlying thing thus allows being to be composite, and its composite character means that both being and non-being are specific or definite: to be is to be something in particular, and the same goes for not-being. Thus, for Aristotle, all coming-to-be is coming to be something, and all being in the primary sense is being-something in particular. The basis for the claim that being is many is not language, or not only language, since the distinction between underlying material and form depends on change.

In claiming that change is the basis of the argument for the multiplicity of being in *Physics* I, I do not intend to make a strong claim about the history of Aristotle's thinking on the subject. Given the range and diversity of his work, it seems unlikely that he came to formulate this fundamentally original ontological position by following just one line of thought. It is much more plausible that he arrived at it by having traveled many pathways. For this reason, it seems unlikely that the idea of a plural ontology came to Aristotle solely through the examination of change, and for the same reason, it also seems unlikely that it came to Aristotle on purely logical or metaphysical grounds. But telling such a story was not my aim. What I attempted to establish was, instead, that change offers the strongest available reason for thinking that being is multiple in aspect. *Physics* I.7–9 provides the best and clearest argument for ontological multiplicity that is available in the corpus.

For all of its accomplishments, the argument of *Physics* I only opened the door to the claim that change *is*. The analysis dealt with change, but it neither defined what change is, nor established *that* it exists, because it was made within the constraints of categorical being. To define change, and show that it *is*, it is necessary to establish a different sense of being entirely, in *Physics* III.1–2.

CHAPTER 2

The Demonstration of Change in *Physics* III.1–2

Chapter 1 developed what I called the Descriptive Argument for change in *Physics* I. I argued that Aristotle's distinctions between the aspects of change—underlying thing, form, and its opposite privation—made it possible to describe changes coherently, without mixing being with non-being. These same distinctions, he claims, are his argument for how many elements there are, and thereby how many being is. Thus, change both requires being to be many, and specifies some of the ways that it is many. However, the descriptive argument is *only the first part* of a demonstration that change exists, since while it marks out the parts involved in change, it does nothing to define change itself.

This chapter examines the *second part* of Aristotle's argument for the existence of change. *Physics* III.1–2 fills in what was missing from the Descriptive Argument in *Physics* I by defining change and demonstrating its existence. To do this Aristotle must do two things: he must make an even higher-level distinction between aspects of being than he did in *Physics* I, namely between categorical being and what I will call the dynamic-energetic sense of being, and he must make potency and being-complete (*entelecheia*) ontological terms, so that together they can establish that change is real. The success of this demonstration will retroactively legitimate his use of change in *Physics* I to distinguish between underlying material, form, and privation.

In this chapter my focus turns to the sense of being that is most of all related to change, namely the dynamic-energetic sense. This sense of being is composed of a cluster of terms all related to operation (*ergon*) and completion (*telos*): potency (*dunamis*), being-at-work (*energeia*), and being-complete (*entelecheia*). Subsequent chapters deal with these terms, building up Aristotle's argument that sourcehood determines what is primary in being (*ousia*).

The Argument of *Physics* III.1–2

Let me recap the reasons why a second stage of argument is required to establish the existence of change, and then outline how the second stage works. The importance of change to physics and ontology was well established in *Physics* I-II, which argued that being is multiple, and that nature is an internal source of change (*Phys.* II.1 192b22–24). But what change itself is went unexamined. Aristotle says as much when he turns to the subject of change in the first lines of *Physics* III (*Phys.* III.1 200b12–15). Through the analysis of change itself, we are meant, implicitly, to find what it is to be a source of change, and thereby to understand the kind of source that Aristotle calls a nature.

Whether change exists could not have been resolved in *Physics* I or II because the terms that Aristotle distinguished there presupposed change and described only the predicates and other categorical beings involved. Change still lacked a definition. Without knowing what it was, no demonstration was possible. Aristotle pointed to a further argument in *Physics* I.8 when, after finding his way out of the argument against the existence of change, he noted that there was more to say: "That is one way of handling the matter [i.e., the existence of change]; another is to point out that the same things [i.e., underlying material and form] may be spoken of either as potential or as at-work. That, however, is dealt with in greater detail elsewhere" (*Phys.* I.8 191b27–29).[1] Aristotle recalls this promissory note in *Physics* III.1 in distinguishing between two of the four primary senses of being, namely, the categorical and the dynamic-energetic (*Phys.* III.1 200b26–27). In the definition of change that follows he makes use of the concepts of potency and complete being (*entelecheia*) (*Phys.* III.1 201a9–11). Moreover, he concludes his explanation of the definition with the claim that although change is difficult to see, it does in fact admit of being (*Phys.* III.2 202a3–4). I take the bulk of *Physics* III.1, therefore, to be the second stage of the argument for the existence of change. Because it is a single argument, this chapter will present and analyze its stages step by step.

Now, Aristotle spends a quarter of the chapter setting up the distinction between the categorical and energetic senses of being (*Phys.* III.1 200b27–201a10). This, I contend, is the most important distinction in the definition of change. Though it is usually overlooked, this section makes two points central to the project of the *Physics* as a whole: it serves both to show that change is describable by the categories, and that change itself is defined not through them, but through being-potent and being-complete. The key to Aristotle's argument for the being of change is that he uses potency (*dunamis*) and complete activity (*entelecheia*) in an ontologically meaningful way: it is because each is a certain meaning of *being* that they can establish the being of change.

The definition of change (at *Phys.* III.1 201a9–11) is followed by examples that show the relationship between its terms (lines 11–19) and then an examination of consequences of the overlap between the terms, namely, that they can account both for how things change one another, and for unmoved movers (lines 19–29). Aristotle then identifies what the subject of change is by distinguishing the categorical concept of the underlying material, (e.g., a being insofar as it is a bronze thing) from the being-in-potency (e.g., the being insofar as it can be a statue) (lines a29-b5). Having shown that being-in-potency is a definite way that particular beings are, Aristotle closes with the argument that change exists: it exists because the being of identifiable, discrete, potent beings is necessarily connected to change, which completes their potency (lines b5–15). By marking out how change comes from being, and how obviously existing beings require it, Aristotle clinches the argument against Parmenides's refutation of change.

It is important to note that Aristotle does not define change by reference to space and time. He argues that change is ontologically prior to time, and that time is the number of change (*Phys.* IV.11 219b1–2). Recent scholarship has shown that he does not presuppose time in his account of change, and this chapter upholds that claim; in his account, change has a continuity and order that is independent of time.[2]

Categorical and Energetic Being (*Phys.* III.1 200b26–201a9)

Aristotle sets the stage for his definition of change by insisting on the distinction between two of the four primary senses of being: the categorical and the energetic (*Met.* V.7, VI.2 1026a33–b2, IX.1 1045b27–35, etc.). This distinction is pivotal, since no account of categorical properties can give a definition of change; it can only specify the features a particular thing has at a certain point in the change, or define a continuum along which change occurs. But most of this section consists of an argument that, although change is not a categorical being, every change is categorically definite.

The first, most important task is to distinguish between the ways that being is said: "There is, on the one hand, what is something by being-in-completion [*entelecheiai*] alone, and what is [something] by being-potent and being-in-completion, and on the other hand there is the *this*, the so much, the such kind, and similarly with the other categories of being" (*Physics* III.1 200b26–29, my trans.). Speaking of something as being-complete or being-potent, on the one hand, and of something bearing categorical properties, on the other, is to address it as possessing two fundamentally different, mutually irreducible sorts of being. Of categorical beings, Aristotle lists primary being ("this"), quantity ("so much"), and quality ("such kind"). Categorical beings are either "said of" things as subjects, the way that being Socrates or being human is said to be his being, or they are said to be "in" things as dependent (*sumbebēkos*) beings or properties, the way a size or a color is *in something* or *belongs to it* (*Cat.* 2). Essential properties are not, of course, equivalent to dependent properties: the former *are* what underlies, but the latter *belong* to what underlies. This relationship between subject and predicate is the structure of categorical being.

Now, the import of this distinction is that the terms by which Aristotle will define change—*dunamis* and *energeia/entelecheia*—*are not categorical beings*, and they are not assimilable to categorical structure. He brought up the distinction between categorical and energetic being in order to clarify that it is energetic being which defines change. Aristotle underscores the importance of this distinction when, after a brief discussion of the relationship between change and categorical being, he reemphasizes that we are using the energetic sense of being to define change: "Making sure [*diēirēmenou*] to divide being-in-completion and being-in-potency by each kind . . ." (*Phys.* III.1 201a10, my trans.).³ A primary task for his discussion of the definition of change (most notably, of the "as" clause, as I will show) is to clarify what it is to grasp something as being-in-potency and being-in-completion.

Potency and being-at-work are neither the names nor the species of something, nor are they attributes said to be in or to belong to a thing. This is an important point: the capacity to dance is not a *property* of things, nor is it a class or category that beings have, and the activity of dancing is an expression of a being, the way the being *is being something*. It may be that certain properties are essential conditions to be able to dance, for example, having limbs that allow for self-movement, but unlike her attributes, her being-able-to-dance *just is* her being-a-dancer.⁴

The distinction, then, between categorical and energetic being is a topographical remark that helps us to locate the account of change among the senses of being. It elicits a host of misconceptions, however, of which two must be addressed. The first of these is the idea that "actuality" (*energeia*) is the only way for something to be, or that potency could not in some sense be on its own. Since being-potent is not the same as actively being, we might be tempted to identify not-being with potency, and object to the idea that a potency could be on its own; we might think, then, that a thing cannot be at all by being only potent. But Aristotle clearly takes potent beings to be in their own right. To take just one example: "it is clear that, of what appear to be primary beings [*ousiai*], most are potencies" (*Metaphysics* VII.16 1040b5, my trans.). This strongly suggests that being a potency is a distinct way that identifiable beings are what they are.⁵

My claim, then, is that Aristotle's distinction between potency and being-complete or being-at-work (*energeia*) describes two distinct ways of being something identifiably independent: being a French speaker is to be a whole person considered insofar as you are capable of speaking French, a being considered, as it were, from the point of view of this function. This means that "being-capable" names a functional complex of one's physiology, psychology, politics, and history, for example. Being-complete and being-at-work are not the only words for "reality." A thing can be-potent in the midst of the world without us needing to re-describe this as "actuality." My claim here is that, while it is true that a person must *also actively* be, say, human, in order to be a capable dancer, the one subject is not derived from the other: they are two aspects of the same being. Thus, it is correct to describe the subject as *being a dancer in capacity* in her own right.

The second misconception is the related idea that, for Aristotle, potency and "actuality" cannot be at once. Those attributing this view to him hold that the two operate as alternating actual states.[6] But to say "what is [something] by being-potent and being-in-completion" is clearly to suggest that they *are* at one and the same time (*Phys.* III.1 200b26–28). Potency and being-complete are not mutually exclusive modal states of categorical properties: it is not Aristotle's position that at a given time a woman is six feet tall in *only* one of two ways, either actually or potentially. It is a mistake to attribute this view to him. If Aristotle did believe this, it would be hard to find a place in his works where it would be more important than here for him to say so explicitly, in the course of the definition of change. He should have said that each property belongs to the categorical subject *either* potentially *or* actually, and not at once, but he did not do so.[7]

Another passage that indicates this clearly is in *Metaphysics* VII.16: "the parts that are intimately related to the parts of the soul . . . have being both in full activity [*entelecheiai*] and in potency [*dunamei*], by having sources of change stemming from something in the joints" (*Met.* VII.16 1040b5–14).[8] In *Metaphysics* IX.3 1047a11–29, Aristotle gives his sharpest argument for both the difference and compatibility of potency and activity: the absence of a capacity is incapacity, and while a thing is active, it cannot be incapable.[9] This is especially clear for living things: a thing is alive only while it is capable of being alive: living things must be both in-potency *and* in-completion at once, with respect to the capacity to live, or they would not be alive.

Change Is Categorically Determinate (*Phys.* III.1 200b27–201a9)

In the next stage of the preamble to the definition of change, Aristotle makes three points in quick succession, without announcing their subject matter or purpose. The preamble is so densely formulated that it is often quickly and carelessly read, which leads readers to blend the three points together.

Although these points do form a single argument about the definiteness of being, to understand this they must be distinguished:

(1) In the category of relation, change is definite rather than indefinite (*Phys.* III.1 200b27–33, compare V.2 225b10–13).
(2) The properties of changing things are categorically definite, that is, they are articulated by quality, quantity, relation, and so on (*Phys.* III.1 200b33–201a3).
   a. change is grasped in and through each category, not outside of the categories
   b. but change cannot be defined by these categories, but only through the energetic sense of being.
(3) Categorical predicates are said to be or not to be (*Phys.* III.1 201a4–9).
   a. being and not-being are the poles of change[10]
   b. potencies are for both poles (*Phys.* III.1 201b, *Met.* IX.3 1047a28–29, IX.9 1051a10–12)

The first point is a discussion of the category of relation. It establishes that change relations are determinate. Change is not itself a relative being. Moreover, relation cannot give us a definition of change, because describing one of the things in the relation as the agent and the other as the patient is to presuppose change. From the argument about relation, Aristotle immediately draws the conclusion that all change occurs within the categories (*Phys.* III.1 200b33–201a3):[11]

> For (1) what changes always changes either in being [*ousia*], or in amount, or in quality, or in place, and (2) there is nothing to take hold of which is common to these, and is neither, in our manner of speaking, a *this*, nor a this much, nor an of-this-kind, nor any of the other categorical beings: so that (3) neither motion nor change will be anything apart from the [categorical] things named, since there is, in fact, nothing other than the things named. (*Phys.* III.1 200b33–201a3)[12]

If change were completely unrelated to the categories, then determinate knowledge of it would be impossible: if change had nothing to do with the categories, then how could you say that a flower gained a quantity of heat from the sun, or that its color changed from green to white? But change is not *defined* through categorical being: change is not the quantity itself, but its *increase* or *decrease*. Change, and by extension the energetic sense of being, thus never exist apart from the categories; all changes are articulable in categories. Since change is defined using the dynamic-energetic sense of being, it does not demarcate a different *realm* of being, it articulates the same being, the same world, but in a different way or aspect.

Point (2) says that there is nothing common to change that we do *not* take hold of determinately in a specific category. Put positively: we *do* grasp what is common to change, but this is not by grasping it separate from the categories. It is not the case that each change is completely and adequately grasped in categorical terms, nor is it the case that change transcends categorical predication altogether or blends categories together. There is something that is the same between change in different categories, but we grasp this one category at a time. We grasp change as something common, which differs from the categories, but we only ever do it by grasping each change within a particular category. This being so, we *can* grasp change itself as a whole; it is not divided up into parts or dispersed among the categories. Change is not broken into pieces, one in each of the categories; it is not partially in each category, it is complete in each. Aristotle uses the same concept of immanent differentiation to describe common sensibles in *Soul* III.1 425a14–425b10.

Aristotle says, instead, that what is *common* to changes is not itself graspable in terms of this or that predicate category, but only *in* and *through* it. We can grasp change as something that happens in each different category, but whenever we say that something has changed, we always begin and remain with something determinate, that is, with a change in place, kind, amount, and so on.

Yet, although we grasp that change occurs by noticing that a thing has changed in size or position (categorically), Aristotle is claiming that change is not definable through size or position or through any of the other categories. Although change is determinate and happens within the categories, it is not defined by the categories, but by *dunamis* and *entelecheia*. These are grasped *within* the categories, but they are neither derived from, nor subfeatures of, nor even subordinate to the categories. Change is grasped within the definite categories, but is not reducible to them.

After these remarks, Aristotle observes that things belong to the categories in two ways: by either being or not being each of them (*Phys.* III.1 201a4–9). Again, this is a description of the categorical sense of being, namely of privation and form, so it is a mistake to substitute "being-potent" and "being-at-work" for "not-being" and "being."[13]

In the preamble to the definition of change, then, Aristotle has done two things: he has contrasted the categorical and the energetic way of speaking of change, noting that each sense of being speaks of change differently. In addition, he has demonstrated that change is categorically determinate. Potency and being-complete are not reduced to modal states of the categories. These senses of being are, instead, ways of considering independent beings as manifesting different sorts of structure altogether: the categorical sense addresses a being as a subject bearing a collection of properties, whereas the energetic sense addresses the entire being in view of its functions.

The Definition of Change (*Phys.* III.1 201a9–21)

Using the energetic sense of being, Aristotle gives his definition of change: "Making sure to divide being-complete and being-potent by each type [of change],[14] the being-in-completion [*entelecheiai*] of the being-in-potency [*tou dunamei ontos*], as such, is change" (*Phys.* III.1 201a9–11, my trans.). For each of the kinds of change (e.g., alteration, locomotion, learning, ripening), change is the being-complete of the potential being, as potential being. The parts of the definition that require interpretation are (a) what *entelecheia* means, (b) the meaning of "the being insofar as it is in-potency,"[15] and (c) the meaning of the "as" (*hēi*) clause. Thankfully, the rest of *Physics* III.1 addresses each of these, either implicitly or explicitly.[16]

A more English-sounding definition would run: "Change is the fulfilment of a being insofar as it is capable" (*Phys.* III.1 201a9–11, my trans.). Aristotle gives a sense of what he means by the terms by substituting other terms in subsequent passages. For instance, he will speak of "the being-complete of a potent [thing] *as* a potent [thing]" (*Phys.* III.1 201b4–6, my trans.), or say that "the being-complete of the alterable, as alterable, is alteration" (*Phys.* III.3 202b25, my trans., compare 201a11–12).[17] His examples range from rather general types such as alteration and growth (*Cat.* 14) to richly specific ones like learning, ripening, rolling, and leaping (*Phys.* III.1 201a11–21). Change is always specific. Grasping it requires us to use the terms appropriate to each particular change. Each type of change has a potency and completion proper to it.

To be the sort of *entelecheia* specific to each particular potent thing is to be change: the words that substitute for *entelecheia* include "building," "carrying," and "alteration." Some scholars argue that *entelecheia* is the wrong word, apparently motivated by the idea that "actuality" (a misleading translation of *entelecheia*, as I argue in chapter 3) means something static in opposition to change. There are signs that this is a problem: Ross renders *entelecheia* here, and here alone, as "actualization," thereby including change in its own definition.[18] Anagnostopoulos makes a case that Aristotle should have used *energeia* instead of *entelecheia*.[19] And yet, with very few exceptions, Aristotle uses *entelecheia* to define the different kinds of change.[20] But if *entelecheia* does not mean "actuality," then the motive for modifying or replacing it loses its force. I take *entelecheia* to be the culmination, success, accomplishment, or completion of the potency.[21]

Next, several sorts of expressions stand in for the "being that is in-potency" (*to dunamei on*): from substantive adjectives such as *tou alloiōtou*, "the alterable," and *tou oikodomētou*, "the buildable," to *to dunaton*, "the potent [thing]."[22] Understanding this term will be one of our main goals in what follows, since the demonstration of change hinges on it.

Now, to interpret the definition and its explanation, we need to grasp what it is meant to accomplish. I shall argue that what is at stake is whether change can be said to be at all, and that this gives us the most natural reading of *Physics* III.1–2. Brague and Anagnostopoulos come close to arguing for this position in arguing that in the definition Aristotle is responding to Parmenides, but they each read the definition as establishing the conceptual consistency of movement rather than its being, which appears to be a distinction without a difference.[23]

Current scholarship on the definition takes its task to be to distinguish between change and either the product of change, actuality, or being.[24] Scholars usually derive the potency from its end state.[25] Some scholars distinguish between the potency for change and the potency for being (i.e., the product of the change).[26] While my view is compatible with such a distinction between capacity for change and capacity to be, it adheres to Aristotle's argument at *Metaphysics* IX.3 1047a30–35 that the capacity for change naturally implies being. If a capacity for change necessarily *is*, then the being of change depends neither on a further product nor on a distinct end state. Other scholars argue that it is only during a change that potency actually is.[27] But this view leads to several complications: first, this view holds that potencies only exist while the actuality exists,[28] a view that Aristotle argues makes change impossible (*Met.* IX.3 1046a29–1047a29).[29] Second, the motive for these scholars is to avoid the so-called Product Puzzle—the idea that the definition of change is primarily concerned with distinguishing between change and its finished product. The existence of this Puzzle has been challenged on textual and philosophical grounds.[30] There is good reason to think the Product Puzzle is not important to Aristotle, since he clearly contradicts the idea that change and its product must be mutually distinct phases: "house-building . . . comes to be and *is* at the same time as the house" (*Met.* IX.8 1050a28–30).[31] I hold, instead, that potencies have a way of being that is meaningfully independent of actuality.

There are, therefore, two common assumptions that we must set aside: first, if to equate "actuality" with "being" we made actuality the opposite of change, then it would be self-contradictory to use the word to define change. Therefore, we must avoid opposing the two concepts. Second, a similar problem emerges if we oppose actuality and potency: doing so makes the definition incoherent. If something in-potency does not qualify as being, then we must either constitute exotic beings (i.e., actual potencies), or make potency a modal state that alternates with actuality, either of which would make Parmenides right that change blends being (*entelecheia*) and non-being (*dunamis*).[32]

Let this suffice as an overview of other views and their problems. What is needed here is not a repetition of the diagnosis, but a cure. So, instead of directly taking on the puzzles these views confront, it will be more useful to set out a positive account, in the hope that it solves or dissolves these puzzles.

How a Definition Can Demonstrate the Existence of Change

After giving the definition of change, Aristotle outlines the demonstration he will give in the final passage of the chapter for the existence of change (*Physics* III.1 201b5–13): "That this is change is clear from this. Whenever the buildable [*oikodomēton*], as the very thing we say it to be [namely "buildable"], should be-in-completion [*entelecheiai*], it is being built [*oikodomeitai*], and this is building [*oikodomēsis*]" (*Phys.* III.1 201a17–19, my trans.). Put generally, whenever the thing-insofar-as-it-is-capable has the completion proper to its capability, it is being changed, and this is what change is. Aristotle says that examples should be sufficient to show the truth of this definition. In showing what change is, Aristotle also shows that it exists.

The claim that Aristotle aims to show *that* change exists is important to my argument in this chapter, and there are several things to say in its support. First, in *Physics* I.8 Aristotle announces that a way to reject Parmenides's argument against the existence of change is to describe it using potency and activity, and in *Physics* III.1–2 he does exactly that. Second, as I argued in chapter 1, distinguishing the (static) elements of change, as Aristotle does in *Physics* I.7–9, does not define change, which means that it does not establish the existence of change. Until it is established, he cannot use its analysis to argue that the sources of being are multiple. Third, he gives a definition: change belongs to the "genus" of things being-complete (*entelecheia*) and is differentiated or specified by being *of* something being-potent (*dunamei on*). Fourth, he says in *Physics* III.2 that this definition shows that change admits of being.

The *if-it-is* question is not just about contingent things, but "is ultimately asked and answered at the level of metaphysical analysis."[33] But *if it is* and *what it is* are intimately related: "it belongs to the same act of thinking to make clear both what something is and whether it is" (*Met.* VI.1 1025b16–18, compare *Post. An.* II.1 89b21–35, II.8 93a4).[34] Definition has an important role, then, in establishing the existence of a being on a metaphysical level.

Or rather, perhaps it is closer to the truth to say that *some kinds* of definition have an important role. For there are several types of definition, and only some definitions establish both that something is and what it is.[35] So for example, when considering things that have a cause outside of themselves, a definition of what something is can show that it exists because the definition is also a demonstrative syllogism (*Post. An.* II.8 93a15–27).[36] The same formula can answer two questions: for example, "What is thunder?" "The quenching of fire in a cloud" (definition); and "Why does it thunder?" "Because fire is quenched in the cloud" (demonstration). The definition is displayed in the demonstration, and vice versa.[37]

Such a demonstration, Aristotle says, is dialectical. It is not a *deductive* demonstration, but the kind of demonstration that *manifests* what something is: "Although there is no . . . demonstrative syllogism of what it is to be by nature, it is through demonstrative syllogism that *what it is* by nature is manifested. So we conclude that, for anything that has a cause distinct from itself, what it is to be cannot be known *without* demonstration, nor can it be demonstrated" (*Post. An.* II.8 93b15–21, my trans.). For things that have causes distinct from themselves, the only way to know them is *through* such a demonstration or showing forth (*Post. An.* II.8 93b15–21). Such a manifestation of *what it is* is also a manifestation *that it is*.

But does Aristotle's definition of change fit this description? Yes. He argues that such demonstrations must provide a middle term or outside cause. Any of the four causes—material, form, outside source, and purpose—will do. In the demonstration of change, Aristotle provides the material cause as differentia: change is x, there are subjects of change, that is, beings whose being is inseparable from change, therefore change *is*.

Potency Extends Beyond What Is the Case
(*Phys.* III.1 201a19–201a27)

The definition of change also distinguishes the different aspects of change precisely enough to make possible the science of causality involving multiple beings. It thus allows Aristotle to make good on the promise, in the opening of *Physics* II, that such a science is possible: "Since some things are both in potency and in *entelecheia* not at once or not according to the same thing, but for example hot in *entelecheia* and cold in potency, then many things will already be doing [something to] and undergoing [something] because of one another, so that all will be at once doing and undergoing" (*Phys.* III.1 201a19–23, my trans.).[38] Most beings are capable of being or doing things that they are not doing at present, and Aristotle shows from this that things mutually affect each other. A single potency is *for* opposites that cannot actively be at the same time. What can be wet can also be dry, but it cannot be both at once (see *Met.* IX.9 1051a5–15). This means that a thing's capacities extend beyond its current condition. But if something is capable of being different than it actually is, *it can be affected by other things at the same time as it affects them*, as when a hot thing heats a cold thing, and is at the same time cooled by it. Thus, the passage reads roughly this way: in the ways that they are not potentially and actively the same thing at the same time, but are instead able to be something they are not actively being now, things will act on each other and be acted upon by each other at the same time. Thus, he concludes, "everything which causes change is also changed, as has been said" (*Phys.* III.2 202a3–5).[39] In a word, the disjunction between being-potent and being-completely implies that change extends beyond individual beings to involve several beings mutually affecting one another. Still, Aristotle says, not all sources of change are changed in return, most notably, what changes things by being desired.

Because the same potency is for *both* opposites, a thing can both be capable of φ-ing and be-completely-φ-ing at the same time. This means that *dunamis* is compatible with and overlaps with its proper *energeia* and *entelecheia*. When potency extends beyond what is the case, beings affect one another. Having just examined how his definition accounts for the mutual affection of different beings, he turns to the problem of self-movement: why do some things move themselves, while other things do not (*Physics* II.1 192b22–24)?

The "As" Clause: Potency and the Underlying Thing (*Phys.* III.1 201a29-b4)

In the passage that follows, Aristotle explains the meaning and role of the "as" (*hēi*) in the definition: it specifies what it means to be a being capable of change. The passage begins with a distinction between being bronze and being able to be a man, and it culminates in a distinction between the being that underlies change and the being insofar as it is potent, showing these to be phenomenally distinct, independent aspects of a being.

The way Aristotle concludes the section on the "as" clause shows how it contributes to the definition of change and gives us the clearest view of what being-potent is: "Since they are not the same, just as color is not the same as visible, it is clear that change is the being-in-completion of the potent thing [*tou dunatou*], as potent" (*Physics* III.1 201a29–b4, my trans.). The color of the thing is a what-sort or quality, a categorical property said to be in the thing. A thing's being-colored is a property that obtains simply because the thing is what it is. Insofar as a thing is a being with properties, it does not depend on other beings, but coincides with itself, and it is discursively simple. By this I mean that the articulation of the colored being needs to refer only to that being for its being-colored to be evident. It is this apparent self-coincidence of categorical being that would lead to the claim that being is self-identical presence and inspire so much criticism in the twentieth century.

On the other hand, as visible the thing is named in and through its relation to potential and actual perception, that is, in relation to an other. To talk about a thing as visible is to grasp it through a different sense of being rather than to grasp it through its categorical properties. A being addressed in this way is not grasped according to a property that inheres simply and in its own being, but through its being as a communal and active thing. It is thus grasped *transitively*. Potency is potency *for something*, through which it depends on another. As visible, a thing is grasped through a transitive aspect, through an active relationship between it and something else, or itself as something else. This transitive aspect of a being, namely its being-potent, is most clearly visible in changes accomplished by the action of one thing on another, but is not limited to those.

Aristotle argues for the distinction as follows:

> By "as" I mean this. [1] Bronze is in potency a man [*dunamei andrias*]; [2] all the same it is not the being-complete of bronze *as* bronze that is change. [3] For it is not the same to be bronze as to be something in-potency [*dunamei tini*], while [3] if it were the same, simply and according to *logos*, [2] change would be the being-complete of bronze *as* bronze, but it is not the same thing, as has been said . . . [3] Since they are not the same, just as "color" is not the same as "visible," it is clear that change is the being-in-completion of the potent thing [*tou dunatou*], as potent. (*Physics* III.1 201a29–b4, my trans.)

In the standard view, the "as" or *qua* phrase is meant to prevent the definition from applying to the product of change. But nothing resembling this worry comes up: "the idea that the *qua* phrase neutralizes a subsequent threat of picking out the products of change is in tension with the grammar of Aristotle's definition and incompatible with his own explanation of the phrase's function."[40]

Aristotle's worry is this: if "bronze" *itself* meant "being potentially the shape of a man," then it would move itself. Bronze *is* clearly capable of being shaped like a man. A piece of bronze is completely being (*entelecheia*) bronze. So if *being bronze* meant *being potentially shaped like a man*, then the being-potentially-shaped would be completely, that is, the being-in-potency would be-completely, so it would change spontaneously into the shape of a man. Thus, by *modus tollens*, what it is to be bronze, is *not* what it is to be potentially a man.

The empirical question that motivates this passage, then, is the question "why does bronze *not* change itself?" In the standard view, the answer is that its potency is dormant.[41] The preamble, however, set up a much sharper answer: it is different to address them as categorical beings (i.e., bronze) than it is to address them as energetic and capable of something (i.e., capable of changing itself).

Aristotle means the "as" clause, then, to distinguish the thing's potency from its character as an underlying thing. The distinction here is not between layers of change (as though bronze were "under" the potency) or phases of change (as though the important thing were that change happened before the product appeared), but between the being of the bronze underlying thing, and its being-potent. Bronze does not move itself because being bronze is not being potent, and being potent means to depend on another, in this case, a craftsman.

Now, there is no such distinction between being a natural being and being a source of change.[42] When what something is (its categorical being) includes being a source of change (its dynamic-energetic being), it will move itself (*Met.* IX.1 1046a28–29). Such self-moving beings include elements, living things, and heavenly bodies (*Met.* IX.8 1050b18–28).[43]

To understand what is at stake in this passage, and therefore what it accomplishes, it will help to say why this is a difficult distinction to make. For the self-moving bronze to be a problem, two things must be the case: first, being bronze must be a way to be complete (*entelecheia*). If not, there would be no possibility that it would change itself. Second, bronze and its being-capable of being a statue must be hard to discern without the "as" clause. Addressing this difficulty clarifies what being-in-potency (*to dunamei on*) is.

Disentangling Categorical and Energetic Being (*Phys.* III.1 201a35–b3)

The quotation above omits a dense parenthetical remark that explains, more thoroughly, the distinction between the underlying thing (*to hupokeimenon*) and its being-able-to-be something (*to dunasthai*) (*Phys.* III.1 201a35–b3): Aristotle argues that unlike the underlying thing, which is one, a single potency is capable of opposites. The difference in number shows that the underlying thing is not the same as being-potent.

To understand what this contributes to our understanding of being-in-potency, several remarks are in order. First, the underlying thing is inseparable from being-potent. In chapter 1 we saw that the underlying thing is one in number, but two in form: in addition to the categorical attribute that it has, the underlying thing also has its *own* form, for example, bronze or flesh (*Phys.* I.7 190b23–24; see *Met.* VII.11 1036a30–35). But it can have opposite attributes at different times: "The most distinctive mark of primary being [*ousia*] appears to be that, while remaining numerically one and the same, it is *capable* of admitting contrary qualities. . . . for it is by itself changing that it does so" (*Cat.* 5 4a10–11, 4b3).[44] What distinguishes the primary underlying thing (*ousia*), Aristotle argues, is that it is capable of being opposites, and potency is what makes this possible: one bronze, two potencies (to not be a man or to be a man).

However, and secondly, this means that, like the underlying thing, being-potent is *also* said doubly (*dichōs*): it is one in number but two in meaning, articulation, or form. For, elsewhere, Aristotle describes the capacity for opposites as a single capacity: a thing that is at-work being healthy is *both* potentially healthy *and* potentially sick, and being able to be healthy *necessarily implies* being able to be sick (*Met.* IX.9 1051a6–10; see chap. 4, "The Being of Potency"). This is why potency extends beyond what is actually the case, as we saw (*Phys.* III.1 201a9–201a27). The conflict between the single and the double character of potency is more apparent than real, since although the potency for these opposites is one, the potency is nevertheless two in respect of what it is capable of doing.

The point here in the *Physics* is that the underlying thing—a categorical being—is one in number, but its single potency is for either of two opposites. In artificial things, the capacity for opposites distinguishes the being-potent from the unitary thing underlying its formal properties (the *eidei*). For natural beings, by contrast, the distinction appears to collapse. This is one thing we can learn about nature from the inquiry into change: that the underlying thing is identified with the nature.

Nevertheless, third, the inseparability of potency from being an underlying thing does not collapse the distinction between categorical and energetic being. Being a woman and being a mother are inseparable but not identical; two aspects of being can be inseparable from one another without being the same. The distinction between categorical being (the bronze underlying thing) and energetic being (able to be a man) is not a distinction between essential and accidental categorical predicates. Potency and being-at-work are *not properties*, and this is because they are neither said to be *in* a thing as properties are, nor are they said *of* it. They are inseparable but not identical.

This point is hard to grasp because Aristotle's account of energetic being is in profound disagreement with our typical way of speaking of properties. For us, properties are more or less what we can say truthfully about something, so for us this includes potency and actuality. But for Aristotle, potencies and activities are not essential or accidental properties that categorical beings could ever have, because they are not properties at all: they are a way of understanding beings in and through how they operate.

It is understandable that people would confuse the categorical being with its potencies: certain attributes (hardness, shapeability, etc.) appear to be required for a thing to be potent in a certain way. Similarly, being-potent implies that something has particular attributes; for example, being a runner (the being-as-potent) implies that one has legs, and conversely, bronze is, *because* it is bronze, able to be a statue of a man, whereas water is not. The difficulty is that when you grasp the one, you grasp the other.

Again, however, this does not imply that being a potency or activity is just to be a set of categorical predicates. The reason why is clear if we ask what it is that determines the set of categorical predicates relevant to the situation. Some of these categorical predicates can be substituted for others: for example, unlike bronze, wood cannot be melted and poured into a mold shaped like a man, but both can be cut into that shape. What sets the substitution criteria? Not an attribute, but the operation by which something is made into and maintains this shape. Wood *behaves* differently than bronze: when pressure is put on it at a certain angle, it is more flexible than some sorts of metal, more rigid than others. In short, its active tensile strength has different affordances because it has a different structure. To describe its behavior is to address its energetic being. *Being-potent is different than being an object with properties.*

To sum up: the "as" clause in the definition directs us to the being insofar as it is potent, that is, insofar as it is organized in relation to a function. This distinguishes it from the being that we name insofar as it is the bearer of categorical properties. Though they are numerically one, the underlying being and its being-potent are different in meaning, different kinds of being. The inseparability and even their mutual implication does not mean that they are the same in being. Their difference is fundamental.

Clearly, energetic being is concrete, possibly even more concrete than an object bearing properties, because activities and potencies cannot be abstracted from particular beings. But despite (or because of) their concreteness, energetic beings do not simply show up on their own, because they do not simply coincide with themselves. They are, instead, related to one another, and their potency extends beyond what they currently are. The parenthetical passage points out the structural difference between potency, which is related to others, and categorical being, which is self-coincident. What is crucial in the whole passage is that the subject of change is evident to us, and that it is *not* the bronze categorical being, but a being insofar as it is in potency.

The Demonstration of Change (*Phys.* III.1 201b5–13)

The opening arguments of Physics III were that change is categorically definite, and that energetic being must differ from the categorical for it to define change. After giving an overview of the definition and how a certain way of giving a definition can at the same time demonstrate something, we returned to Aristotle's categorical/energetic distinction to specify the subject of change. The next step is the demonstration that the *entelecheia* of this subject is change.

The passage states its aim, and pursues it in two rounds of argument, which I indicate with numbers below:

> [Thesis] That, then, [change] is this [the being-complete *of* the being-in-potency as potent], and that being moved happens whenever the being-complete should be this, and neither before nor after, is clear. [1] For each [thing] admits of either being at work or not, as the buildable thing [does], and [2] the being-at-work of the buildable thing, as buildable, is building. [1] For building is either [the] being-at-work of the buildable thing, or [building is] the house,[45] but whenever the house should be [at-work], the buildable thing is no longer [at-work]; [2] but the buildable thing gets built. It is necessary, then, for building to be the being-at-work [of the buildable thing]. [3] And building is some change. (*Phys.* III.1 201b5–13, my trans.)

The aim of the argument is to establish that when the *entelecheia* is of what is potent, as potent, change is occurring. By showing that change *only* occurs when this is the case, Aristotle confirms that change is an *entelecheia* and that it is genuinely *of* the being-as-potent, not incidental to it. Thus, he argues that the being-complete (*entelecheia*) of being-as-potent is, properly speaking, change, rather than anything else.

Before this passage, the preamble distinguished eidetic categorical being (i.e., the bronze) from energetic being (i.e., the thing insofar as it is potent), and the "as" clause specified the aspect in which a being is the subject of change. This involves arguing that there are such beings, namely, beings-as-potent. Now, in the culminating claims of this argument, Aristotle establishes that (2) these beings-in-potency have an *entelecheia* proper to them, and (3) that this is change. The demonstration *that change is* amounts to showing that there *really is* an *entelecheia* that is specifically of such beings, and that this *entelecheia* is change.

The argument can be paraphrased as follows:

(Thesis) Change happens only when there is an *entelecheia* of a being insofar as it is potent.
(1) Each thing, for example, the buildable thing (*oikodomēton*), can either be at work (*energeia*) or not. What is 'building'? It could either be the being-at-work of the buildable thing, or it could be the house at-work. But when the house is at-work, the buildable thing is not what is at-work. So what about the being-at-work of the buildable thing?[46]
(2) The buildable thing has an activity (*energeia*) and completion (*telos*) proper to itself, namely to get built. A buildable thing is a being considered insofar as it is capable of being built, not insofar as it is capable of being a house. The being-at-work of the buildable thing, as buildable, then, is building. The activity of building completes it just insofar as it is capable of being built.
(3) Building is a change. Change, therefore, happens only when there is a subject of change that is currently being-complete, for example, a buildable thing getting built. Change is therefore an *entelecheia*.

Why construct the argument in this way? The attempt to show that change admits of being confronts an acute difficulty. For change, too, is not a self-evident categorical being (*to on*), nor is it even a being-in-potency (*to dunamei on*) that you can point to; it is the potent being's completion *as potent* (*hē entelecheia tou dunatou, hēi dunaton*) (*Phys.* III.1 201b4–6). This means that change depends both on others insofar as they are potent *and* on the *entelecheia* of their relationship. So Aristotle's strategy for demonstrating *that* change is cannot be direct; he cannot demonstrate it by means of ostensive reference. So he constructs a demonstration that begins by exhibiting a discrete, categorical being, a being that *shows up as what it is*, as an *eidos*, but which has the distinction of being something we naturally grasp as a being-in-potency: construction materials.

The evident distinction between two concrete beings—houses and construction materials (both based on the root *oikia*)—leaves something unexplained, namely this: what is it that makes construction materials *construction* materials? In the previous passage, Aristotle distinguished between two pairs: the potent being and its activity, and the matter and the form that are separated out from it (*Met.* IX.6 1048a30–b9).⁴⁷ The construction materials (*oikodomēta*) are potent beings with their own completion (*entelecheia*). Their being construction materials is not something they are on their own; they are construction materials because of something else. They are therefore *incomplete*, and what completes them *is the activity of constructing them* (see *Met.* IV.2 1003a32–b18). Thus, for these things to be construction materials, something else must also be real, namely, the activity of construction. We can tell this activity is specifically *of* these things *insofar as* they are construction materials, because when those same materials are a house, they are not construction materials any longer since construction can stop. But the activity of construction is a change. The direct consequence is thus that evidently real, tangible beings depend for their being on change. In a word, Aristotle argues that change exists by showing that there are things that undeniably are, which cannot be what they are unless change is real. These are things whose being implies change, and which have their full meaning only in change.

This passage, then, is the conclusion of the argument for the existence of change that Aristotle promised in *Physics* I.8. Immediately after this passage, Aristotle underlines his accomplishment: "[change] is a certain being-at-work . . . of such a kind as we have described, difficult to bring into focus [*idein*], but admitting [*endekhomenēn*] of being" (*Phys.* III.2 202a1–2).⁴⁸

The Buildable Thing

This demonstration needs to be unpacked. The first concept to work through is the being of the buildable (*to oikodomēton*). An *oikodomēton* is a being grasped in its concrete aspect of being-potent, while *entelecheia* is used here to name its focal sense.⁴⁹

The word *to oikodomēton* is a substantive adjective that is ambiguous between "what can be built, the buildable" and "what has been built." In this context, it is clearly "the buildable thing." What is the buildable? The "as" clause gives us an answer: it is not a categorical being, such as wood or bricks, but the same being grasped in and through its potency to be built. This means the being is not just wood: to grasp what it is, we do not perceive the wood and only subsequently infer its ability to be built. Instead, we grasp the wood to the extent that it is potent: the buildability of the wood is *in* the wood and belongs to it by means of the wood's very being: it is one of its ways of being something. Some pieces of wood are less workable than others but its fibres are stronger or less susceptible to rot, some bricks are more brittle than others but lighter or more porous. To name a potency is to take up the complex of these properties as oriented toward some action. Potency is thus not a separable property, nor is it a set of properties. It is the plank or this pile of bricks here, considered in its entirety insofar as it can be taken up in the activity of building.[50] When we say that something is potent, we are not naming a part of it, or a feature of it; we are naming the being considered through and through, that is, the whole insofar as it is susceptible to change (*GC* I.8 326b29–33).

Thus, the buildable thing (*oikodomēton*) *is something*. But "the buildable thing gets built": to be a buildable thing *just means* to be the subject of the activity of getting built. So the buildable thing can be something at all only if building is something.

The phrase "For building is either [the] being-at-work of the buildable thing, or [building is] the house" (Phys. III.1 201b10–11) could have as its subject either building or being at-work. If the former, the question is, What is building? Is it the activity of the buildable thing, or is it the house? At a certain point, once there is a house, housebuilding can stop. This means the activity of the buildable thing, as buildable, is not the house. But the buildable thing has its own proper way of being at work, namely to be built. So building is the activity of the buildable thing getting built.

If the subject of the sentence is being-at-work, the question is, What is the *energeia* of the buildable thing (*oikodomēton*)? We are tempted to answer that it is the house that the materials become. After all, once planks have been assembled into walls and floors, then they have come to be a work (*ergon*). A thing is most potent when it is at work doing that which it is potent for. So if the purpose of building in the first place is to have a specific product, this product would have to be the *energeia* of the *oikodomēton*. Indeed, it is difficult to see how else buildable things could be related to the product of building.

However, unlike a growing, budding tree, a pile of wood lacks its own character and direction. Unlike trees in a forest, the pieces of wood in a pile do not differentiate themselves, but are indistinct. Unlike being wood, which has inherent resilience, their being as planks, that is, as capable, does not actively maintain itself: left alone, the planks will rot and cease to be. They have been *made ready* by the sawyer, have become such beings by being sawed and planed into boards, and yet what they have been made ready *for* is unclear:[51] they could be a wall, a door, or a floor, but they do not have this function (*ergon*) yet. A plank has a definite range of capacities: it does not have the capacity to run or sing. But within this range, the plank's capacity is indeterminate and flexible: it could become a floorboard, part of a wall, or a piece of paper. Lying there, no end-shape is in them that is specific to them as boards. As long as they are not currently being built into something, the product's shape is not actively being incorporated into them by the builder. Construction materials are neutral about ends, so their being-at-work (*energeia*) will not be a house. What is their proper sort of activity?

The builder cannot build a house without a site for building, the necessary tools, and buildable things, *oikodomēta*. The activity of building is therefore the complex of potent beings that includes the builder and the *oikodomēta*. It contains within it and implies an assemblage of definite beings and their purposes, ranging as far as architectural drawings and zoning laws, all without leaving the circuit of its proper activity: all of its conditions are included. The activity of building (*oikodomēsis*) is the whole complex. Building is an *entelecheia*. Since *energeia* converges with *entelecheia*, the two terms are both the same and different (*Met.* IX.8 1050a22–24). The being-at-work (*energeia*) in this case is change considered as the operation or exercise (*energeia*) of the building materials (*oikodomēta*), which means it is slightly different in meaning than *entelecheia*, which encompasses the whole operational context.

Since there are a great many things that are *oikodomēta*—nails, planks, bricks, paint—it follows that *oikodomēsis* exists. Thus, Aristotle shows that there are things whose very being requires change to be. There is an *entelecheia of* these things; therefore, change must be.

The Meaning of "The Buildable Is No Longer"
An objection to this reading comes in the form of the so-called Extinction Hypothesis. This hypothesis takes Aristotle's phrase, "When the house is, the buildable thing is no longer" to assert (without argument) that potency and actuality are incompatible and cannot be at the same time. The potency, it holds, is *for* being a house, but extinguishes itself in accomplishing its goal. If true, this claim might give the Product Puzzle some textual basis as a rival reading of the passage. Others have shown that the puzzle is not found in the passage, and I have argued that it cannot be Aristotle's position (see *Met.* IX.8 1050a28–30).[52] What is necessary is a reading of the phrase to replace it.

What, then, *does* Aristotle mean by the words "the buildable thing is no longer"? Grammatically, it could mean that when the house is there, (i) the buildable thing is not there any longer; (ii) the buildable thing is no longer *the being that is at work*, since a different object—the house—is the being that is at work; or (iii) the buildable thing is no longer *at work as buildable* but as something else—as a wall or door.

Answer (i) means that a certain aspect of a thing is no longer there. Answer (ii) collapses into (iii): if the house is the being that is at work, this implies that the planks, which are part of the house, are at work as something other than buildable.

Answer (iii) is that once the building materials have been assembled and the house is there, the planks in it will not be at work as planks, for they are only at work as planks while being changed into the house. They will instead be at work as something else. But this is a change in their *being*. If they are at work as a different color, they can, of course, still be planks. But if a plank is at work as part of a house, what is there is no longer a plank, but *part of the house*, such as a floor, a kitchen, a hallway. Unlike planks, these higher-order parts have new functions and new capacities that come from being fit together into operative wholes; for example, parts of a wall require other parts to work together, or the wall will fall down. The identity of the whole operation, namely the house, determines the identity of the parts (see *Met.* V.26 1023b25–29, *Met.* V.25, VII.17 1041b11–33).[53]

Thus, for the underlying thing to be at work as something *other than* as buildable (e.g., for buildable wood to become part of a house) is not for it to be a plank, but to be a floor surface, a beam, or a threshold. Indeed, since the buildable is an underlying thing grasped as what-is-able-to-be-built, what is at work as a house would not be the buildable, but the underlying thing grasped as what-is-able-to-be-a-house. The same underlying things might be there, but their being is different. Therefore, option (i) is the correct one: the planks, the buildable thing, are no longer.

And yet, while the compound house is in-activity something other than its constituent beings, "the constituents . . . neither (a) persist in activity, as 'body' and 'white' persist: nor (b) are they *destroyed* . . . for their 'power of action' is preserved" to the extent that the alteration allows (*GC* I.10 327b30–33, 328b17–18).[54] Thus, a builder could repurpose the planks in a barn as good building materials for a floor.

In sum: before they were built, they were workable things here and there. Now, together, they are capable of holding up a roof. As buildable, they did not have a proper product as their object, since they could become many different things. The buildable things were not intrinsically related to the product. Their defining feature was their shapeability, workability, buildability. As part of a house, by contrast, they have a distinct function and a distinct name: a floor, a wall, a beam. As long as we are addressing what they *are*, we will not call them buildable any longer.

And yet the stones of this temple can, after all, be used to build a church. It is clearly possible to address those same things as though they were different beings. It *is* possible to look at a forest or at a floor as *oikodomēton* (the converse of iii), but this is not to see them as a forest or as a floor, but instead to see pieces of wood able to be made into something, such as a chair, a picture frame, or, indeed, a floor. So a carpenter examining a floor could say, "These planks would make a great floor if we sanded them down some more." As any homeowner knows, it is not because it cannot be built any more that a house is not under construction, but because people are no longer at work building it. You would get strange looks if you asked what it is about the materials of a house that ended construction. *Building stops not because the potency has run out, but because people have stopped working on it.* The builder's purposive activity determines what gets made and whether it is complete.

Aristotle's thesis, after all, is that it is *entelecheia*, not potency, that determines when change happens and when it does not: each thing admits of either being at work or not being at work, and there is change only when the right *entelecheia* is there. We may therefore add the following passage from the *Metaphysics* in support of this reading: "A house, as well as the activity of building, comes from the house-building power . . . [while] the activity of building takes place within the thing that is being built, and it comes into being and *is* at the same time as the house: (*Met.* IX.8 1050a26–29).[55] This passage makes two points. First, the potent thing is not internally oriented toward being a house; the potency that produces the house is not the buildable thing, but the builder. The builder's activity of building is the process of organizing such things into the shape of the product. Thus, the builder gives rise both to the activity of building and to the house. Second, it follows that both the activity of building (and therefore the *oikodomēta*) and the house are not mutually exclusive, either on a physical or metaphysical level. Whether something is at work depends on whether the agent is at work on it.[56] There is no need to appeal to a metaphysical idea of self-destructive potencies.

In my reading, then, an Exclusion or Extinction Hypothesis is neither required nor implied, and it conflicts with Aristotle's argument in *Metaphysics* IX.8. We do not need to say that the potency has vanished or been exhausted or replaced by its actuality. Neither extinction nor exclusion is the metaphysical event afoot in a change. Aristotle is not concerned here to draw a precise temporal limit between a change-phase and a house-phase, but to use the distinction to confirm that there is indeed a being-complete (*entelecheia*) proper to the buildable as buildable, and to show that this being-complete is change, thereby confirming that change exists. The point is that in the world there is something that makes beings-as-potent meaningful, a single, focal meaning on which they depend: a being-complete that is a change.

* * *

Physics III defines and demonstrates the being of change, but also contributes to our understanding of being. We saw that categorical and energetic being are decisively different. Categorical being is the sort of being that shows up, that presents an individual look or form (*eidos*), while being as being-potent, being-at-work, and being-complete are collectively the active, energetic sense of being. Although change is categorically determinate, it can be defined only using energetic being. Energetic being is not a subtype of categorical being.

Having distinguished these senses of being, we can work out the complex relationship between the two. We saw that, although it is hard to grasp, their difference is concrete and robust: "the being-in-potency" (*to dunamei on*) and "the buildable thing" (*oikodomēton*) name a being that is individual and categorically identifiable, that is, the bronze or a plank or a brick, but they name it *only insofar as it is able to be built*. What distinguishes *this* sort of being is its potency, not its categorical features; as potent, even its categorical features appear in the light of its ability to change or to hold together as a house.

Physics III.1, then, defines and uses an ontological sense of potency and being-complete (*entelecheia*). Each of these is a way of being that is neither implied by nor derived from categorical being. Potency here is not just a capacity; it names a being considered insofar as it can accomplish something. This distinction is what establishes the subject of change. The subject of change is, properly speaking, not the bronze, but the being insofar as it is changeable, that is, the being-in-potency. This discovery makes it possible to demonstrate that change exists.

There is being-complete specifically of beings-in-potency, and change occurs only when these are being-complete. If buildable planks exist, then their buildability refers to something, or something makes them buildable. A house is not what makes them buildable, because when they are part of the house, the capability they are exercising is different: they are complete doing something else. Since being a buildable thing means to get built, building is what completes (*entelecheia*) buildable things. Building is a change; therefore, change admits of being. Building stops when the *entelecheia* is not there, that is, when the builder stops building, not when the capacity is used up.

There is much more to be said. Aristotle's inquiry into change uncovers much more about the terms of the energetic sense of being—*energeia*, *entelecheia*, and *dunamis*—than we have seen in the exhibition of the existence of change. For one, *dunamis* and *entelecheia* are not derived from one another, despite the fact that *dunamis* points toward *entelecheia*. Moreover, Aristotle will argue that each of the terms is a source (*archē*), and therefore a being, in a particular way, and that each has a different relationship to completion or accomplishment (*telos*). He will claim, ultimately, that sources are fundamental in ontology. The rest of this book is devoted to examining these claims.

CHAPTER 3

Energeia, Entelecheia, and the Completeness of Change

Perhaps the greatest consequences of change for ontology came to light through Aristotle's development of the concepts of activity (*energeia*), fulfillment or actuality (*entelecheia*), and potency (*dunamis*). The use of these terms in Aristotle's demonstration of the existence of change showed a great deal about them: they are not categorical concepts, but make up a different sense of being altogether; they differ from one another, since, although fulfillment is the focal being of potency, beings-in-potency are meaningfully independent of their fulfillment; and the same term can include or refer to multiple beings.

In this chapter I begin with a philological exposition of *energeia* and *entelecheia*, and then, in the latter part of the chapter, I elucidate their meaning in the demonstration of the existence of movement. Since the prevailing winds of scholarship on the subject push us toward the conclusion that *entelecheia*, since it is complete, is incompatible with change, which is, in a way, not, my primary concern will be to restore the relationship between *entelecheia* and change. The next chapter will turn to potency, fleshing out its independence from "actuality"-concepts and arguing that it diversifies and modifies Aristotle's conception of being.

The Controversy over Activity and Actuality

There is no reason to think that the words *energeia* and *entelecheia* were commonly used in Aristotle's time; in fact, scholars broadly agree that the words are Aristotle's own coinage.[1] In *Metaphysics* IX Aristotle hints that the words are his own design, explaining the motivations behind their composition: "the name being-at-work, which is composed to converge with [*suntithemenē pros*] being-complete . . ." (*Met.* IX.3 1047a30, my trans.).[2] There is also widespread agreement that *energeia* is closer to words in common usage at the time, and that if the works of Aristotle can be dated, it would have been coined earlier in Aristotle's career than was *entelecheia*, as early, in fact, as the *Protrepticus*.[3]

63

The current debate about the meaning of *energeia* and *entelecheia* follows, in part, from the resurgence of interest in Aristotle's definition of change; out of this interest comes the question of their proper English translation. While almost everyone agrees that *entelecheia* should be translated by "actuality," there is an ongoing dispute over whether *energeia* means "actuality" or "activity." Often the debate proceeds by analyzing certain passages and testing to see whether it is "actuality" or "activity" that best fits in the relevant context. For instance, Anagnostopoulos's analysis of change subserves two more specific points: first, that *energeia* means "activity," and second, that Aristotle used the wrong word when defining change using *entelecheia*, which he translates as "actuality."[4] Beere takes a more conservative approach, arguing against translating *energeia* with either word, since, he asserts, it means *both* "activity" and "actuality."[5]

That Aristotle uses the word *entelecheia* to define change is a problem for interpreters such as Ross, Heidegger, and Kosman, who take *entelecheia* to mean "fixed and finished off."[6] To preserve this interpretation they need to either alter the definition of change (e.g., in the definition, Ross translates *entelecheia* as "actualization" instead of "actuality," as he translates it elsewhere), find another sense (Kosman takes the definition to mean that potency becomes something actual when change occurs), or else argue that the terms distort the being of change. Some declare that what Aristotle meant by *entelecheia* is clear, but criticize him for failing to consistently apply the term he coined.[7]

Scholars increasingly hold that the word *energeia* must at least be translated differently than *entelecheia*. For example, Kosman and Anagnostopoulos argue that it should be rendered as "activity" instead of "actuality." They present the issue as a major advance in scholarship on Aristotle. Kosman writes, for example:

> What I saw as an emblem of my misunderstanding, or perhaps constitutive of it, or perhaps as a cause of it, was the fact that I had, like most people, almost always rendered *energeia* in English as *actuality*. I was in good company in this choice of translation, but I had come to recognize it as a mistake . . . The translation of *energeia* as *actuality* fostered the representation of that concept in modal terms, terms that contrast the *actual* with the merely potential and lead us to think of realization as the making actual of a *possibility*. That representation, I came to see, obscures what is fundamental in Aristotle, and it must yield to one in which the paradigmatic realization is the *exercise of a capacity*.[8]

In supposing the distinction between *energeia* and *entelecheia* to correspond, respectively, to "activity" and "actuality," Anagnostopoulos argues that "actuality" should replace "activity" in the definition of change.[9] Beere takes a more nuanced view:

> The two translations of *"energeia"* ["actuality" and "activity"], so very different from one another, suggest that the word is ambiguous. But I will argue that it would be disastrous to see *"energeia"* as ambiguous, since the very point of the term is to capture what these diverse cases have in common. On the other hand, if we insist on seeing *energeia* either as activity or as actuality, then we seem forced into absurdity.[10]

Beere is right that we ought not to assume that, for Aristotle, activity and actuality are different. But there is still a problem with thinking that the relevant cases are "activity" and "actuality," at least as we commonly understand those terms.

The controversy over activity and actuality has produced important and useful work, but, speaking generally, operates under two major methodological flaws. First, part of the goal has been to assimilate Aristotle's Greek to our familiar concepts of actuality and activity. Graham, for example, argues that the tradition correctly understands the concept that *entelecheia* was created to express—perfection or being at an end—and concludes that Aristotle's own characterization of its meaning and derivation is false.[11] But such views elide the fact that our understandings of these concepts have shifted since Aristotle's time. Moreover, the terms changed as they descended through Latin into modern languages.[12] For these reasons, questions over whether *energeia* and *entelecheia* mean "activity" or "actuality" operate under unwarranted assumptions that narrow or distort their semantic scope.

Second, and more importantly, by framing the debate as a decision about which of our familiar concepts to use, we act as though we already firmly grasp the meaning of "actuality" or "activity." This framing is motivated by the methodological principle that we should get clear about our concepts before we start. But the attempt to do so pulls us away from the question of what Aristotle could have truly meant by these terms, which are among the highest, and most philosophically complex in the corpus, and are therefore among the last to be understood. So it may not be possible to call *energeia* and *entelecheia* familiar or common-sense terms at all. They were not, after all, Greek words until Aristotle coined them. The reason to coin *two* words was that there were no readily available Greek words or meanings that expressed what he meant to say. In his own time Aristotle was neither using ordinary concepts nor ordinary language.

Moreover, Aristotle's method is explicitly at odds with the idea that we could discern the pristine and precise meanings of philosophical terms in advance. We do not start off with clear concepts at all. We begin, he says, with a sense of what is the case, a familiar, general whole (*to katholou holon*) of things jumbled-up or poured-together (*ta sugkechumena*). The only method he offers for discovering knowledge from this—though it is a powerful one—is to take these undistinguished senses (*adioristōs sēmainei*) and define (*horizei*) and distinguish (*diorizei*) them from the others (*Phys.* I.1 184b13).[13] But process occurs, of necessity, *in and through the investigation itself*. Neither we, nor Aristotle's contemporaries, understand in advance what the words *energeia* and *entelecheia* express, what problems they solve, and what they imply. To get to them we have to start from our familiar meanings, and allow these to change and even leave them behind and grasp whatever comes to light in the course of rigorous dialectical inquiry.

It will serve us well, then, to restrain ourselves from thinking that we know or can intuit in advance what Aristotle must mean by these core terms. We should adhere to Aristotle's dialectical method: we begin by assuming that we do not know what these terms are, and seek to understand them by examining what distinctions come up in the course of the investigation, and why they are necessary.

With this in mind, in the first part of this chapter, I will present what we can figure out about the meaning of these terms from their etymologies and from general features of how they are used. The most rigorous way to understand the meaning of *energeia*, *entelecheia*, and *dunamis*, however, is to examine Aristotle's arguments individually in order to see what work the terms do, and what they therefore must mean in each case for the argument to work, as I did in chapter 2. So in the second part of this chapter, I will draw out the meaning of a crucial feature from the examination of change, namely its incompleteness, by analyzing an important passage in *Nicomachean Ethics* X.4, before presenting the relationship between incompleteness and change systematically.

Energeia

When Aristotle draws attention to the way *energeia* and *entelecheia* are composed in relation to each other, he invites us to work out their similarity based on their syllables. Etymologically speaking, the common noun *energeia* comes from the root *erg*, which means "work" or "deed." This explains why *energeia* has been translated not only by "activity," as we have seen, but also by "function" and, more recently, by "operation" and "process."[14] But as we have noted, *ergon* resembles the English "work" in its twofold meaning, referring both to the activity of working and to the thing produced by this activity. For this reason, it can also be translated as "the work," "the thing," "the matter."

The adjective *energon*—"active, at-work, working"—was not very common at the time of Aristotle. Its prefix *en-* has several meanings, which correspond to dative prepositions like "in," "at," "with," or even "by." In the word *energeia* Aristotle turns the adjective into a substantive that emphasizes the meaning "at-work" while retaining the meaning of "thing." Literally translated, *energeia* means both "at-work-ness" and "being-in-work." Sachs's translation, "being-at-work," is thus the most usable literal translation currently used. I take the word "being" in the formulation to cover the substantivized sense, both the nature of "at-work-ness" and the being that is this working, while the "at-work" clarifies that this being is an activity, a thing that is precisely activity. The translation of *energeia* by "actuality," as long as the word is not reduced to common usage, and the word "act" is clearly heard in it, might suffice in situations that call for a looser, more traditional approximation. But this obscures both the active character of *energeia* and its relation to the accomplished work (*ergon*)—the key term in Aristotle's argument that *energeia* converges with *entelecheia* (*Met.* IX.8 1050a22–25; see "The Etymological Argument" in chap. 6). This is another reason why "being-at-work" is superior.

There have been several attempts to reconstruct the path Aristotle took to coining the term *energeia*. Menn argues that, in the so-called early texts, the *Protrepticus*, *Eudemian Ethics*, *Topics*, and *Magna Moralia*, Aristotle uses *chrēsis* and *energeia* interchangeably to mean the exercise of a potency (*dunamis*) or disposition (*hexis*).[15] Blair thinks that Aristotle coined *energeia* to express the "immanent activity" of an agent, in contradistinction to the change accomplished in the object. Aristotle, he argues, considers several words to communicate his meaning, and settles on *energeia*: the word *chrēsthai*, "use," is too passive, while *ergon* can mean both the doing and the thing done; but *energeia*, he contends, has the advantage of potentially including both "achieving" or "doing" (*poiein*), and "undergoing" or "being affected" (*paschein*) within it. At the same time, *energeia* avoids the sense of "making" in the word *prattein*. So, Blair argues, Aristotle ultimately derives the word from the active form of the verb *ergazesthai*, but because he wants to express activity or what is working in the agent, instead of using the word *energia*, which could come from *energos*, "effectiveness," or "what works" in the thing acted upon, Aristotle changes the spelling to *energeia*.[16] Thus, Blair argues, *energeia* excludes the sense of "inert, passive," on the one hand, and "external" on the other.

But this line of interpretation, while laying out the linguistic terrain, has a critical flaw: Aristotle cannot have meant to exclude from *energeia* the ability for it to be the activity of the patient, since the patient has a capacity (say, to be hot) that gets exercised and is at that time at-work.

Kosman is right to be concerned that "actuality" refers us to modality rather than to the use or activity at the root of *energeia*. Beere is right that, while "activity" is clear in its content, it risks being misleading to the extent that it leaves out the sense related to "actuality." Sachs's "being-at-work" solves both problems.

Entelecheia

The philological background of *entelecheia* is much more complex and suggestive than that of *energeia*, consisting as it does of words for "in," "completion," and "having." It is thus surprising that most scholars do not hesitate to translate the word with "actuality," including scholars who are scrupulous in rendering *energeia*. Still, among those who reject the traditional translation, there is a fruitful debate over what rendering *would* best express its verbal richness.[17]

The word "actuality" in English means "in fact" and applies to whatever happens to be the case, as in "they actually call this meat." Thus, Sachs argues, translating *entelecheia* as "actuality" impoverishes its meaning:

> The things Aristotle called *actualities* are limited in number, and constitute the world in its ordered finitude rather than in its random particularity . . . The only actualities in the world, that is, the only things which, by their own innate tendencies, maintain themselves in being as organized wholes, seem to be the animals and plants, the ever-the-same orbits of the ever-moving planets, and the universe as a whole.[18]

Unlike the commonly used term "actuality," Aristotle's complex, carefully constructed term expresses a precise meaning.[19] This is a strong reason to resist rendering it as "actuality." Any translation of *entelecheia* must fit its status as an apex concept.

"Actuality" does get something right about the proper sense of *entelecheia*: as we saw from the demonstration of the existence of change, Aristotle does hold that to be *entelecheia* is to be. It is thus necessary to make sense of why Aristotle thinks that saying something is *entelecheia* is the same as saying it is, that it has being (*Phys.* III.1; *Met.* IX.3 1047a30–b3).

The word *entelecheia* does not seem to have any synonyms in Greek, because of the complex relationships between each of its three parts: *en-*, *telos*, and *echein*. The meaning of *entelecheia* cannot be captured in a single elegant English word or phrase. In what follows I shall argue that there is a fruitful ambivalence in the term that makes it flexible and more useful than a single English rendering can give it.

The *en-* prefix is crucial to the word's meaning, and the longest section of Aristotle's argument for the convergence of *energeia* and *entelecheia* concentrates on it (*Met.* IX.8 1050a23-b2). The core of the word is *telos*, meaning "fulfillment" or "completion," or "accomplishment"; however, since potencies can be complete as well, *telos* also means being completely ready for action or use (*Soul* II.5 417a22–31). Moreover, Aristotle resists a common reading of *telos* as the end of a sequence, in favor of its sense of completion. But the word *echein* is no less crucial. If it was not, then he could have used *entelēs*—"complete," "full-grown," "perfect"—as an adjective, or as an adverb: "at last." But as Ross notes, although *entelēs* was used in Aristotle's time, it was never used by Plato, and only once by Aristotle.[20] I shall take each part in order.

En-

The prefix *en-* has the meanings we set out above, notably "in" and "at" in the sense of being "there," coinciding with the being that is there, rather than in the sense of being "at an end." Kosman argues that the *en-* is locative, drawing an analogy between the phrase "to be complete" (*entelēs einai*), which means "to have one's end within oneself" (*en heautōi telos echein*), and "to be god-possessed" (*entheos einai*), which means "to have a god within one" (*en heautōi theos echein*).[21] Aristotle clearly uses *en-* as a locative prefix at *Metaphysics* IX.8 1050a17–24 (see "The Location Argument" in chap. 6). But in addition the prefix turns the word into the dative of substance, relating it to being.

Telos

Telos means "completion," "accomplishment," or "readiness." Aristotle takes the sense that it is the "end" of a sequence to be derivative. Aristotle's lexicon entry on *telos* in *Metaphysics* V.16, says that its proper sense is "excellence lack[ing] no part of the fullness it has by nature" (*Met.* V.16 1021b22).[22] Excellence here is not an end point in a sequence, but an ongoing virtuous potency. Discussing happiness in a complete life response, Aristotle argues against the idea (derived from Solon) that *telos is* an end point: what is primary is the ongoing condition of being *teleia* (*NE* I.10). Thus, it is not determined by its being opposed to something; it is not logically or ontologically dependent on its opposite. Rather, the opposite, as well as the continuum between the two, derive their meaning from the *telos*: a lack is only a *telos* by transference, so something can be "completely ruined" or destroyed: "even death is by a transference of meaning called an end, because both are extremes, and the end for the sake of which something *is* is an extreme" (*Met.* V.16 1021b21–30).[23]

The primacy of the completion-related sense over the sequence-related sense of *telos* is reinforced by Aristotle's use of *telos* to mean *source* (*archē*). The completion-related sense is evident in the phrase *hoi en telei*, which refers to a governor or magistrate; so *telos* suggests "origin" (*archē*): a source of action, events, or being that directs or structures what arises from it. Aristotle argues for the identification of *telos* with *archē* in *Metaphysics* IX.8 and XI.1: to be a *telos* is primarily to be that for the sake of which, which is different than (though not exclusive of) being an end point of change (*Met.* IX.8 1050a6–8, XI.1 1059a35–37).

When we speak of teleology, we normally mean the Scholastic concept, which assimilated the Aristotelian idea to the Christian historical concept of Divine Providence. Teleology thus takes on the sense, for us, of a kind of goal set for a creature in advance, external to it, and toward which it is confined to strive. By contrast, at a minimum, *entelecheia* in Aristotle means the *inherent* completeness or wholeness of a thing, a completeness that can coincide with, and be the thing itself. *Telos*, for Aristotle, does not primarily mean "ended," or "finished." It means "complete," "fully there," "whole," "entire"; and in the definition of change it means "having its complete sense." Its finality is akin to what makes us say "at last," as in "at last we find water."

Echein

The word *echein* means "to have" or "to hold on" to something. The "grip" of having, as it were, is "being in charge of, keeping," or even "holding in guard, keeping safe," and in a related sense, "holding fast, supporting, sustaining, or staying." The infinitive can mean "to be able." When a location is specified, *echein* can mean "to dwell" there.

The word *echei*, "have," is important to *entelecheia* because it expresses a particular way of relating *telos* to being. Aristotle uses *echein* to say: "Those things are said to be complete [*teleia*] for which a good *telos* initiates activity from within [*huparchei*], since it is by *having* the *telos* that they are complete" (*Met.* V.16 1021b23).[24] "Having," then, stands in for the term "initiate from within" (*huparchei*), a word often translated as "belong to" or "be present." A thing is complete (*teleia*) by *having* or *holding onto telos*. *Echein*, then, is another way to express the inherence of the *telos*.

Perhaps the most revelatory sense of *echein* for our current context is that in ordinary Greek the verb can substitute for "be": in response to a greeting, *kalōs echei* means "it is going well."[25] Now, "having," "holding on," and "sustaining" are ongoing conditions or activities. Using *echein* as a synonym for being, then, suggests that being is not static or passive, but a continual accomplishment.

Energeia and *Entelecheia*
If Aristotle assembles *energeia* and *entelecheia* to converge in such a way that they illuminate one another (*Met.* IX.3 1047a30–32, IX.8 1050a17–24), they must, clearly, have related meanings. This is one reason why Blair's claim about their mutual interchangeability seems initially plausible.[26] Yet if they were the same, Aristotle would not have created *two* of them. Moreover, there would be no need to argue that their meanings converge (see "The Etymological Argument" in chap. 6).

But by announcing that he composed *energeia* and *entelecheia* to tend toward one another, Aristotle invites us to think through their parts. Instead of the root *erg-* in *energeia*, we find *telos echei*. Sachs writes:

> [Aristotle] chooses a common noun (*energeia*) built on the root *erg* that signifies work. He finds the same meaning in the common verb *echein* that means to be by continuing or holding on in some way, and attaches it to an adjective (*enteles*) that signifies completeness, to form the coinage *entelecheia*, which redoubles its meaning by punning on a common word (*endelecheia*) that means continuity or persistence. [And drawing on the phrase *ti en einai*, Aristotle] remakes Socrates's favorite question *ti esti* (what is it?) by changing the verb to the past tense (*-en*), in which alone its progressive aspect can be made unambiguous.[27]

The word *entelecheia* expresses the being of something, insofar as it is both complete and ongoing. If *entelecheia* is a pun on the word *endelecheia* ("to persist or continue on, to endure") then the word would suggest "continuing" and "holding on."[28]

The Word as a Whole
Based on these considerations, it seems clear that the standard practice, which translates both *energeia* and *entelecheia* with the word "actuality," should be abandoned. *Energeia* should be rendered "being-at-work" or "activity," but could also be translated "being insofar as it operates." For its part, *entelecheia* can only be rendered by several nearly equivalent phrases. The *en-* literally makes the

word mean "being in the *telos*," and *telos* is not conceived horizontally as "at the end of a sequence" or "finished off," but vertically, as fulfillment, completion, or accomplishment, while *echein* means both ongoing capability and activity, and being. In general, *entelecheia* should be rendered by "being-complete," with the word "being" a translation of "having" (*echein*), and understood as an ongoing accomplishment. Less versatile translations are "staying-fulfilled," "holding onto completion," "holding itself in completion," "holding its completion in itself," "in active completion," and other such formulae.

Energeia and *Entelecheia* in Change

Now that I have described the words *energeia* and *entelecheia* themselves in general, I return to how they are used in Aristotle's account of change to resolve an apparent self-contradiction in the use of "being-complete" (*entelecheia*) to define incomplete motion. I shall argue that *energeia* applies to individuals, while *entelecheia* applies to composites, a broader class of things that includes individuals.

In the demonstration of the existence of change, *energeia* and *entelecheia* are used differently: being-built (*oikodomeitai*) is the being-at-work (*energeia*) of what is built (*oikodomēton*), while building (*oikodomēsis*) is change (*kinēsis*) and the being-in-completion (*entelecheia*) of what is built as built:

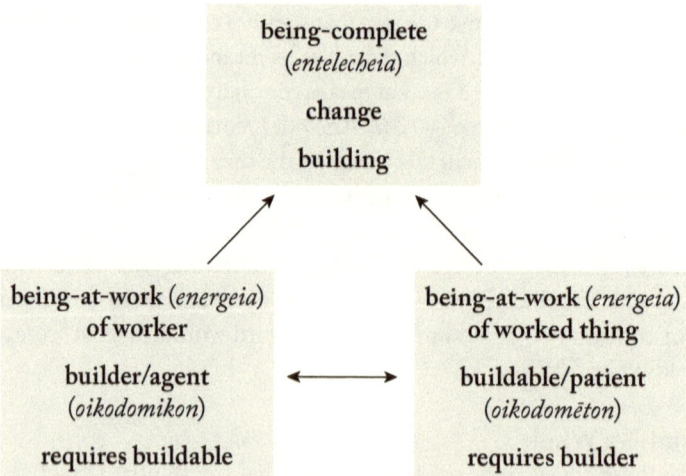

Energeia as being-built (*oikodomeitai*) means the activity of building happening to something: the *energeia* is of that which undergoes the change, though it is at the same time the activity of the builder. On the other hand, *entelecheia* as building (*oikodomēsis*) does not describe something insofar as it is distinguished into an active thing opposite another passive thing; it is only "building," a complete articulation of the complex of builder and built. Unlike being-built (*oikodometai*), building (*oikodomēsis*) refers neither to the agent-patient nor to the completeness-incompleteness of the elements; rather, it is just the complete change of building, in which the agent and patient are not separable.

The distinction between the activity of the agent and patient is complex. On the one hand, considered as the activity of the builder or teacher, the activity is not considered a change in a typical sense, that is, a change out of what it is, but as the activation or use of a skill for building or teaching. But on the other hand, considered as the activity of the buildable or the student, it is a change. In other words, a single *energeia* has two aspects, two meanings, two definitions depending on which being you consider. It is in a way one, and in another way two:

> For things are not identical to which the same things belong in some particular way, but only those of which the being is the same. And it is by no means the case that to learn is the same as to teach, *not even if the activity of teaching is the same as that of learning*, just as the separation from here to there is not one and the same as that from there to here, even though the interval between the things set apart is one. And to speak generally, teaching is not the same as learning in the highest and most proper sense, nor acting the same as being acted upon, but *that to which these belong, the change, is the same*. For the being-at-work of this in that, and the being-at-work of this by the action of that, differ in meaning. (*Phys.* III.3 202b16–26)[29]

Things are only the same in being, Aristotle argues, when their sense is the same. So they can be the same in number, but different in orientation. And in this case the underlying thing that is the same is the *change*. But the meaning and therefore the being of the *energeia* differ for each being involved: for the teacher it is teaching, for the learner, learning.[30] There is no translation that captures this structure. But "actuality" clearly does not.

The Problem of Completeness and Incompleteness

It is conspicuous that change is defined as being-complete (*entelecheia*) almost without exception (*Phys.* III.1 201a6, 201a10, 201a25, 201b4, III.2

202b25, 202b26), even while it is described as incomplete (*atelēs*) (*Phys.* III.2 201b31–33, VIII.5 257b6–9; *Soul* II.5 417a16–17, 431a6–7).[31] Since *entelecheia* already means "complete," change is therefore an incomplete being-complete (*entelecheia atelēs*) (*Phys.* VIII.5 257b6–9). This contradiction motivates some scholars to argue that change is a self-contradiction, and others to argue that Aristotle used the wrong word to define it. To solve this contradiction, it is necessary to work out how change is related to completeness, that is, the meaning of the *telos* in *entelecheia*.

The most common view is that what it means for change to be "incomplete being-complete" is for a changing thing to be on its way to, but not yet having reached its end.[32] Thus, the motion of running from Marathon to Athens consists of the runner being potentially in Athens, while not actually being in Athens. (I shall use "actuality" and "potentiality" here, since this is how it is expressed in the literature.) For a moment, this appears to solve the problem of contradiction, since potentiality and actuality are not the same aspect of a thing. But we are left with a contradiction between potentiality and actuality, and this is a problem if motion is the actuality of a potentiality.[33]

I think, however, that this view misrepresents the problem. Moreover, the solution—relocating the contradiction in the relation between potentiality and actuality—seems more problematic than the problem, since it opposes the terms on an ontological level. The problem of incompleteness seems vexing if we think it concerns how to describe the location of a changing thing on a continuum between a categorical form and its lack. But such a description, I argued, uses the wrong sense of being. If I say "at 1:00 the runner was at Marathon, at 2:15 he was between Marathon and Athens, and at 3:35 he was in Athens," I have described the static properties of an object; no motion-like being has been articulated. This is not at all where the problem of incompleteness of change is located.

The sort of incompleteness that applies to change itself will belong to potency and being-at-work, that is, it will be within the sense of being that can define change and sources of change. If I am right that the *telos* in *entelecheia* does not mean being-at-the-end, but being-complete, then we will be able to find our way through the impasse.

Wholes and Parts of Changes

To understand what it means for change to be something "incomplete being-complete," the best start is to examine Aristotle's most thorough passage on the subject: *Nicomachean Ethics* X.4.[34] Here he argues that change *is* complete *as a whole*, but *incomplete* in its *parts*.

Beforehand, it is useful to rehearse, once again, Aristotle's rejection of the argument that change is inherently self-contradictory (as discussed in chap. 1). If it is a blend or identity of being and non-being, change is ontologically self-contradictory. But since Aristotle endorses the Parmenidean premise that things either are or are not (*Phys.* I.8 191b12–20), change is not such a blend. If it were, he would then be committed to Parmenides's rejection of the existence of change. But he is not. Therefore, Aristotle's conception of change will be ontologically positive, not at all mixed with non-being.

In *NE* X.4, Aristotle argues that change can be a complete being (*entelecheia*) while its parts, each of which is potentially a being, are not complete. Broken into steps, the passage reads:

(1) For every change (e.g., that of building) takes time and is for the sake of an end,
   (a) and is complete when it has made what it aims at.
   (b) It is complete, therefore, only in the whole time or at the final moment.
(2) In their parts and during the time they occupy, all changes are incomplete, and are different in kind from the whole change and from each other.
   (a) For [example]
      (i) the fitting together of the stones is different from the fluting of the column, and these are both different from the making of the temple;
      (ii) and the making of the temple is complete (for it lacks nothing with a view to the end proposed), but the making of the base or of the triglyph is incomplete; for each is the making of a part.
   (b) They [the whole and part] differ in kind, then, and it is not possible to find at any and every time a change complete in form, but if at all, only in the whole time.
      (i) So, too, in the case of walking and all other changes. For if locomotion is a change from here to there, it, too, has differences in kind—flying, walking, leaping, and so on.
      (ii) And not only so, but in walking itself there are such differences;
         (a) for the whence and whither are not the same in the whole racecourse and in a part of it, nor in one part and in another,

(b) nor is it the same thing to traverse this line and that; for one traverses not only a line but one which is in a place, and this one is in a different place from that.

(iii) We have discussed change with precision in another work, but it seems that it is not complete at any and every time, but that the many changes are incomplete and different in kind, since the whence and whither give them their form. (*NE* X.4 1174a13–b23)[35]

As the opening and closing sentences show, Aristotle's argument is not that change is itself intrinsically incomplete, but that, as (1a–b) and (2a) and (2b) make clear, its categorical form *is* complete "in the whole time." The *parts* of a change are incomplete, since for each the *telos*, limit, or place is different (3a–b).[36] When we examine the changing thing, we find the *parts* of the change to be constitutively complex, multiple in such a way that each is incomplete: the act of putting mortar on bricks is not the same as putting the bricks on top of each other; but neither of these is on its own the complete act of building. In other words, the whole change itself can be divided, and its sequences distinguished.[37] So although change is an *entelecheia*, it is *of* several parts.[38]

The "whence and whither" of a change, or its privation-form structure, is what determines whether the *parts of the change* are incomplete. The form can differ for each part of the change, just as that of each part can differ from that of the whole change.[39] Being-complete (*entelecheia*), then, does not mean being complete in every respect: it can simply mean being the completion or accomplishment of parts, insofar as they are incomplete and depend on one another. This is how the soul can be the being-complete of a complex body, one that has life as a potency (*Soul* II.1 412a20, 27, 412b4). It follows from what change is that it constitutes within each of the categories a divisible continuity, and as divisible, its parts are incomplete, while as a whole it is complete.

Completeness and Incompleteness of Sources

But since this passage concerns the categorical attributes of changing things, rather than the energetic terms by which change itself is defined, this passage does not address what would make change *itself* essentially either incomplete or complete. I contend that completeness has a different meaning for categorical being than it does for energetic being.[40] Incompleteness becomes an intractable problem for change only when the distinction between the two kinds of being is collapsed.[41] Since potency, being-at-work, and being-complete are dynamic-energetic *sources* (*archai*), it is necessary to examine sources.

After Aristotle defines change, he says that it is incomplete, not because it is on the way from a privation to a form, but because the *potency* is incomplete (*Phys.* III.2 201b33–34). There are several sorts of incompleteness that potency-like sources appear to have: a potency can be incomplete if (i) as a source of change, it lacks an *other* necessary for it to set to work, for example, a violinist without a violin; or (ii) the source itself is not yet complete, for example, one who is not yet a German speaker; or (iii) the source is incomplete because the being points toward and requires change in order to be what it is, for example, the relation between the buildable thing and building; or (iv) the source is incomplete because it generates something beyond it, for which it acts, for example, the activity of production yields a table.

I shall address (i) to (iii) in order. Aristotle sets aside (iv) in *Metaphysics* IX.8 1050a21–b2.[42] Note that, just as change is not a transition from the underlying thing to the form, change is not a transition from potency to being-complete (*Soul* II.5 417b8–17).[43]

(i) Since potency is a source of change in an other, one potency depends on another in order to act, unlike, say, a nature (*Met.* IX.8 1049b8–10).[44] Since change is the being-complete of potency, and potency always requires such supplementation, it follows that change is incomplete.

This sense of incompleteness can be found everywhere in Aristotle, from logic to biology: some things depend on others:

> It is clear then that a deduction is formed when the terms are so related, but not a perfect one; for the necessity is not perfectly established merely from the original assumptions; others also are needed. (*Prior Analytics* I.5 27a15)[45]

> All other oviparous fishes produce an egg of one colour, but this is imperfect, for its growth is completed outside the mother's body by the same cause as are those eggs which are perfected within. (*GA* III.1 749a)[46]

> Eggs that are perfect include the yolk, so they can feed themselves. (*GA* III.2 754a1)[47]

In each of these examples, "imperfect" means "requiring supplementation" or "needing an outside source."

(ii) Among potencies, some can be completed, that is, *entelecheia*, and among these, some are not complete (*Soul* II.5 417a22–b2). These are unable to accomplish their goal at all, or consistently, or they are not able to accomplish it on their own without an outside source; for example, a student who can only complete geometry problems with the help of a teacher. The completion of such a potency can be the *telos* of a process of change, just as building a temple is the *telos* of change (*Soul* II.5 417a30–35). A completed potency is commonly referred to as "Second Potency" (see "Complete Potencies" in chap. 4).

(iii) As we saw in the demonstration of change, a potency does not just (i) depend on an other, it also depends on the activity it accomplishes together with others. In order to be what it is, a potency depends on change. This is a different sort of dependence—a focal (*pros hen*) dependence, and a dependence on a different sort of object, than (i) and (iv).

Since incompleteness in sense (i) and (iii) are permanent features of potency, whereas in (ii) only some potencies can be completed, it follows that (ii) will not be the sense of incompleteness that is native to change. Since the incompleteness articulated in (iii) also, necessarily, admits of completion, it follows that it will not be the sense of completeness at stake. This means that the relevant sense in which changing beings are incomplete is that they require outside sources in order to change.

* * *

My argument so far leads to some conclusions about the meaning of being-at-work (*energeia*) and being-complete (*entelecheia*) for change. We saw in the demonstration of change that the changeable thing depends on change to be what it is. This dependence means that the changeable is incomplete (*atelēs*), since it lacks a source that could set it in motion. But the changeable thing thus refers to *two* other things: the changer, and the change that comes about when changer and changeable are together. The same is true of the changer, with the difference that it is responsible for bringing about the change when the agent and the changeable thing it affects are together.[48] The agent and patient are complementary and therefore incomplete elements of the change. However, the change, that is, the *entelecheia*, is a complete, unified action toward which the changer and changeable point and upon which they depend. *Entelecheia* in this case is the *telos* of a composite, that unity toward which the parts point (*pros hen*). It is because *entelecheia* means this that Aristotle can demonstrate the existence of change. Far from being opposed to change, *entelecheia* applies precisely to what is *ateles* (incomplete) on its own.

Entelecheia, then, is the *concrete* term for change precisely because it is the complete, single event of change, while insofar as individual things are involved in a change, they are abstract because they get their meaning from it: the buildable thing gets its meaning from the change, while a builder and her activity of building are both what they are because of the change that they bring about in the buildable thing.[49]

Yet if *entelecheia* means that an individual *this* is in a *telos*, or has the *telos* in itself, the individuals can, in a sense, be *entelecheia*. So we must account for how the term can apply to individual parts. Insofar as they are *parts*, the parts of the whole change are related to the whole; because the whole and part are, together, one thing (see *Met.* V.26 1023b25–29, VII.17 1041b12–33), when change is underway it is possible to describe the *entelecheia* (i.e., the whole) as belonging to a part. Thus *entelecheia* has a native use and an extended use: (1) it is the focal or *pros hen* meaning of both agent and patient, since the builder and buildable are what they are by pointing to a single change that unifies them, and makes them "agent" or "patient." (2) *Entelecheia* is the full being or completion of either agent or patient, since when an individual, insofar as it is in-potency, "has" (*echei*) its completion (*telos*), that is, insofar as it is *entelecheia*, then as a changing thing its being is complete, and it possesses its full sense by being part of this whole. In both cases, *entelecheia* is a being's focal sense or completion, and to be *en-tel-echeia* is for a thing to have (*echei*) this completion (*telos*).

In several passages, Aristotle seems to refer to a sense of being-at-work that is more complete than change, such as the activities of skills and the capacities to see and know (e.g., *Soul* II.5 417a16–17, III.7 431a6–7). We have no reason to believe that Aristotle is speaking loosely when he does so. Since potency has a definite diversity of senses, surely being-at-work can as well. In the *Nicomachean Ethics*, Aristotle uses the phrases "the complete being-at-work" (*hēi teleia energeia*) (*NE* X.4 1174b14–17) and "being completely at-work" (*teleiotatē energeia*) (*NE* X.4 1074b20, 22). This suggests that being-at-work can be incomplete, but not that this is a contradiction. Now, *energeia* is the genus, and motion or change is a species of it.[50] So complete and incomplete *energeiai* will be complete or incomplete depending on what they are *of. Energeia* does not, then, have a fixed relationship with *telos*; it is not simply, or by definition, complete (see "The Problem of *Telos*" in chap. 6). But this means that it is not the same in meaning as *entelecheia*, which *is* inherently complete. This is why Aristotle needs to argue in *Metaphysics* IX.8 that *energeia is* in fact a completion, *telos*, in order to show that it converges with *entelecheia* (*Met.* IX.8 1050a17–1050b, see "The Etymological Argument" in chap. 6).

The distinction between potency and being-at-work, then, is not a distinction between incompleteness and completeness. Potency and change are not incomplete sorts of being in the midst of integral being; they are not flaws in being. Insofar as it is potent, a being can be complete (e.g., a complete soccer player, a geometer) or incomplete (a student of soccer or geometry). Activity, similarly, will be either. But every time, it will be *a certain kind of completion*, namely the exercise of its potency.

From this analysis of incompleteness, we can see a further way that change determines how being will be manifold. For change requires us both to distinguish agent from patient, and to distinguish parts of change from one another. Change, whether its sources are complete or incomplete potencies, is necessarily composite, and insofar as the parts of change depend on and differ from the other parts, they are each incomplete when distinguished from the whole change. Nevertheless, a change itself is a complete whole, and it is on the basis of this whole that parts are distinguished at all; that is, it is with respect to the whole change that they relate to one another. *Entelecheia* is not pristine and selfsame. It is the focal sense of heterogeneous parts that are related to and distinguished from one another in and through the reality of change.

CHAPTER 4

The Being of Potency

Aristotle's concepts of potency (*dunamis*), activity (*energeia*), and being-complete or fulfillment (*entelecheia*) are among the greatest contributions of change to ontology. But the question of the relation between change and being gets fought out within the concepts of potency and activity themselves. The previous chapter examined *energeia* and *entelecheia*, and argued that the way potency is incomplete is compatible with the way that change *is a completion*. This chapter examines what change contributes to ontology through the concept of potency. It clarifies what potency is and how it is related to change, and describes what sort of being it has.

Chapter 2 examined the use-meaning of being-in-potency in the demonstration of change, but we have yet to examine the *definition* of potency. In its authoritative (*kurios*) sense it is a source of change in an other, or in the same thing as other (*Met.* IX.1 1046a10, *Met.* IX.8 1049b7–9). Being a source, potency sets directly to work when its relations with others are right.

Potency's importance for ontology, I aim to show, lies both in the fact that it names a distinctive way that a being, as a whole, *is*, and in the fact that it sets conditions for what is and what can be in other ways as well. If we conceive of ontology as an account of what it is to be an *actual* being, and of the types of relationships between such beings, potency would change ontology because it is a sort of being that is *not* actuality, but which both *sets relationships between actual beings*, and the *meaning of actuality* (*energeia*). Potency contributes to ontology by moving it beyond being merely an account of what is actually the case.

The core claim of this chapter is that the change-related sense of potency is the bearer of its ontological significance. First, I aim to show, through a description of the scholarship on potency and activity, that this claim is plausible and attractive. Then I make the positive case for the ontological importance of potency by providing an account of what it is for potency to be a source of change and rest, what its structure is, and what sort of being it has. Only in this way will it be clear why it is possible and worthwhile to extend change-concepts to material, form, and primary being (*ousia*) (in chaps. 5 and 6). This chapter examines what it means, ontologically, for potency to become complete, and sets up the claim, in the next chapter, that to be in the primary sense is to be a source (*archē*).

Potency and Activity, Change and Being

In book IX of the *Metaphysics*, Aristotle examines the change-related senses of potency and activity, which he calls their primary senses (*dunamis*: *Met.* V.12 1020a4–6, IX.1 1045b25–1046a1, 1046a10, *energeia*: IX.3 1047a32). Yet, he argues, "potency and activity are said in more cases than those referring to change alone" (*Met.* IX.1 1046a, my trans.; see *Met.* IX.6 1048a17–30, b8).

The key scholarly contributions in this area tend not to focus on the being of potency and its importance for ontology, but on what other things the words *dunamis* and *energeia* extend to. Most scholars think that Aristotle extends these words from their change-related sense to a distinct being-related sense, thereby minimizing the importance of change for ontology. They translate this so-called ontological sense of *dunamis* and *energeia* as "potentiality" and "actuality," or "possibility" and "reality." I shall argue that this is misguided, and that the natural reading of the text is that potency and activity are extended not to second, "higher" senses of these terms themselves, but, instead, to the categorical concepts of material and primary being (*ousia*).

It is not possible here to review all the interpretations of potency and activity in Aristotle, but since our primary question concerns what they are and how they are related to being, it will suffice to examine what scholars say about whether potency and activity are themselves split into change- and being-related senses.

To clarify what is at stake, and to sharpen the point I am making in this chapter, it will be helpful to track out how scholars think change relates to being within the concepts of potency and activity. The most prominent views are (i) that potency's ontological sense is possibility, and that for something to be possible is for it to depend on the real powers of existing things; (ii) that a thing's change-related potency implies that it has a certain kind of reality, which means that it *is* a potentiality; (iii) that the two senses of potency and actuality are, on the one hand, causal powers and their activity, and, on the other, being-in-capacity and being-in-activity, where the latter pair are alternating modal states of categorical predicates; (iv) that the ontological sense of potency and actuality is not potentiality and actuality but material and form; and (v) that actuality means presence, disclosure, or manifestation, while potency is bound up with the negativity of non-disclosure.

I will make the following key points: the ontological sense of *dunamis* and *energeia* is not (i) possibility-reality, as Charlton and Menn claim. Instead, (ii) as M. Frede argues, potency's claim to reality is implied by and entangled with the capacity to act, that is, to start a change. (iii) The modal interpretation of *dunamis* and *energeia* makes potentiality and actuality into mutually exclusive states of being, so this view ought to be set aside. Moreover, (iv), as Anagnostopoulos has shown, *Metaphysics* IX does not extend the concepts of potency and actuality to potentiality and actuality, but to material and form.[1] This dismantles the textual basis for the claim that the words themselves have a separate ontological sense. Meanwhile, (v) some argue that the change-related sense of potency is already ontological, but the most notable proponents of this view, Heidegger and Agamben, define potency as a negation of actuality, which they also call "presence."

I make the case, below, for a position suggested by this overview of the literature, that the change-related sense is already ontological in the relevant sense, and that once this positive sense is fully grasped, it has become clear that it extends to and reinterprets material and form. In other words, by rejecting the distinction between the change-related and the ontological senses of potency and activity, we can understand much better the ontological meaning of the two concepts.

I shall address these views in order.

(i) One way to interpret the respective meanings of potency and activity is to say that it corresponds to the distinction between two pairs of terms: power-exercise, and possibility-reality. Thus, Menn argues that the extended sense of potency is to be merely *possible* through the real *power* of some other thing: a house is in-potency, that is, possible, through the power of the builder to build it.[2] Charlton similarly argues that "existing *dunamei* and existing *entelecheiai* . . . should be understood as the contrast between the kind of existence which attaches to possibilities and the kind which attaches to fulfilments of possibilities."[3] In their view, the relevant sense of potency is its minimal common sense, namely the most rudimentary thing that every case shares, rather than the sense that distinguishes the most robust exemplar.

We should resist reading the being-related sense of *dunamis* as possibility: as Witt shows, Aristotle argues that possibility is secondary to and depends on the primary sense of potency (*Met.* IX.3 1047a13–17, IX.4 1047b2–30).[4] Moreover, it is unlike Aristotle to argue that being is a minimal or derivative concept. As Brentano argues, conceiving of potency and activity this way makes them merely relative concepts, or features of a subject's rational mind, instead of real beings.[5] So my approach will be to examine what full, non-subjective reality they have in Aristotle.

(ii) Frede's view starts from the claim that change implies being (*Met.* IX.3 1047a30–b1).[6] Thus, although this view also distinguishes between change-related *dunamis* and *energeia*, on the one hand, and a further, being-related potentiality and actuality on the other, this further sense is not, in his argument, a distinct "kind" of potency, but an aspect of *all* potency: it highlights the way that potency and actuality each imply that something has a degree of reality.[7] But, Frede argues, it is not obvious that potency implies being. To see that it does, he says, Aristotle elevates *dunamis* to an ontological status by pairing it with actuality.

(iii) Instead of claiming that potentiality and actuality are modal in the sense of being possible or actual, Witt and Beere claim that Aristotle uses the terms as modal *beings*. This view holds that being-in-potency and being-in-activity are modal states of categorical properties. The analysis of *dunamis* and *energeia*, they claim, is different in kind from categorical analysis, and they both claim that potentiality and actuality are modes or ways of being subdividing the categories.[8] Potency is real in a sense different than actuality, and they conceive of the two as alternating modal states of categorical properties; for example, a thing is either red in-potency or in-actuality.[9] According to this view, it is the categories that are unqualified senses of being, while potency and actuality are senses of being insofar as they are modes of the categories. In this view, a change-related sense of power and activity still differs from the ontological terms "potentiality" and "actuality."

Now, I have argued elsewhere against the view that potency and *energeia* are binary, alternating, mutually exclusive states.[10] Chapters 2–5 offer reasons for the positive view that potency persists as itself, as a source, even while it is at-work. But one criticism should be added: this modal categorical reading, in my view, conflicts with Aristotle's repeated assertion that potency and being-at-work are senses of being *simply* or without qualification (*Met.* VI.2 1026a34–b1). In my argument, a categorical property is an unqualified sense of being because it applies to the whole being; for example, the weight of a being is the weight of all of it, it is the whole being insofar as it has weight. Similarly, potency is the whole being insofar as it is able to accomplish a particular act. Now, to be a modality of categorical being is to be qualified by a category. But if potency and activity are unqualified senses of being, their claim to being will not depend on their relation to categorical being.

(iv) There are, however, other ways of understanding what the further things are to which potency and activity extend. Anagnostopoulos showed recently that the extended sense of *dunamis* and *energeia* cannot be potentiality and actuality.[11] He agrees with Frede, as I do, that the terms do imply reality, but argues that no special sense of potency or activity is required for this to be evident.[12] He argues, against Menn, Frede, and Witt and Beere, that potency and activity are not extended to potentiality and actuality, but are extended instead to new kinds, namely to matter and primary being (*ousia*).[13] Finally, he argues that the motion-related sense and the extended sense are analogous because they have a "point of sameness," but he does not say what this point of sameness is.[14] Below, I provide an answer: the point of sameness that connects change concepts to material, form, and *ousia* is precisely *the change-related sense, once it is fully understood*. In my view, the analysis in *Metaphysics* IX follows the methodology of *Physics* I.1 184a–b6, moving from rudimentary and confused but familiar concepts of change to a philosophically clarified grasp of the being of change. The clarified principles provide insight into being beyond what we normally link to change (*Met.* IX.1 1045b33–1046a3).

(v) The view that the ontological sense of potency and actuality is related to change has many adherents as well. But its most notable proponents, Heidegger and Agamben, and their school take what I shall call a negative-dialectical view, in which potency implies its own opposite.

For Heidegger this was not a foregone conclusion.[15] In *Aristotle's Metaphysics Θ 1–3*, he argues that "the actuality of the *dunamis* as such remains completely independent of the actuality of that of which it is capable."[16] To work out the meaning of potency, independently considered, Heidegger distinguishes between different senses of its actuality: (1) the capability on its own, as potency, which he says is opposed to its enactment (*energeia*);[17] (2) capability in its enactment, which he says is compatible with its enactment; and (3) capability as expressed in its product, which he says manifests the capability most of all.[18] But he takes the key determination of potency *as such* to be (1): being opposed to *energeia*. As Brogan observes, for Heidegger, "*dunamis* as affirming is always also denying, *adunaton*, so that this sense of *dunamis* involves an *enantion*, a contrariness or opposition."[19]

Heidegger is right to claim that the being of what is capable is independent of the being of its product. But his elaboration of this claim runs into several difficulties. First, he assumes that the way potency has being is through actuality, which he calls "presence," which appears to collapse the distinction between the two concepts.[20] Second, there are textual difficulties with opposing potency and its enactment.[21] Third, Heidegger reads potency as a force being restrained, and released into enactment. But Aristotle nowhere describes potency as a pressure or force.[22]

The opposition that Heidegger articulated in this passage becomes the theme of Agamben's interpretation of potency in Aristotle. Agamben, analyzing *Metaphysics* IX.8 1050b8–14, argues that potentiality "is not simply the potential to do this or that thing but potential to not-do, potential not to pass into actuality," and because, in his account, potency must be able not to be, he concludes that this ability not to act is the decisive feature of potency: "To be potential means: to be one's own lack, *to be in relation to one's own incapacity*."[23] Yet since some kinds of potency are always at work, for example, the heavenly bodies (*Met.* IX.9 1050b20–28), it seems clear that potency is not essentially a negation. Agamben's account, founded as it is on a contradiction, might be called a "speculative" negative dialectical account.[24] If it is possible to give a positive account of potency that does not depend on self-contradiction, and accounts for the same phenomena, as I aim to do, then both the virtues of, and the need for, this dialectic of self-negation dissipate.

We can sum up by drawing these views into groups: on one side are those who hold that the extended sense of potency, that is, potentiality, is its ontologically relevant one, and they take this either to be its minimal modal sense, a modal sense subordinated to the categories, or a bare marker of reality. On the other side are those who take potency to be an ontologically robust concept in its change-related sense, but define it by negation or self-negation. Anagnostopoulos does not take a strong position: he agrees with M. Frede's view that potency implies some kind of reality, but offers only that its reality must have some other basis than a concept of potentiality.

There is, therefore, an opening for a new position: it is possible to hold that the change-related sense of potency and activity implies being, and that this already constitutes the ontological contribution of these terms. Before turning to the details, allow me to demarcate this claim.

I hold that the extended sense of potency and activity is material and form, not potentiality and actuality. Since material and *ousia* concern the primary sense of categorical being, extending potency and actuality to it clearly has ontological relevance. But the ontological relevance of the terms is not limited to their applicability to material and form: because a discussion of potency and activity is already a discussion of one of the four primary senses of being, namely the energetic, the terms are already implicitly ontological. Aristotle does not need to lift the terms *out of* a change-related sense and *into* an ontological register because, as we saw in the demonstration of change, something that "has" a capacity can, for that reason, be described as a *being*-in-potency. Thus, I contend, a further sense of potency and activity is not necessary for these concepts to have ontological meaning.

My claim, then, is that the analysis of potency and being-at-work in *Metaphysics* IX is, from beginning to end, an analysis of change. If this is right, then the project of that book is not to extend non-ontological concepts to ontological ones. The ontological importance of potency and being-at-work in fact emerges from, and is continuous with, the change-related senses of these terms.[25] This thesis makes sense of the centrality of change in the argument of *Metaphysics* IX. In contrast, by maintaining a distinction in kind between the change-related and being-related senses of the words, scholars make it difficult to understand why Aristotle requires us to go through their change-related senses to get there. In doing so, they implicitly rely on the fact that change *does* have ontological import. The confusion, I think, is that they have not yet properly grasped the respect in which potency and activity are *extended*: they place an extent between being and change, when it should be placed between energetic being and categorical being.

According to my account, then, the different senses of the terms "potency" and "being-at-work" that we find in the text actually evidence *their evolution* through the course of Aristotle's investigation. What scholars think is a distinction between the change-related and being-related senses of potency and activity is actually a distinction between a jumble of familiar concepts of the words earlier in the inquiry and the philosophically clarified understanding of what they are by nature later on. This is the cornerstone of Aristotle's dialectical methodology (*Phys.* I.1 184a–b6). I read *Metaphysics* IX as one of the key sites of this archaeological process, where Aristotle analyzes change in order to deepen and clarify the notions of potency and activity. This brings into view their suitability to describe phenomena, like the relation between material and *ousia*, which are not normally characterized as changes. This discovery is valuable because, at a minimum, change concepts offer us new and useful ways to describe categorical being.[26] Therefore I shall concentrate, at least at first, *not* on what potency and activity are extended to and how, but on the concepts through which Aristotle says we need to go to understand this: the concepts related to change.

In the course of my argument, I also aim to show that potency and *energeia* are not alternating states; potency is not opposed in any way to *energeia*, neither as possibility, nor as insistence, nor as privation. Potency is instead a distinct and independent way of being that is *compatible* with being-at-work. It is a permanent aspect of things that accounts for their propensity to get to work. All of this shall demonstrate how the change-related sense of potency has inherent implications for ontology.

Potency as Source

Potency is, for Aristotle, a particular kind of source. So in order to grasp its core sense, I will describe the being of sources in general, and then what distinguishes potency as a source, first by examining the conditions in which it acts, and second by examining its complex relationship to what it achieves. Finally, the chapter turns to the question: if potency implies reality, what is this reality like?

To be a source is to be something in particular that necessarily and immediately sets to work. "What is common to all sources is to be the first thing from which something is or comes to be or is known; of these some spring up within [*enuparchousai*] while others [are] outside [*ektos*]" (*Met.* V.1 1013a18–20, my trans.). Aristotle distinguishes the sorts of things that count as sources, referring to nature (within) and potency (outside), but he does not provide a general description of what sources are or how they act. This makes sense if a source is always a *particular* source. But we can infer what sources are through the analysis of potency and nature.

Potency has the following character: when the right conditions are met and the right beings are together, it necessarily and immediately sets to work (*Met.* IX.5 1048a4–6, *Soul* II.5 417a5–10). Things that have come to be as natural wholes (*sumpephuken*) already meet the right conditions, since there is no other on which they depend, and so they are immediately at work (*Met.* IX.1 1046a27–29). Potency and nature differ in the conditions in which they act, but they share what it is to be a source, namely, to set to work when these conditions are met.

The conditions of action are part of the structure or form that defines the source. The structure of the source is what determines what happens, when, and how, for "a thing will do the things it is capable of in the way it is capable of them" and not in any other way (*Met.* IX.5 1048a23):

> It is never necessary to add to the definition [of a potency] "when nothing from outside obstructs it," for having a potency or being potent is being capable of acting, and this is not in every way but when things are in certain ways, in which ways the obstructions from outside will be distinguished or cast out, since these are removed by some things in the definition [*diorismō*]. (*Met.* IX.5 1048a16–22)

The conditions in which a potency sets to work are part of what it is to be a particular potency. Obstructions are reduced to a failure to meet the potency's inherent activation conditions. Whenever those conditions are met, it is at work.

While the activation conditions of a potency are *part* of its structure, they do not define that structure because they precisely do not account for the sourcehood of the potency. The nature of potency is not determined by these activation conditions; these conditions are determined by the source. Saying that a rubber band is defined by how fingers pull and release it misses exactly what makes it a rubber band, namely, the way it responds to stretching by pulling itself back together.[27]

Potency has this structure whether it is natural or acquired. Natural potencies, skills, and crafts are ultimately the same in this respect:

> But always, whenever what can act and what can be acted upon are together, what is potential comes to be at work, as the one learning, from being something potentially becomes something potentially in a different way ... and once he is in this condition, if nothing prevents it, he is at work and contemplates, or else he would be in the contrary condition, that of ignorance. And these things are similar with natural things; for what is cold is potentially hot, but when it has changed [i.e., become hot], by the time it is fire, it burns, unless something prevents it and gets in the way. (*Phys.* VIII.4 255a31–b9; see *Soul* II.5 417a5–10, *Met.* IX.5 1048a4–6)[28]

Aristotle says three things in this passage that are relevant for our purposes: first, although knowledge is acquired, when it is complete it is potent the way other natural things already are, and is immediately at work just as earth falls and fire burns.[29] So all sources have this propensity to act, whether the source is nature (*phusis*), desire (*orexis*), or choice (*prohairesis*) (*Met.* IX.5 1048a10–16).[30]

Second, activity is not something that happens to potency: the activity comes from the source, that is, what is at work is the source. This is clear even in the way Aristotle describes material as "a co-cause with the form of the things that come into being, like a mother," which "inherently yearns for [*ephiesthai*] and stretches out toward [*oregesthai*] it [the form] *by its own nature*" (*Phys.* I.9 192a13–18).[31] Its nature "yearning for" and "reaching for" metaphorically express the being proper to potency, namely, the tendency to be-at-work immediately unless prevented. What this means is that the agent-patient relationship is not the fundamental character of sources, but a derivative feature. The basis of agent-patient relationships, as we shall see below, is not force, but mutual affection.

Third, there is a distinction between potency and activity, for a thing can be potent without being at work *if its conditions are not met*. This means that it is possible for something to be fire while not currently burning—that is, be fire in-potency—just as a builder is still a builder even while he is having lunch.

Potency as a Source in an Other

Now that I have marked out what it is to be a source, what distinguishes potency as a kind of source is next. Potency has two aspects that we need to describe: the source itself, and the kinds of things it accomplishes.

Aristotle defines the primary kind of potency as "a source of change [*archē metabolēs*] in some other thing or in the same thing as other" (*Met.* IX.1 1046a10, *Met.* IX.8 1049b7–9). This structurally distinguishes it from nature, which he defines as "a source of change [*archē kinētikē*], though not in something else, but in a thing itself as itself" (*Met.* IX.8 1049b8–9). So, while potency depends on an other to act, natural sources do not. Aristotle writes: "insofar as something has developed as a natural whole [*sumpephuken*], it cannot be passive to itself, since it is one thing and there is no other" (*Met.* IX.1 1046a27–29).[32] Some potencies, such as perception and procreation, can be natural in a derivative sense by being capacities natural beings have, but I am concerned here with what kind of sources potency and nature are in the primary sense.

The dependence of the potency on its other is evident, for instance, in the comparison Aristotle makes between sense organs and burnable things: "The perceptive potency does not have being as a being-at-work, but only as a potency, and this is why the sense organ is not perceived, just as what is burnable is not burned itself by itself without something to set it on fire" (*Soul* II.5 417a7–8).[33] Perception, like unlit wood, *is something* on its own, but requires an active outside source to light it up and complete its ability to perceive. Potency is the name for how things are incomplete by themselves insofar as they need other beings to act. This sort of incompleteness is true even of the "completable" potencies that can be mastered, like the skill of building, which requires buildable things, or tennis, which requires rackets, courts, and so on.[34]

From this definition, Aristotle builds an account of the way different potent beings interact with one another, framed in terms of an agent-patient relationship. It trades, that is, on a distinction between a potential-to-affect and a potential-to-be-affected. But he takes a somewhat counterintuitive stance on that relationship. For it would seem reasonable to expect that the relationship is based on the agency of the agent, that *agency* is the source of the ability to be acted upon. After all, potencies to act upon others are more responsible for what happens than potencies to be acted upon; for example, a builder decides when the materials will change, and what they will change into. Thus, being an agent takes causal precedence. But it does not follow from this that agency is the basis for the relationship between beings. For both the agent and patient are still required in order to act.

Aristotle argues that the capacity to act and the capacity to be acted upon are, in a way, one potency, and then adds that in another way it is differentiated by its location. He puts the first point this way: "There is a sense in which the potency of acting and being acted upon is one (since something is potential both by means of its own potency to be acted upon, and by something else's potency to be acted upon by it)" (*Met.* IX.1 1046a20–21).[35] The primary capacity is for such bodies to be heated by one another. The power of heating is the capacity of bodies to be heated by one another. Things belong to the same domain of changes, say, having heat or location, because they are all able to be affected in that particular way. In this way, separate things have the same potency. This is what makes all agent-patient relationships possible: for bodily agency to be possible at all, the agent must be able to be affected in the way it affects the patient.[36] This means that potency, too, like all sources, is not constituted by agency, or even by an agent-patient relationship.[37] The relationship between beings that distinguishes potency is constituted through two things having the same potency to be affected. The problem with having a bull in a pottery shop is that the bull and the pottery are both bodily things that can be moved by one another. House-building can happen only because the builder's body can be moved by the construction materials, and those materials by his body. While he is building, the builder may not be moved insofar as he is a builder, but his hands and body must be movable for other things to be moved by them, that is, they must be bodily things to move anything else bodily. Of course, Aristotle argues that there are things that move without being affected, for example, things that are desired.

Aristotle's point here is another reason to resist the Extinction Hypothesis (the idea that, for example, a hot stone loses its ability to be heated when it gets hot). The first reason we examined was that potencies extend beyond what is actively the case (*Phys.* III.1 201a19–27, see "Potency extends . . ." in chap. 2), and are therefore always open to being affected, even in the ways that they are currently affecting other things. Aristotle's point here in Metaphysics IX.1 1046a20–21, by contrast, is that an agent has the ability to be affected in precisely the way that it actively is, for example, a hot stone retains the ability for its heat to be changed, and this connects its capacity to other things and gives it the ability to heat them up.[38] When the temperature of two things reaches equilibrium, they still both have the capacity to be heated or cooled. This means that when heating stops, it is not the capacity to be heated which has vanished, but the activity of heating, because the activity of being hot, namely, that one thing is hotter than the other, is no longer there.

Potency in this sense is shared; it cannot be isolated in a particular being, and marks out a way that many things are one. This positive nature of potency—that a thing is potent because of a way it is the same or one with others—shows that potency is, but is not itself *a being*, because it is one thing *in* two beings.[39]

On the other hand, in spite of this unity between acting and being acted upon, there is another sense in which they are not one, but two:

> ... there is a sense in which they [acting and being acted upon] are different. For the one is in the thing acted upon
> (for it is by virtue of having a certain kind of source, and even because its material is a certain kind of source that the acted-upon thing is acted upon, even though it is one thing and is acted upon by the action of another—for something oily is burnable and something that gives way just so is crushable, and similarly in other cases),
> but the other is in the thing acting,
> as heat and the house-building power are in, respectively, something that confers heat and someone who can build houses.
> (*Met.* IX.1 1046a21–29)[40]

The potency of acting differs from the potency to be acted upon, first of all because they are *in* different beings. But this makes their potencies much more specific: the bull can be bruised, but the plates can be smashed. By contrast, a builder's shaping power is quite different from the potency of buildable things: the buildable things are changed into something else, whereas the builder becomes more skilled at building.

These distinctions have a counterpart in *energeia*. Two things can have the same activity; for example, the activity of teaching *just is* the student's activity of learning. When we locate it in a particular being, however, it is clear that the same activity belongs to both things without being the same for each; for example, the activity of the teacher is not a change, while the activity of the learner is (*Physics* III.3 202b6–25, see "*Energeia* and *Entelecheia* in Change" in chap. 3).

To sum up: potency is necessarily other-related, but this relation has two aspects. In one, beings are one with respect to their common passive potency and common activity, while in another beings are many, differentiated by their location and distinguished into agent or patient.

The Accomplishments of Potency

To be a source, however, is to be the source *of* something (*Phys.* I.2 185a4–6), that is, to complete or accomplish (*telein*) something. Different kinds of sources will have different relationships with what they accomplish, so we need to examine what distinguishes potency's relationship with the sort of accomplishment (*telos*) to which it is directed.

Potencies are distinguished, then, by this key structure: they aim at accomplishing something. This feature of potencies receives the most attention in the literature: potency is normally described as being defined by its ends.[41] But just as potency is not defined by the conditions of activation, it is not defined by its ends. Still, we can understand potency through the complex of relationships that it has with its accomplishment (its *telos*).

Potency is related to its accomplishment in three ways: (i) It is able to accomplish opposites (e.g., health or sickness), (ii) It is only able to do one thing at a time, and (iii) It is able to act or not to act. I shall treat each of these in turn.

(i) Aristotle argues that what distinguishes primary being (*ousia*) most of all is that it is capable of changing into opposite categorical predicates, for example, hot and cold, large and small (*Cat.* 5 4b16–19). So one sense of potency is to have "a potency to change in any direction whatever, whether for the worse or for the better," where "worse or better" stands in for any pair of opposites (*Met.* V.12 1019b2–3). The key here is that, in some respects, the potency is indifferent to which of the things it is. I shall call this the Any Opposite Principle.

The question arises, however, whether the potency to be hot is different altogether than the potency to be cold: why is it one and the same capacity that is capable of opposites? Aristotle says:

> So far as [something] is meant as a potent thing, that very thing is capable of opposites. For instance, the very thing that we say to be potentially healthy is the same as what [is potentially] sick, and [also] at the same time, for the same potency is of being healthy and falling ill, or of being at rest and of being at change, or of building up and of knocking down, or of being built and of falling down. Therefore, being capable of opposites obtains [*huparchei*] at the same time, though the opposite things are unable [to obtain actively] at the same time, just as the [opposite] activities cannot obtain at the same time, for example being healthy and being sick. (*Met.* IX.9 1051a5–13, my trans.)

A single potency, the *same* potency, is capable of accomplishing opposite things. Potency is not an actual state or a mode of being a quality or quantity. It is the name for the fact that someone at-work being healthy can also be sick; and because of this, that health or sickness will necessarily belong to this being here at different times.

This description of potency is periphrastic for a reason: it avoids characterizing potency in terms of an abstraction like temperature. The continuum marked out by the opposites is an abstraction derived from the poles of change. But the continuum is not a being: what is there is only, for example, something hot; its ability to be hot includes, implies, and is also at the same time the ability to be cold. Potency is immanent and concrete; it is not related to a transcendent type: the potency is for being hot or cold, not for having a temperature.

(ii) Speaking abstractly, however, we say that potency lays out a range of things that can be the case—say, a capacity to be hot, lukewarm, and cold. But potency is also what limits a thing to a single accomplishment along this range:

> Even if one wishes and desires to do two things at the same time or to do contrary things, one will not do them, and there is no potency for doing them at the same time, since a thing will do the things it is capable of in the way it is capable of them. (*Met.* IX.5 1048a21–25)

A being can only be one thing at a time in the same respect. The phrase "there is no potency for doing them at the same time" shows that Aristotle is presenting this fact as a feature of potency, not of activity: *potency* is finite in this way. The capacity to be actively hot means that when a thing is hot it is not capable of being actively cold at the same time and in the same respect. Thus, the capacity to be hot or cold is the capacity to be *either* actively hot *or* actively cold, not the capacity to be *both* hot and cold. Capabilities are only capable of one thing at a time. Negatively put: being capable means being unable to be at work in more than one way in a certain respect at a certain time. Positively put: being capable means being able to do things in the way that one is capable of doing them. Potencies are causally specific: they narrow what a thing can *do* to one thing at a time. I shall call this the Singularity Principle, since it is an outcome of the singular specificity of potencies.

(iii) I shall call the third point, that the same potency admits of being active or not active (*Met.* IX.9 1050b8–16), the Binary Principle. It rejects the idea that the capacities for action and inaction are different.

The Binary Principle follows from the combination of the Singularity Principle and the Any Opposite Principle: the same thing at the same time will be contrary things potentially, but not in full activity at the same time

(*Met.* IV.5 1009a33). This allows Aristotle to say that the same thing (e.g., a statue) can both be (i.e., potentially), and not be (i.e., at-work) at the same time (*Met.* IV.5 1009a22). A stone is *both* hot *and* cold in the sense that it *can* be either hot or cold while it is at-work being only one. So in a certain way the statue comes to be out of not-being (at-work), but in another sense it comes out of being (potentially).

The principles can now be combined. We may say that a thing possesses a potency just in case

(1) the very thing that is able to be healthy is also at the same time and *for that very reason* able to be sick,
(2) the thing with this ability can only be *one* of these at any one time, either healthy or sick, or something in-between,
(3) the thing with this ability *must* be one of these.

These propositions are inseparable from one another: in the concept of potency, they *imply one another*. They are the same, and the name for this single complex is potency. Potency is specific and inseparable from the actual constitution of a particular body (as [2] and [3] show). Yet the potency implies that this body has something about it that can be abstracted, namely a continuity between hot and cold, healthy or sick (as shown by [1]) that can be marked off in speech. Put more precisely, in this description, potency expresses the inseparability of a singular body from a structure that necessarily refers to something counterfactual, namely, what it is not and cannot be right now. Potency makes room in being, it relates things that can be to what is the case. In this way, potency as a source is a structure that has implications beyond what actively is.

This principle reveals a structure of being that is hard to characterize. It follows from proposition (2) that different accomplishments of a single potency exclude others, so that it is not capable of simultaneously being at work in every way that it is potent: a thing cannot, for example, be all temperatures at once. More narrowly, one potency cannot be at work in every way it is capable of all at once *because one of its own aspects* is at work being the case. Through this we can grasp the finitude of potency and *energeia* (on the singularity of *energeia*, "The Basis for Ontological Multiplicity" in chap. 1).

To recap, the Binary Principle is an outcome of the Singularity and Any Opposite principles: since the same potency, ranging over several possibilities, is nevertheless only an ability to do one at a time, potency is necessarily limited with respect to its own range of potential acts. This conception of potency differs from the concept Agamben puts forward, that incapacity essentially *constitutes* what it is to exercise a capacity, in other words, that every action is at the same time an inaction in the same respect (or of a potency held back from its own enactment, as Heidegger has it). Since things can be potent for things they are not currently doing, the Binary Principle follows necessarily.

The Being of Potency

Now that I have described what it means to be a source, and described what distinguishes a potency as a source, I will examine what sort of being potency has. The first task is to show that potency has an independent claim to be. Then we will examine the most conspicuous way that potency is.

Aristotle argues explicitly that potency entails being: "[If we] take the being-potentially [*dunamei*] in the same way as if something were potentially [*dunaton*] a statue, [then] this will also *be* a statue" (*Phys*. III.6 206b19–22).[42] Examples of potencies we have seen so far include buildable things and builders, visible things and perceivers, knowers and things known, and fire and burnable things. Potencies are prominent among beings:

> And it is clear that most of what seem to be primary beings [*ousiai*] are potencies [*dunameis*], not only the parts of animals . . . but also earth and fire and air. (*Met*. VII.16 1040b5–10)[43]

> Now since being [*ousia*], in the sense of what underlies a thing as material, is acknowledged, and is in potency [*dunamei*], it remains to say what the being [*ousia*] of perceptible things is in the sense of being-at-work. (*Met*. VIII.2 1042b9–11)[44]

Aristotle in this way regularly foregrounds potencies as the most readily acknowledged sort of independent things (*ousiai*), to the point that being-at-work seems to be a less obvious candidate for being (*ousia*).

As we saw in chapter 2, the demonstration of change depended on the fact that potent beings are evident on their own. Aristotle takes the existence of the ability as evidence that what makes the ability what it is—the activity—must admit of being, at least at some point. This move depends, then, on the assumption that reality can be extended (*contra* M. Frede) from potency to activity.[45] Of course, this argument depends on potential beings having a legitimate claim to be. We examined in chapters 1 and 2 how this legitimacy could be established through a phenomenology of aspects. Put in linguistic terms, the adjective "potent" (*dunaton*) and the noun "potency" (*dunamis*) in fact point us toward a fundamental way of grasping a being concretely, by grasping the being itself insofar as it is potent (*to dunamei on*). Aristotle switches back and forth between the adjective and the noun to emphasize their interrelationship. In the passage specifically addressing when something is in-potency, for example, Aristotle says: "there is something that is potent [*dunaton*], and this is what is healthy in potency [*dunamei*]" (*Met.* IX.7 1049a3–4, my trans.). Viewed in this way, potency and its activity make up one of the several basically distinct aspects or senses of a concrete thing, alongside categorical beings (e.g., size, kind, position) and truth.

The advantage of the dative formulation (i.e., "being-in-potency," "being-insofar-as-it-is-potent," "potential being") is that it avoids the risk that potency would be mistaken either for a property (*dunaton*), as it could be in some common phrases, for example, "His best features are his red hair and his ability to make me laugh," or mistaken as having a separate being (*dunamis*), for example, "Michael Jordan acquired the ability to shoot three-pointers." The dative forces us to confront a being in its aspect of being potent: the being *in* its potency, or *insofar as* it is potent, or *as* potent.

Complete Potencies

I have briefly set forward the case for the independent being of potency. Now I turn to the most obvious way that potencies are related to being: some beings themselves are named after them, which means the being is viewed *as potent*, or in-potency. Aristotle's most detailed description of when something is in-potency is in *Metaphysics* IX.7, where he examines three cases: *technē, poiēsis*, and *phusis*:

> *Technē*: "not everything can be healed, by either medical skill or chance, but there is something that is potential [*dunaton*], and this is what is healthy in potency [*dunamei*]. But the mark of what comes to be in complete activity [healed] out of what has being in potency [*entelecheiai gignomenou ek tou dunamei ontos*], as a result of thinking [i.e., done by a doctor], is that (a) whenever it is desired it comes to be [*gignetai*] when nothing outside prevents it, (b) and there, in the thing healed, whenever nothing in it prevents it." (*Met.* IX.7 1049a3–8)[46]

Aristotle sets aside the sort of healing that the body might do by itself, and looks only at the case where the activity of a doctor—that is, her *thinking*— brings about the healing. To be healthy in-potency is for health—that is, the product of change—to come to be (a) whenever it is desired and nothing in the doctor or the patient prevents it. Furthermore, in a medical context, (b) a body is in-potency whenever it will set to work being healthy when the conditions are right and the doctor has removed the obstacles to healing. Aristotle gives another example of artificial change:

> *Poiēsis*: "And it is similar too with a potential house; (a) if the builder desires it, [and] (b) if nothing in this or in the material for becoming a house stands in the way, and there is nothing that needs to have been added or taken away or changed, [then] this is potentially a house, and it is just the same with all other things of which the source of coming into being is external." (*Met.* IX.7 1049a8–13)[47]

This second example closely resembles the first, but specifies that the materials need to have been changed or already completely capable for them to be called a house in-potency. Once the materials have a fully developed capacity to hold together as a house, that is, as the product of change, then they are in-potency that house, for example, once the wood has been cured and shaped, and joints have been cut. Something is in-potency the product, properly speaking, at the *end* of a change, not at the beginning.[48] As Brentano argued, change constitutes a new potency, namely the ability to be a house.[49] But the being in-potency in this case is viewed as the source of the *product* (e.g., being healthy or the house) rather than as the source of *change* (e.g., the buildable). Unlike in the case of doctoring, in which the body's ability to heal is aided and organized by the doctor, in *poiēsis*, the source of change in the materials is itself *generated* by an outside source of change.[50]

This pattern can be extended to natural sources by putting the source of change into the thing itself. This is how Aristotle formulates being-in-potency in the case of *phusis*:

> *Phusis*: "And of all those things in which coming into being is by means of something they have in themselves, (a) those are in potency which will be on their own if nothing outside blocks their way, for instance, the semen is not yet potential, since it has to be in something else [the womb], and to change, but (b) whenever it is already such [i.e., when it has come to be in-potency] by its *own* source of change [and not by another source], it is from that point on in potency, though in that previous condition it has need of another source." (*Met.* IX.7 1049a13–17)[51]

Whereas, in the first two cases, the source of change requires an outside source to set what is in-potency to work, for natural things, once they are in-potency they are already at work. As long as a natural thing still requires an outside source for it to be what it is, it is not yet in-potency. This confirms my argument in chapter 3 that the reason why capacities for change are incomplete is that they require an outside source.[52] Semen, for Aristotle, is not the material that constitutes an embryo, it is an auxiliary, an outside agent that organizes the materials to generate the embryo (*PA* I.1 641b30–37, *Gen. An.* 734b28–735a3). Semen is not capable of generating an embryo on its own, and therefore it is not yet in-potency: it requires an outside source—for example, a womb, warmth, nourishment—for its potency to come to be. When it has come to be in-potency, it is from then on the source that brings the embryo into being.

Similarly, for a body to be able to live is just to live, unless something gets in the way (*Soul* II.1 412a27–28). To remove the potency is for a body to die. Being-in-potency does not alternate with or resist being-in-activity: it is the very source that is at work. There is no separation, opposition, or contradiction between ability and activity; still, they are two different aspects of the same being: the activity arises continuously from the potency. Living beings thus belong to the class of *self-changing beings*: things that are continuously changing in and through themselves, or because of their being (*Met.* IX.8 1050b28–34). Their being is not, then, potency, for potency is a source of change and rest *in another*. So self-changing beings have themselves as their source *and being*. And since to be a natural being is to be a source of change in itself as itself (*Met.* IX.8 1049b8–9), these things move in and through themselves, as heavenly bodies do.[53]

In sum: if we distinguish between capacities for change and capacities for being, as some scholars do, we must allow the following case: some beings include capacities for change in their very definition.[54] Something whose being is named through its potency, namely a complete potency or a being-in-potency, is distinguished from mere potency by the fact that *a complete potency is a source*, not just of any result, but of a particular result—health, a house, an embryo, life.[55] This important claim is the subject of the next chapter.

A Map of Potency and Activity

I have now made two distinctions that overlap with one another: first, for a being to be *merely* potent is not the same as for it to be *completely* potent. These do not exist in the same way. We need to examine how they are different and how they are related. Second, a capacity can be completed in two ways, either by itself becoming complete, for example, becoming a violinist, or by acting, for example, playing the violin. This means that complete potencies *still* require a further completion. To understand the being of potency, then, we need to examine the relationship between these two sorts of potency, and two sorts of completion. These distinctions overlap, but only in part, so "one must divide up the senses of potency and being-complete," that is, distinguish the senses in which things are potent, and the senses in which things are complete (*Soul* II.5 417a22–24).[56] They can be laid out topologically as follows.

(i) Something is called merely potent when it is a being that belongs to the class of things that have the potency. Mere potency is traditionally called "first potency." For example, a human being who has never done geometry or played the violin is called "capable of geometry" or "capable of being a violinist," while unarranged stones are capable of being a house, but only because they are the sort of thing that is typically capable of being part of a house.

While a student's capacity to do geometry is incomplete, she is more or less indifferently capable of opposites: she might not even recognize whether she succeeded or failed. She can only do geometry with the assistance of others. While we could say that she is a geometer in the sense that human beings are the animals capable of geometry, we would not describe her in particular as a geometer.

(ii) Something that has a complete potency is a being-in-potency. It is traditionally called both "second potency" and "first actuality" because it is an overlap or fusion of potency and "actuality" (being-complete, *entelecheia*). A being-in-potency is, for example, the woman who has learned the capacity to do geometry, and is completely capable of doing it whenever she so desires. This means that she no longer needs outside help, and in the right conditions she sets to work immediately. She always does geometry successfully and well (*Met.* IX.1 1046a17). She is not indifferently capable of opposites: the capacity to fail at geometry has been removed from her. She completely expresses what it is to do geometry, so her being is properly described by the potency: she is a geometer. Finally, her capacity remains whether it is at work or not: she remains a geometer whether she is sleeping or doing geometry. In fact, her condition of being a geometer resists being undermined: she does not easily forget how to do geometry, even when she is hungry, sick, out of practice, or drunk (*Met.* IX.1 1046a13–15).

(iii) Something that is at-work exercising its potency is complete in another, higher sense. This is traditionally called "second actuality." The geometer who is currently working on a geometry problem is fulfilling the meaning of her capacity. This fulfillment is a different sort of being than the potency. It is the enactment, activity, completion, or being-at-work of her ability to do geometry. This activity comes to be and ceases to be depending on the conditions and the geometer's desire to do it. Conceiving of potency and activity this way allows Aristotle to reformulate all change as an event of becoming what one already was; change is not an event of negation, it is the proper activity of nature.

Now that I have drawn this map, there are several important observations to make. First, although it is easiest to present these distinctions as a sequence, each is a distinct sort of being, rather than a phase in a temporal development. They stack. For example, because something merely potent is potent based on its *species*, it follows that the first kind of potency is *not eliminated* when the capacity is brought to completion. Since the potential geometer only possesses that potency by means of her *humanity*, the elimination of that sense of potency would amount to eliminating her humanity altogether. Since the geometer remains human, the first potency remains as well.

Second, the distinction between (ii) and (iii) means that potency has two sorts of completion: on the one hand, it itself can be completed, and on the other hand, a potency is completed in a further way by acting. To be a complete potency is not to be an activity. To be a complete potency is to be completely ready oneself to set to work when the conditions are right. For example, no outside source is required to provide a geometer with the internal source of motion to complete a geometrical proof. Still, activity is the completion (*entelecheia*) of potency.

Third, because of the other-related structure of potency, it will remain true in each case that the actor requires others in order to act, as a violinist requires a violin, or a builder requires tools and materials. In this respect, completed potencies resemble all other potencies.

But, fourth, complete potencies have a different structure from those which are indifferently capable of opposites; for example, the ability to be either hot or cold, standing or fallen down. For whenever the potency is used, the same thing happens: someone able to count does so correctly every time, someone able to play the violin does so well every time, and an animal continues to live, unless they are obstructed. Such a capacity means that it will succeed every time, unless something interferes. In an abstract way, the geometer remains capable of failure, but this is due either to imperfections in her capacity or to interference, so they will be incidental rather than essential to her potency.

This is because, while a student could have all the materials and not know what to do, or be just as likely to fail as to succeed at his task, the accomplished violinist or builder's *agency* is complete, so when the things that get acted upon are there, they will accomplish what their potency aims to accomplish. Whereas one sort of natural potency is symmetrical—for example, one thing heats another while the other cools it—this sort of potency is asymmetrical, based upon the agent who possesses them, for example, the violinist who only plays well, or the body that keeps living. That potency can establish this asymmetry bolsters its claim to ontological independence.

Fifth, all of this will only be the case if being-in-potency *continues to be at the same time and in the same respect* as being-at-work. A violinist (i.e., a being-in-potency) remains a violinist, but her violin-playing (i.e., her being-at-work) comes and goes. The persistence of potency gives it a strong claim to primacy in *being* (*ousia*) over activity (*Met.* V.11 1019a8–15).[57] Aristotle both argues for this point, and resists the conclusion that potency is thereby ontologically primary (*Phys.* II.1 193a9–b18; *Met.* IX.8, XII.6 1071b23–1072a18; and "The Argument of Metaphysics IX.8" in chap. 6). Being-in-potency is not, as Witt and Beere hold, a modal state that alternates with actuality.[58]

In sum: potency is used in two basic ways, which correspond to two levels of completeness. Some things are *merely* potent: for example, the newborn baby who is in a distant way a being capable of speech, the ability to go camping. These have a kind of reality because change can bring them about (*Met.* IX.3 1047a33–35). But other things are potent in the proper sense, as when someone is fluent in French, or everything is packed and ready for the camping trip (*Met.* IX.7 1049a5–13). In both cases, what has the capacity can be articulated as a being insofar as it is capable: for example, a French speaker, camping gear. The difference is that the baby is a French speaker, but only in an abstract way, while this mess of stuff is still camping equipment, but when their capacities are complete, they *are* in a different way.

Changing Into Oneself

I have demarcated complete potencies from others, and mapped out the relation between mere potency, complete potency, and activity. But to understand what sort of being potency has, it is necessary to describe what it means to complete a potency, in ontological terms. How do we describe, on an ontological level, what happens as a potency is completed?[59] Seen in one way, Aristotle says, the process of completing something is (1) a change into something it is not, but in another way it is (2) a change into something it already is in a certain respect (*Soul* II.5 417a30–35, b17–28). In this analysis, Aristotle's primary concern is not the concept of change in general, but specifically the concept of alteration (*alloiōsis*), a change in the sense of something becoming other than it is.[60] The concept of completion as (1) a change into something it is not will turn out to be, in a key respect, empty. Therefore, completion is better viewed as (2) a thing becoming what it already is.

I shall take the two in order.

(1) In this approach, the completion of potency is an alteration of what a thing is. The potency is generated by something acting on what is *unlike* it. The completion of potency is a change insofar as an outside source repeatedly changes the subject *from* the privation *to* the form; for example, in learning, a teacher repeatedly moves the geometry student out of not-knowing into knowing. All this time, the student's potency is incomplete, since she requires the outside source in order to do geometry. But in the process of alteration (*alloiōsis*) the form (*eidos*), that is, the knowledge in the teacher, destroys what is unlike it, namely, its contrary privation (*sterēsis*), that is, ignorance and the ability to fail. In this description, the alteration is the activity of destroying this opposite.

The change in the student's *disposition* that eventually occurs happens on a higher level than the destruction of the privation: what is merely potent changes into something completely capable. The completion of its disposition is gradually accomplished by many smaller changes away from the privation and into the form. When it is complete, the disposition either keeps itself in the form, or can take on the form without outside help.

(2) In this approach, the completion of potency is not an alteration out of itself into something else. The potency emerges through the action of something on what is *like* it. The being in-potency (*tou dunamei ontos*) is therefore *preserved* through the change by the complete being (*hupo tou entelecheiai ontos*). In fact, the activation (*energeia*) of the potency is not a change at all, but a free development (*epidosis*)[61] toward itself and its completeness (*entelecheia*) (*Soul* II.5 417a22-b9). The only thing that distinguishes this from a natural process of maturation is that an outside source is required for the potency to become what it is.

The most striking feature of (2) is that the generation of a complete potency *preserves* the being, much as enactment or activation do. As we saw in the previous section, Aristotle does not consider the activation of something that is in-potency to be an alteration at all: the activity of building is the expression of the builder's capacity. That is, since the builder is merely doing what he is able to do, the exercise of the potency does not involve a change into something *else*.[62] This is the same in the case of completion.

But the most striking feature of (1) is the fact that what is destroyed here is *non-being*. This leads us to think that the process of completion is not an alteration at all. A capacity is completed by negating a negation. How are we to understand this negation? Recalling *Physics* I.7–8, we can say that what is negated is something inessential, incidental to the potency. Thus, the completion of the ability to be a geometer destroys something that is not (i.e., something without its own being or character, for example, ignorance of geometry), insofar as it is a negation. Ignorance of geometry had no ontological status on its own; this privation (*sterēsis*) is projected backward as the negation of the form that comes to be, so it is not something on its own, it is *precisely something that is not*. So, as Parmenides said, in attempting to think about non-being, we are led back to being.

This strange situation suggests that processes of completion are best understood without negation. The thing alters—the marathon runner builds slow-twitch muscle—but what is left behind, namely the inability to run marathons, never was anything itself. What happens, then, is that the runner's abilities become more what they are.

If our earlier analysis of the "causal space" of potencies is right, however, a richer way of understanding the removal of the opposite emerges. Let's recall that potencies for opposites (the Any Opposite Principle) are constitutively incomplete, since at any one time only one part of their dual capacity can be at work (the Singularity Principle). Now, if the capacity for one of the opposites is removed, the potency will no longer be at odds with itself, and will coincide with itself. Such a potency is entirely what it is, and is therefore complete.

This means that mere potency is neither converted into complete potency, nor destroyed. For to the extent that the process of completion involves the negation of an *opposite*, the mere potency will not change at all. This leaves it to be what it will be on its own.

In sum, Aristotle distinguishes between the two possible accounts of the process of completion. If it is viewed as an alteration, he argues, it involves destroying something that is not. The emptiness of this idea naturally leads us away from this idea toward an understanding of alteration as preservation. There is ultimately only one viable account of completion: that a thing becomes what it already was in potency. We only call the process of completing a potency an alteration because we lack another name for becoming what one is (*Soul* II.5 417b7–9, b29–418a6).

Thus, when Aristotle distinguishes the three ways that he has articulated change, it is clear which sorts of description are superior:

> That which, from being potential, learns and grasps knowledge
> through the one who is complete and able to teach either (a) must
> not [be said to] be acted upon, or alteration [must be said] to be in
> two ways: (b) a change [*metabolē*] into a condition [of] privation,

and (c) [a change] into dispositions [*hexeis*] and the nature. (*Soul* II.5 417b11–16, my trans.)

Aristotle's analysis of the completion of potency shows that it can be described in three ways, which reduce to the best one. The completion of learning is either (b) the rearrangement of something to deprive it of a privation—an option that cancels itself out and leads to (c) coming into one's own potencies and nature, or (a) a process that is not initiated by an other, but by a source setting itself to work. This analysis can be generalized, that is, all change can be described in these terms.

Modal Consequences of Potency

To this point, this chapter has concerned itself with both what potency is and what its being is. In so doing it has concentrated on the authoritative (*kurios*) sense of the word *dunamis*, namely, being a source of change in an other (*Met.* IX.1 1046a4–12). But as Brentano remarked, the concept of "possibility"—a distinct meaning of the word *dunamis*—has become prominent in ontology.[63] I will briefly point out two features of the potency-possibility distinction, in Aristotle's account: that possibility is anchored in the real potencies of particular beings, and that potency pervades modality.

First, Aristotle subordinates possibility to the more robust sense of potency, examined above, by arguing that "it cannot be true to say that such-and-such is possible, but will not be the case," that is, that a thing will not be possible unless a real potency can accomplish it (*Met.* IX.4 1047b2–30).[64] But this subordination affects the meaning of modal concepts: they are located in the real potencies of particular beings. It is uncontroversial to point out that Aristotle's physics is not an account of universal laws applied in particular situations. But this means that possibility is not an independent universal concept; possibilities, regularities, and necessities are expressions of the character of particular potencies

Second, potency matters to ontology in at least three modal situations: when a thing is actively being a certain way and able to be so, when it is not active in this way, but able to be so, and when it is incapable of being so. Although potency is most conspicuous when a thing is both able to be the case and not at-work being that way, the most central insight is that potency is there and contributes to each of the three modal situations. When a thing is the case, potency is what allows it to be and at the same time determines whether what actually is will be necessary or contingent. When something is not the case but able to be, potency is responsible for its contingency. When something is not able to be the case, potency is responsible for the necessity that it cannot be.[65]

Broadie concludes her work on Aristotle's modality as follows: "no proposition or set of propositions is necessary, contingent, or impossible unless something is actual, and although this too may be described by a proposition, its *actuality* finds no place in any propositional set."[66] She is certainly right that the actuality of the actual is not part of the domain of categorical assertion. My suggestion is that, due to the sort of reality that belongs to potency, she could also have said ". . . unless something is *potent*."

Potency is not only an unexercised ability, nor is it a mere possibility that evades being impossible by reference to something actual. It is a positive way of being that persists in its own right, a principle of the structure of being. Potency does not get its reality from actuality, it is not a mode of actuality, and it is not a negation or derivation from actuality. Its positive character is to be the source of activity.

* * *

This chapter opened with an argument that the change-related sense of potency and activity is also their ontological sense. Aristotle's dialectical method takes us from confused concepts of change to clarity about the sources of change. This allows him, in *Metaphysics* IX, to extend these energetic concepts to categorical being. Potency and activity are not, therefore, extended from change to being, as though there were a gap between change and being. Instead, the potency and activity have an inherent ontological importance.

The chapter then turned to examine the being of potency, first by distinguishing it from other kinds of sources. The first step in doing this was to show that, while a source immediately sets to work when conditions are right, potency is a source that requires others, which can be differentiated into agent and patient. The second step was to show that potencies can accomplish opposites (the Any Opposite Principle), but can only do one at a time (the Singularity Principle), which means that at any one time, part of a potency will not be at work because another is (the Binary Principle).

The chapter then turned to examine what it means for potency to be, and in particular the conditions under which potency provides the name of a being. We first examined the reasons for thinking that what is potent is, and what it means for it to be. It turned out that while "potent" and "potency" both imply being, the word "in-potency," because it picks out beings *insofar as* they are potent, most clearly points out the being of potency. By examining Aristotle's account of when something is in-potency, namely, when the being is complete with respect to its potency, I gave a topology that laid out the relationships between overlapping registers of potency and activity. This set up an examination of what it means to complete a potency. The process of completing a potency is not a process of alteration into something else, but a free development (*epidosis*) into what a thing was already capable of being.

CHAPTER 5

The Ontology of Epigenesis

This chapter draws the discussion of potency to an important conclusion by examining what it means for sources of change to come to be. Its main task is to work out the ontology of the genetic process. This brings us to a major insight about the ontological status of sources (*archai*) and of completions (*telei*).

Chapters 3 and 4 examined the terms "being-at-work" (*energeia*), "being-complete" (*entelecheia*), and "potency" (*dunamis*), and showed that for Aristotle potency is incomplete (*atelēs*) in one respect and can be complete (*teleia*) in another. If, with Aristotle, we distinguish between a source (*archē*, e.g., potency) and the kind of completion that it accomplishes (*telein*), the description of their relationship will be called *teleology*.

Teleology has been widely regarded as the antithesis of automatic material processes.[1] This chapter shows, to the contrary, that "spontaneous" or automatic generation is a paradigm case of Aristotle's teleology. For Aristotle, sources are emergent or epigenetic, that is, they emerge out of more rudimentary processes and patterns. Certain combinations of material sources can give rise to complete (*teleia*) forms whose determinate structure is a governing principle of change, a higher-order source, a nature or potency. But what is generated in this way becomes a fully fledged *being* only when it becomes a *source*, and it is a source only when it is *complete*.

The argument, then, is that *being a source is being an accomplishment* (*telos*). Moreover, *potency has a claim to being because it is a source*. Altogether, Aristotle's underlying claim is that *being in the primary sense means being a source*. This sets up the argument in chapter 6 that being-at-work takes priority because it is a source in a more governing sense.

To make the case clear, it will be helpful to follow Aristotle's lead and mark out his position in relation to reductionism. Although he draws heavily from his materialist predecessors, he puts forward his account of *genesis* in explicit disagreement with them. Since a single chapter cannot address the entire dispute between kinds of materialist reduction and teleological causation, I shall concentrate on Aristotle's relationship with the reductionist view of one of his predecessors, namely Empedocles, whom Aristotle often presents as representative of reductive materialism. According to Aristotle, Empedocles was right to say that material nature amounts to mixture, but he argues against Empedocles that some such mixtures—the complete ones—are ontologically and "causally" robust.[2] Thus, Aristotle disagrees with Empedocles about material processes *only* in holding that what emerges from them can itself be an origin of organized changes. But this makes all the difference.

But since the concept of teleology is burdened with philosophical concerns, before turning to this analysis, it will help to outline the concept of *telos* in general terms to clarify what is at stake, and specify how I approach Aristotle's argument in what follows.

Teleology: Scope and Issues

One of the most important and distinctively Aristotelian contributions to ontology is the claim that being admits of completion or fullness. The meaning and legitimacy of this teleological claim is one of the enduring questions, and major philosophical and scientific positions have sometimes pivoted on their adoption or rejection of teleological concepts. The idea remains important both for philosophical work, ranging from ethics to philosophy of mind and mereology, and for sciences that deal with emergent complexity, from mathematics and computer science, to biology and chemistry, to neuroscience. Meanwhile, the concepts of teleology, namely potency, activity (or actuality), completion, and the relation between wholes and parts, are practically inescapable. It is, as Witt argues, through the discussion of potency and activity that teleology has a presence in ontology.[3] Expressed through its core concepts, teleology is the study of how the potencies of individual things come to be complete or active.

The strong claim is that to do ontology we must, at some point, do teleology, and, conversely, that teleology in the proper sense is concerned with how things accomplish their being. The claim that being *is* teleological has two obvious but important requirements: being must be oriented toward something, and it must be organized. Some parts of beings or aspects of being will not be indifferent to others, but will depend on them and/or on a larger whole from which they get their sense or orientation.[4] But the concept of teleology is often used vaguely, especially by its critics, and the allegation roams freely that the very idea that being is oriented and organized is ethically or epistemologically problematic. In view of these concerns, it will help to describe the core things that *telos* does for Aristotle, and what it explains.

A *telos* is that for the sake of which natural beings act at all.[5] Teleology accounts for how things act for the sake of something, and therefore it accounts for *changes*. It therefore has a wide field of application, since, on the one hand, the "what" of all natural and artificial beings, elements, and heavenly bodies includes change,[6] and on the other hand, the highest good and highest being in first philosophy is the prime *mover*, that is, the source (*archē*) of coming-to-be and change.[7] Aristotle does not use *telos* to describe a fulfillment or purpose of the cosmos as a whole, but primarily to describe individual beings and concrete wholes, for example, a city.[8] Not all natural beings have intentions, and *telos* is not limited to concepts of intention or purpose. The concept of natural teleology that I suggest below, then, does not appeal to the idea of a purposeful designer, but develops the concept of genetic processes that coalesce in a structure, for example, a living organism, that, in turn, is capable of producing specific outcomes.

Teleology is often presented as a normative concept: the *telos* is the goal for which all things *should* strive, according to which they are evaluated as deficient or sufficient.[9] This presentation of the concept originates in ethics and the critique of ethics. But in recent scholarship it is often Aristotle's biological works that have been presented as the authoritative ground for the concept of teleology.[10] In my argument, Aristotle's metaphysical account of teleology resembles the biological concept: it is primarily descriptive, and only derivatively normative. Aristotle uses *telos* to describe epigenesis, in which a natural being, that is, *an organizing source of self-movement*, comes to *be*. Aristotle's analysis of the *genesis* of sources does not yield a normative or prescriptive teleology, but instead, I argue, a descriptive, retrospective teleology.

Telos is conspicuous in the argumentative structure of the *Metaphysics* because it explains how material and form (i.e., part and whole) can be unified; *telos* explains how hylomorphic compounds can be at all (*Met.* VII.17 1041b11–33, VIII.6 1045b8–18).[11] But some aspects of its role in Aristotle's concept of hylomorphism are not immediately clear.[12] To unify a compound, Aristotle has to establish that form is itself the *telos* of material. On what basis does he argue that *telos* applies to material and form (i.e., to categorical being)? I argue that it is based on *genesis*, and therefore on potency and activity (see the section on potency and activity in chap. 4, and on the structure argument in chap. 6). It is on the basis of the dynamic-energetic sense of being that categorical being is called teleological. Genetic teleology is important, then, in two respects: it shows the relationship between sources and being, and it shows how the dynamic-energetic sense of being affects the concepts of material and form.

Teleology in Aristotle, then, is not an axiomatic or free-floating assumption, but has a conceptual home, and a basis in phenomena.[13] I aim in this chapter to articulate the phenomenal basis for Aristotle's metaphysics of teleology, while in the next chapter, I return to the examination of how Aristotle discovers the telic structure of potency and activity, and thereby of sources in general, in this phenomenon, that is, the phenomenon of *generative change*. Together, these chapters show that teleology originates in one of the four senses of being, namely, the energetic sense articulated in the words *dunamis*, *energeia*, and *entelecheia*. Again, I aim to show that the basis for Aristotle's account of *telos* is his analysis of change, specifically of coming-to-be, *genesis*. The only thing that might be controversial about this claim in general is that I take change to be the *inalienable* basis for teleology. I mean that ontology is teleological insofar as beings have sources, and the concept of a source is evident to us insofar as things are constitutively beings that change. The analysis of *genesis*, in Aristotle's hands, gives us teleology by working out the general structure of sources and their achievement. In doing so, it also introduces a way to apply the energetic concepts of source and achievement to the categorical concepts of material and form. It is through teleology that source and achievement come to apply to concepts of part and whole, subject and predicate. In this chapter, concepts of material and form take center stage, but not as narrowly categorical concepts, since they are infused with concepts of potency, activity, and completion.

The Unity of *Genesis* and Its Outcome

Now that I have situated my account in the context of general issues with teleology, we can turn to the first part of the argument of this chapter. The goal of this section is to describe the relationship between *telos* and *genesis*. This relationship is what most of all distinguishes Aristotle's account of nature from his material-reductivist counterparts, and Empedocles in particular.

The first subsection examines the subject of *genesis*: Aristotle argues in *Metaphysics* VII.7–9 that *genesis* is of the composite, not of material or form considered separately. Then it is necessary to face the core puzzle of the genetic process: how is *genesis* both continuous and discontinuous?

Material, Form, and Composite

To specify what gets generated, it is necessary to mark out the concepts of material and form, and how they relate to change. This will also help clarify how they get reworked by the concepts of potency and activity.

Material has two registers: it can mean either "the first material [i.e., ultimate elements] underlying each of the things that have in themselves a source of motion and change" (*Phys.* II.1 193a28–30),[14] or the level of material immediately underlying the relevant form, as we say when we call a table wooden, or an animal bony or fleshy (*Met.* VIII.4 1044a16–25, IX.7 1049a20–b2). As Byrne argues, for Aristotle prime matter is not featureless stuff: it must have properties in order to play its part in the generation and activity of bodily things.[15] For its part, two different words stand in for form: the shape (*morphē*), a term used to pick out the structure of the natural being, and the form or look (*eidos*) that can be distinguished from material in speech, but not in the being itself (*Phys.* II.1 193b3–5). The form can be either general, for example, "human being," or particular, for example, "Socrates."

When generation occurs, Aristotle says, it involves three preexisting things: (1) the outside source of generation, for example, the builder or parent; (2) that material out of which it comes to be, for example, the bronze; and (3) the form it comes to be, for example, the sphere (*Met.* VII.8 1033a24–28). These three causes precisely do not describe the particular composite that comes to be. The *telos*, by contrast, does come to be; it does not preexist.

Neither material nor form are brought into being, for the material is that nonspecific being in which the form comes to be and so must preexist and persist through the change, while the form is not an object but a *kind of thing*, so it cannot be created or destroyed (*Met.* VII.8 1033b20–26).

What comes to be, then, is the concrete particular; that is, being (*ousia*) in the sense of a *this* (*tode ti*), a particular *one* (*Met.* VII.15 1039b20–28). The composite *this*, then, is what is generated, and what is generated by nature is primary being (*ousia*) most of all (*Met.* VII.8 1033a28–b11, 1034a3–5). This is only known directly and actively; for example, the way we know someone as the unique being she is when we encounter her in person (*Met.* VII.10 1036a6–7).

But conceived as a composite, a *this* is always known in terms of something else, that is, as composed of other things. It could be composite in two respects: first, as a material-form composite, since any particular *this* can be distinguished into these two aspects, though only in speech (*Met.* VII.8 1032b10–14). Crucially, Aristotle argues that these must *not* be considered constituent elements or parts (*Met.* VII.17 1041b27–33): they do not fit together like a dovetail joint, because the materials are just the parts, and the form is *their* unified arrangement.[16] Second, a *this* can be materially rather than aspectually multiple, that is, divisible into many material parts or elements (*Met.* VII.17 1041b11–33).

But since material and form have two levels of meaning, general and particular, the composite does too:

> A human being or horse in general, and the things that are in this way after the manner of particulars, but universally [*katholou*], are not primary being [*ousia*] but a certain kind of composite [*sunholon ti*] of such-and-such an articulation [*logos*] with such-and-such material, understood universally, while the particular, composed of ultimate material [*tēs eschatēs hulēs*], is already Socrates. (*Met.* VII.10 1035b27–30; *Met.* VII.7 1033b24–27)[17]

As long as a being is considered universally—and it must be, to have a definition or be known universally (*Met.* VII.10 1036a2–3, 7–8)—it will appear to be a composite of more primary things, that is, material and form, rather than being itself primary. But considered as a particular thing, it is primary being (*ousia*), because it is a *this* most of all (*Met.* VIII.1037a28–35; see *Cat.* 5). Considered this way, the composite primary being (*tēn suntheton ousian*) and the shape (*morphē*) are named by the same name, and point to the same thing (*Met.* VIII.3 1043a29–b4).

This complicates the ontological status of the composite: a logical composite of universal material and a form or essence has no independent being (e.g., platypus as such). Next, when we address a being as a particular material-form composite of preexisting material and form (e.g., a platypus), the composite again does not have an independent status (*Phys.* II.1 193b5–6; see *Met.* VII.3 1029a1–8). Considered in this way, the particular composite thing will still not be the same as what it is, namely, its universal definition or essence. But when we address the particular composite as a *primary being* (e.g., Socrates), not only does it *have* ontological standing, it has *primacy*, for the particular precisely *is itself*; each primary thing is what it is for it to be (*Met.* VII.6 1032a4–7, *Met.* VIII.3 1043a29–b3). It is possible to view such a primary being as composed of material parts (*Met.* VII.17 1041b11–33), as long as these are grasped in terms of potency and being-at-work (*Met.* VIII.6 1045b2–24). To understand *genesis*, then, and through this, teleology, we must examine the composite in the sense of the particular *this* that is a primary being (*ousia*).

Continuity and Discontinuity of *Genesis*

Now that we have sketched Aristotle's account of the material, the form, and the composite that comes to be, we can examine the most basic formal question about *genesis*: is the genetic process continuous or discontinuous?

Aristotle appears to hold contradictory views about this. On the one hand, he argues that coming-to-be is necessarily a divisible process extended in time (*Phys.* VI.6 237b21–22; see *Met.* IX.8 1050a1–2). On the other hand, he says that coming-to-be is not a motion, since there is no process by which something could go from being to not-being (*Phys.* V.1 225a22–b5). Thus, a subject of predicates, for example, a baby, arrives all at once out of its contradictory privation.

Generation is discontinuous because there are no gradations between "is" and "is not." When Mariana passes away, she passes away entirely. She is no longer the being before us; it is false to describe what is in front of us as Mariana. *This* is 5'9", but *this* is not Mariana, it is a corpse; Mariana no longer has a height. When a being passes away, *this thing here* changes from one thing to another as a whole, and nothing perceptible remains of the previous subject (*GC* I.4 319b15–17). No part that remains is part of *her*. It is the same for coming-to-be. Thus, something that is not-Mariana turns into Mariana.

But in another respect, things do not come to be out of sheer nothingness and disappear into it again when they perish. Instead, "every coming-to-be is a passing-away of something else and every passing-away some other thing's coming-to-be" (*GC* I.3 319a6–8).[18] The coming-to-be of wine is the passing-away of grapes, and the coming-to-be of vinegar is the passing-away of wine (*Met.* VIII.5 1044b30–1045a7). This clarifies what Aristotle means by "not-being," namely, the negation of something specific, as we saw in chapter 1. While it is in a way true to say that vinegar comes out of the absence of vinegar, the absence of vinegar was never part of the wine that preceded it, nor is the absence of vinegar part of the vinegar that comes to be. There appears to be no continuity between wine and vinegar, since they are two different subjects. But in retrospect we define a continuity between what is incidentally not-vinegar and vinegar, or between wine and what is incidentally not-wine. The absence of vinegar is apparent only retrospectively, that is, looking backward at the previous stages of generation with the new form in mind. To articulate the continuity between them, we add something incidental to both. Similarly, the absence of the house was never in the building materials, considered as such. What is there is instead (considered categorically) a beam of this size and shape, or (considered energetically) workable material. The categorical being of the house is "read" back into the materials (also considered categorically) from the point of view of the completed house. This is to say, as Aristotle did in *Phys.* I.8: "We too say that nothing comes to be simply out of what is not; but that things do come to be in a way out of what is not, incidentally. A thing can come to be out of the lack, which in itself is something which is not, and is not a constituent" (*Phys.* I.8

191b12–15, my trans.). Thus, the negation, and indeed the whole continuum over which generation occurs, is incidental to what is indeed there before the generation is complete. The continuum becomes apparent in hindsight, and is visible starting from the *telos* that has come to be.

Now let us return to the apparent contradiction between the abruptness of the genetic change and the divisibility of the genetic process. These apparently contradictory views about change can be reconciled because the divisibility argument applies to a different aspect of the genetic process than the instantaneous arrival argument. What is divisible is not the thing that comes to be insofar as it is whole, it is the thing that comes to be, insofar as it has parts:

> What has come into being [before the completion of the process] is not, however, always the very thing which is coming into being [e.g., a whole house], but sometimes something else, as in the case of those things of which it [i.e., what has come to be] is some part, for example the foundation of the house. (*Phys*. V.6 237b12–15)[19]

The analysis of complete changes in chapter 3 helps unpack this argument: the generation of the house can be divided into stages. In the first stage, a hole is dug: this is part of the house, but not the house. Then the foundation is built, and walls are put atop it. There is still no house. Although the walls have some internal structural integrity, they do not stay up well on their own.

But once all the walls are erected, and a roof placed on top of them, the roof holds the walls together, while the walls hold the roof up. Each part of the house at this point begins to operate not just on its own, but together. To describe this, Aristotle uses the word *sun-eimi*, "come together, assemble, coalesce," that is, to go forth into a unity (*GC* I.10 327b28). Until the parts of the house hold themselves together as a house, the house has not yet come to be. In this way, we can distinguish stages of a genetic process over which something is assembled, but the whole still comes into being all at once, when it is *teleia*. Thus, we say the boards in the construction yard are incidentally part of a house while the house does not exist. Strictly, they are not even parts of a house in-potency, since the house is not. But we call them parts by starting our thinking with the house to be accomplished by the process.

The last feature of the continuum that we need to examine is its orientation. Materialists have argued since before Aristotle that earlier stages of the process necessitate later stages, so that the continuum can be said to be future-directed: if you know the earlier conditions, you can reason out the later ones. But Aristotle resists this account, for two reasons: first, he argues that the universe is eternal, so there is no earliest starting point of the processes of generation, no set of starting conditions that could henceforward necessitate such a succession of causes (*PA* I.1 640a7–9). This claim allows him to say that before any given birth (i.e., *genesis*), there was already a parent with the form (*PA* I.1 640a24–27; see *Met.* VII.7–9, IX.8 1049b19–29). Second, he argues that necessity itself points in the other temporal direction: whether a thing is necessary or not is determined by the outcome required:

> It is that which is yet to be—health, let us say, or a man—that, owing to its being of such and such characters, necessitates the pre-existence or previous production of this and that antecedent; and not this or that antecedent which, because it exists or has been generated, makes it necessary that health or a man is in, or shall come into, existence. (*PA* I.1 640a4–7)[20]

Necessity is hypothetical or retrospective in natural science, rather than being progressive or prospective (*PA* I.1 642a9–14). It is because the process of generation gives rise to the form that we need to begin with the form. This is why Aristotle says we need to study the nature of animals that are already formed, and then turn back to examine the process by which they are formed. Empedocles is therefore mistaken, he says, to say that the spine is segmented because it was accidentally broken in the conditions of the womb (*PA* I.1 640a18–28).

Let me summarize this overview of the terms and basic structure of generation. This section began by distinguishing the senses of material, form, and composite, establishing that what is generated is the individual *this* (or its attributes), which is both an aspectual composite of form and material, and multiple in material parts. I then examined the way genetic processes are, on the one hand, discontinuous, since a thing goes from being one subject (e.g., wine) to being another (e.g., vinegar). On the other hand, there is a genetic continuum between not-being (e.g., not-vinegar) and being (e.g., vinegar), which, I showed, is constituted retrospectively. I then reconciled the discontinuity of the subject with the continuity of changes in its parts: although the parts on their own do not form a whole, for the genetic process to reach completion is for them to coalesce into a whole being, that is, to gain the capacity to be a whole. It is then that we say *this particular thing* has come to be. In what follows, I will draw out what is implicit in this discussion, namely, that Aristotle takes both material and form to be *sources*. To do so is to reinterpret the categorical terms as energetic beings.

Empedocles and the Being of Individuals

As we saw, Aristotle holds that individual composite beings can both be generated, and *be* in the primary sense. His predecessor Empedocles, however, rejected the reality of individual beings precisely because they are generated: individuals are momentary accidents in a flux of unchanging elements. Since Aristotle adopts the fundamental principles of Empedocles's account of material processes, we can examine his response to Empedocles in order to grasp why generated beings have, for him, the ontological status that they do. I contend that the reason why Aristotle thinks individual beings truly count as beings is that they are *sources of change*. To establish this, I will analyze, first, Empedocles's rejection of the being of particular things. He rejects the reality of individual beings because they are effects of mixture, giving primacy to their sources.[21] Aristotle's response is to argue that individual beings *are* because they are sources themselves. They are sources, however, only once they have completely come to be.

Aristotle describes Empedocles's position as follows:

> In another way nature means the being [*ousia*] of things that are by nature [*to phusei on*], as those people mean who say that nature is the primary combination of things [*prōton sunthesin*], or as Empedocles says
> > No nature belongs to any of the things that are [*eontōn*];
> > There is only mixture and remixture of intermingled things,
> > and Nature is given as a name by human beings . . . (*Met.* V.4 1015a1–14)[22]

Empedocles rejects the idea that nature belongs to particular things. Still, Empedocles holds that nature *is*, because it is the ongoing mixture of elements. Nature is the being of things because nature's continuous mixing brings them about. We need more precision about what nature Empedocles rejects.

Aristotle quotes Empedocles as saying that being is the process of mixing. We know from other fragments that for Empedocles there are four elements: namely fire, air, water, and earth. These combine according to universal patterns, namely, the character or nature of each of the elements, and also according to a higher-level pattern imposed by Love and Strife.[23] Through these combinations all things emerge. Empedocles holds that Love, Strife, and the natures of the four elements—the six roots—are the primary beings and the real sources of changes and generation. He grants being to these because they are sources (*archai*).

Now, Empedocles follows Parmenides in holding that nothing comes to be or passes away. The plural "things that are" (*onta*) indicates that Empedocles rejects the nature or reality of individuals. Although things *seem* to change, no particular thing really comes to be: *no beings are generated*. This means that any arrangement in a particular shape, for example, a human being, is not itself something. The shape is merely a temporary accident in what is primary, namely, the ongoing mixture of elements. To put it in a word, if *genesis* is the coming-to-be of a *being*, then in Empedocles's account no *genesis* in fact happens. Therefore, even when combined, the elemental parts will remain unchanged. The parts combine without any "whole" influencing the nature of the parts; for example, if hydrogen and oxygen were to combine into H_2O, but both kept their ability to burn. There is, in this account, no "whole" to affect the parts.

Although, Empedocles says, people give the name "nature" to some of these combinations, these beings have no nature. "Nature" does not correspond to any particular *this* (*tode ti*). Individual things are not sources of change or action at all: the six roots are the sources.

In sum: Empedocles rejects natures conceived as individual self-standing wholes, as sources that accomplish their own being. Instead, what are real are the material causal processes of mixture. These produce only temporarily stable combinations. Therefore Empedocles denies that nature belongs to individual "things that are" (*eontōn*) and dismisses the idea that particulars have their own natures as a nominalist fiction.

Agreement with Empedocles

To see Aristotle's response, let us return to the point we left off in the passage from *Metaphysics* V.4. What part of Empedocles's view does Aristotle agree with, and what does he disagree with?: "For this reason, though [as Empedocles holds] all things that are or come to be by nature already have underlying sources [*huparchontos*] out of which they have naturally come into being [*pephuke gignesthai*] or are made [i.e., the material] . . ." (*Met.* V.4 1014a4–6, my trans.). Aristotle begins his response by affirming Empedocles's dynamic materialist view as compatible with his own. He agrees with Empedocles's account of material combination, but disagrees about the status of the products of combination: genuine beings emerge, he claims, and *genesis* actually happens.

When Aristotle introduced the quotation, he approved of it as an illustration of the sense of nature according to which being (*ousia*) and nature are the primary combination of things. In other words, Aristotle approves of Empedocles's grasp of what the *ousia* of natural things is, namely, the primary combination of things, that is, material nature.[24] He repeats his approval in the first part of his response: nature consists of the combination of preexisting material. Individual things arise, emerge (i.e., the verb "nature," *phuein*) into being, with the material already a governing or organizing source within them (*huparchontos*).

Beings are produced by material combining with material. Material itself can be a source of change. Self-moving materials can combine to produce individual things (*Met.* VII.9 1034b5–7). Aristotle describes materials as joint-causes (*sunaitiai*) with the form, and describes the matter as "natured" to yearn for and reach out for (*pephuken ephiesthai kai oregesthai*) it (*Phys.* I.9 192a13–24).

To illustrate how material processes can, of their own accord (i.e., automatically, *automatos*), generate something part by part, Aristotle uses the example of health. Since part of health is being the right temperature, and since the right temperature can be produced naturally in the body, or artificially with blankets, or accidentally by the sun, health can come about naturally, artificially, or automatically, that is, incidentally. The production of living beings is a more complex case, but the description is the same: the right material conditions accidentally combine to produce a distinct thing.

Disagreement with Empedocles

While Aristotle agrees that material can be a source of motion and change, there are plenty of motions that he claims material's own character cannot accomplish: "In some things, the material that starts off the coming-into-being . . . is of such a sort as to be set in motion either by itself or not . . . for many things are capable of being moved by themselves, but not in some particular way, say dancing" (*Met.* VII.9 1034a11–17).[25] Aristotle argues in *On Generation and Corruption* that Empedocles's six roots are too simple (*haplos*) to account for why a wheat seed becomes a wheat plant, instead of an olive tree or a fish or a man-headed asparagus (*GC* II.6 333b4–8). Moreover, Love and Strife cannot act as prime movers (*GC* II.6 333b22–26). The world, Aristotle argues, is full of motions that cannot be reduced to material self-movement. So it is necessary for complex individual things to be sources of change and *genesis*.

Aristotle defined nature as a certain source and cause of being moved in those beings in which it is the primary governing source (*huparchei*), by virtue of itself and not incidentally (*Phys.* II.1 193b22–25). Insofar as a natural thing is itself, nature originates and organizes (*huparchei*) its being changed (*kineisthai*) (*Phys.* II.1 192b21–23). For example, it is insofar as someone is a speaking person that she can decide to act, while it is insofar as she is a body subject to material processes that she can be swept from the ocean onto the shore by waves. This clarifies the part of Empedocles's conception of nature that Aristotle takes issue with: his rejection of the possibility that individual things can be *sources*.

Unlike Empedocles, Aristotle thinks that individual things have natures, but only under specific conditions:

> For this reason, though [as Empedocles holds] all things that are or come to be by nature already have present [*huparchontos*] that out of which they naturally come into being [*pephuke gignesthai*] or are made [i.e., the material], we say that *they do not yet have their natures if they do not have their form and shape* [*to eidos kai tēn morphēn*] . . . and nature is both the first material . . . and the form or being [*ousia*], which is the completion [*telos*] of a thing's coming into being. (*Met.* V.4 1014b34–1015a12)[26]

Empedocles is right, Aristotle implies, to say that it is only when we are apt to name something as having its nature that the nature is there. But this is not, as Empedocles thought, because nature is merely a name. It is because, Aristotle says, before this point, the nature in the sense of the form or being (*ousia*) was in fact not there. A thing only has its nature after it has taken on its form and shape, that is, once its genetic development is complete.

Empedocles's claim is that particular things have *no* nature, that (to use Aristotle's vocabulary) they are not sources, and therefore not beings.[27] Aristotle accepts this for every stage *before* coming-to-be has reached its end. Thus, in response to Empedocles's argument that individual things have neither a nature nor their own being, Aristotle concedes that they do not, up until the point at which an individual thing has its shape, that is, until it has become complete. There is no nature in the sense of being (*ousia*) *until* mixture and remixture have given rise to a source of change and rest. At the very least an animal must be a living embryo containing a nutritive principle of development. Thus, *contra* Empedocles, Aristotle claims that something *does* come to be, a nature, but this is only true for things that have reached their *telos*.

Nature, then, is twofold: primary combination, and the complete form (*eidos*) or shape (*morphē*). When a thing does have its form or pattern, it is a nature, which exists as a structure or shape, but *only* at the outcome of a genetic process, not in or as the process itself.

Why, for Aristotle, does a nature count as a being, and why does what comes to be start to count as a nature all at once? Aristotle's thesis, I argue, is that what makes a generated individual into a nature and a being is that it has come to be a particular kind of *source* of change. The difficulty lies in working out the teleological structure of the genetic process that gives rise to this. In the rest of this section, then, my aim will be to spell out Aristotle's theory of emergence.

Generation of Sources

We need to see what structure Aristotle ascribes to the generation of sources. His most sustained description is in *Physics* II.1. Here Aristotle engages Empedocles's material reductivist position through a surrogate, namely Antiphon. Antiphon's evidence for the primacy of underlying material and the illegitimacy of composites is that if a bed could *generate* something when you planted it, what would emerge is not a bed, but a tree. Nature is not, he claimed, the shape (the bed), but the less structured underlying material (the wood) (*Phys.* II.1 193a10–29). Extending this argument downward yields Empedocles's and Antiphon's claim that all structure or shape is incidental, rhythmic, and temporary, while the underlying material stuff is what really is.

But Aristotle uses the basis of both Empedocles's and Antiphon's argument, namely that what *generates* is what *is*, to argue that the form is also nature:

> Moreover, a human being comes about [*ginetai*] from a human being, but not a bed from a bed. On this account, they say that not the schema [*schēma*] but the wood is the nature, since if it were to sprout, it would become not a bed but wood. But if, therefore, this [material] is nature, then also the form is nature, for from a human being comes a human being. (*Phys.* II.1 193b9–14)[28]

Aristotle picks up on Antiphon's and Empedocles's tacit assumption that *what makes something a nature is its ability to generate*.[29] This would have been intuitive for the Greeks, since the word *genesis* means "birth, generation, coming-to-be," but also "source" or "origin." This means that *what makes something a nature is its being a source*. But if this is so, Aristotle argues, then material is not the only way that nature is a source.

This becomes visible by changing Antiphon's example from an artifact to a living thing. In natural and artificial beings alike, patterns in material arise and fall away. But unlike in artificial things, the *shapes* of natural beings propagate and generate other shapes of the same kind.

The being (*ousia*) that comes to be is a source:

> Since a source is that for the sake of which [*to hou heneka*], and the coming into being is for the sake of [*heneka*] the completion [*telos*] ... [therefore] everything that comes into being goes toward [*badizei*] a source and a completion. (*Met.* IX.8 1050a6–8, my trans.)

The pivotal claim is that coming-to-be *results* in a *source*, that is, the *telos* is an *archē*.[30] Sources emerge through coming-to-be. Shape, therefore, is generative. That Aristotle means the particular composite shape [*morphē*], rather than the universal form [*eidos*] distinguished in speech, is clear from his other uses of the observation that a human being comes from a human being, in rejecting the existence of separated forms:

> There is no need to go to the trouble of providing a form [*eidos*] as a pattern [*paradeigma*] (since they would have looked for it most of all among things generated by nature, for these most of all are primary beings [*ousiai*]), but the begetter is sufficient to produce the things that come into being, and is responsible for the form's [*eidos*] being in the material. But the whole, this particular form in these particular bones and flesh, is already Callias or Socrates. (*Met.* VII.8 1034a2–7)[31]

The form is in the particular material composite, and is the cause of bringing the material into human form. The composite is the source and cause of generation. Each person is a source of generation that itself comes to be. Each is a source in two ways: first, as the outcome *for which* generation is occurring, and second, as the *source of further generation*.

But Aristotle returns to the observation that a human being gives rise to a human being in order to argue that the form is nature *more* than the material is. He has two arguments for this claim. The first reason is that *energeia* and *entelecheia* are prior in *ousia*, an argument we shall examine in the next chapter.[32] The second is that what form generates is more regular and specific than what material does (*GC* II.6, *Phys.* II.4–9). Even if material processes could randomly produce a living being, they could not do so with any regularity.[33] For example, the disorderly movement of wind, sea, or fire exemplifies material movement, while the exquisite detail of oak leaves, almost exactly reproduced millions of times over many generations of trees, exemplifies genesis by particular beings. Moreover, an animal grows rapidly, but then stops growing. Why? Because it has become complete, *teleia*.

To be complete in this way, as a source, is to be a nature, and thereby to *be* in a primary sense:

> So from what has been said, the primary and authoritative meaning of nature is the being [*ousia*] of things that have in themselves a source of change in their own right; for the material is called nature by being receptive of this, and coming-into-being and growing [*hai geneseis kai to phuesthai*] are called nature [*phusis*] by being changes [*kinēseis*] proceeding out of this. And this is the source of change of things that are by nature. (*Met.* V.4 1015a14–19)[34]

Phusis (nature) is a form or *ousia*, but with an important modification, namely, that it is conceived as a source of coming-to-be, that is, considered in the dynamic-energetic sense of being.

Having established that generated shapes are themselves sources of generation, Aristotle describes the genetic structure as a whole. He frames his argument using Empedocles's conception of nature said as generation or birth (*DK* 31 B8):[35]

> Nature said as generation is a road into nature. For it is not like doctoring, which is not said to be a road into the art of doctoring, but into health, for necessarily doctoring [goes] from the art of doctoring, not toward it. But it is not in this way that nature holds by nature, but the growing thing as growing goes from something into something. What is it, then, that grows? Not the from-which but the to-which. Therefore, the shape is nature. (*Phys.* II.1 193b12–19, my trans.)

The process of generation is natural if it is headed toward nature. Aristotle contrasts it with artificial change, in which the change is *from* the source. The contrast means that generation is natural as long as it is on the way *to* nature, whether it comes *from* nature or not.[36] There is no requirement that everything natural come *from* nature, only that nature be that *toward* which the *genesis* is going. What makes a form a nature is its being a certain outcome (*telos*) of generation. This means that if such a form came to be automatically or through artifice, it would nevertheless be natural, as long as the process proceeded into a nature, that is, into a form that is a source of change and rest in its own right. For example, the growth of an embryo in an artificial womb with synthesized nutrients is natural insofar as the embryo is on the way to being a person, that is, because what is being grown is a person.[37] In the proper sense of *telos*, rather than a narrow one rhetorically opposed to automatic generation, something that is generated of its own accord (*automatos*) is in no way opposed to what is brought forth naturally (*phuomai*) or natured (*pephuken*, *Phys.* I.9 192a18), or what grows together into being (*phusei sunestōta*, *Phys.* II.1 192b13).

Aristotle provides, in this structure, the definition of natural change: as long as what emerges through the change is a nature, that is, as long as the *telos* is itself a source of changes and rest, then the *telos* is a nature, a being. Nature as generation is a source of change whose structure constitutes a path toward nature.[38]

In the closing dilemma, Aristotle makes a subtle, but very significant claim: What is the thing that grows (*ti oun phuetai*)? Is it the material, or the adult? The material is that-from-which as the subject of coming-to-be, while the adult is that-to-which as the subject. Which one is the subject of generation? What decides the case is an immanent criterion, namely, the fact that what comes before changes into itself. A sign of this is that what grows is named after what emerges, not after that from which it grows; for example, the oak seed is named after the *oak tree* (*Phys.* V 224b7–8, *PA* I 641b33–36). So that *into which* a thing grows, is what grows, properly speaking. Teleology means that the subject of the genetic process is described retrospectively in view of its outcome, not prospectively in view of the earliest part of the process.[39] Aristotle says, in effect, that Empedocles is right about material processes, but that this entirely misrepresents the meaning of the genetic process.

Moreover, the outcome of natural genesis is a structured being that has, in turn, the ability to generate. For living things, "that to-which," that is, the *telos*, can grow itself and generate offspring, while "that from-which," that is, the material, is not headed toward itself, and neither grows itself nor generates offspring like itself. For this reason, the *telos* is more what it is—a generated source of generation—than the being *from which* it grows, which can merely generate things different than itself. The *telos* or shape, then, is more complete (*entelecheia*) than the material (*Phys.* II.1 193b7).[40] But for a thing to come to be a nature, it must come to be as a whole. This means that being arranged in a particular pattern makes material into a source of a different kind: a unified nature.[41]

Let us summarize this discussion of Empedocles: to argue, as Aristotle does, that to be a nature is to be a source is precisely not to change the basis on which Empedocles and Antiphon account for the processes of the world, but to use it to draw a different conclusion. Mixture and remixture are still basic genetic events, but Aristotle argues that some of these composites are genuine sources of generation. Every source without its own natural shape, for example, material and technical skill, comes from one thing and goes into something else, while everything with a natural shape regularly emerges from genetic processes as their *telos*. Moreover, such shapes can generate other instances of themselves.

Automatic Generation

Aristotle conceives of the coming-to-be of nature, I am suggesting, as the coming-to-be of a form or structure whose coalescence turns it into a source, a dynamic, self-stabilizing structure that initiates change and generation. The Greek adjective "automatic" (*automatos*) means, as Dudley argues, "of its own accord," or "without intervention," and clearly overlaps with natural generation.[42] I take Aristotle's argument to be that automatic causes, no matter how they are constituted (e.g., whether they are independent causes or by-products of teleological causes), are at work in the natural world, and that they can accidentally give rise to complete beings, that is, to natures that are *for the sake of* something.[43] Now I aim to show that Aristotle's acceptance of spontaneous, automatic generation provides a strong motive for such a view, and a useful example of how it works in a way that is compatible with Empedoclean material causality. Even to those who dismiss the idea of spontaneous generation, such a teleological theory matters to the modern account, which holds that life spontaneously emerged from automatic, non-living material processes.

Physics II.1 left open the possibility that natural living things can come from any source, whether artificial or automatic, because it is the *outcome* of generation that determines the nature of the change. Just like Empedocles, Aristotle thinks that automatic generation can give rise to living beings: "some of the same things that come into being from seeds are also produced without seeds" through the combination of materials (*Met.* VII.7 1032a31–33).[44] Aristotle's account is to this extent compatible with Empedocles. This is possible because material, as we saw, can be moved by material: "And those things that come about on their own in nature come into being just as in the case of art, being those of which the material is capable of being moved by itself in the same motion which the seed sets moving" (*Met.* VII.9 1034b4–7).[45] According to Aristotle, material being moved by other material can produce organisms in just the same way that seeds do. For example, seawater froths up and takes on a structure in the presence of heat and gentle change, like bubbles on the top of a pancake, much as the seed and the womb are the ongoing sources of organization of an embryo (*GA* 762a18–27).

What part do material processes have in natural generation? Aristotle distinguishes automatic generation from the sort of generation that is organized by living things. In both cases, material sets what happens in motion just as if it was performed by a craftsman (*Met.* VII.7 1032b23–32; see *GA* 762a37–763b16). A result can come about whether the material conditions are set up automatically, by art, or by something living that is the same in kind as what is being generated.[46] A living thing creates a seed, which is neither the parent nor the offspring, and this seed organizes the process of material mixture to generate another nature like the parent, working much as a craftsman would (*PA* I.1 641b29–37). Natural living beings exist within a world of blind, incidental material processes, but draw on these processes to constitute a lineage of living things.

Thus, the way that materials take hold of their completion (*telos*) or shape (*morphē*) is the way that they come to be alive. The coming-to-life of organic beings, then, resembles the coming-to-be of a structurally unified building: when a wall is placed in an organized relationship with other parts of the house, its internal tensile strength has functional consequences that extend beyond its own boundary: by holding itself together, it holds up the roof and keeps other walls from collapsing outward. Its slight flexibility allows it to bend and move when the rest of the house is pressed by wind and rain, while its porosity allows it to dry out when the rain stops, instead of rusting or rotting. Thus, the wall's own power to maintain itself flows outward into an active shape that it helps to constitute; it is thereby the material of a house, a house in potency. This is an accomplishment of a passive potency to be unchanged (*Met.* V.12 1019a28–32) when it is placed into a completion or shape. Thereby the house holds together in a way analogous to a living thing, though, unlike a nature, it is not thereby a source of change.

Organisms come to be in just the same way, namely, through the organization of material by an outside source until the material's ability to move itself has coalesced into a complete form of activity. This activity of the whole being thereafter takes over from the seed the responsibility of organizing its material parts, that is, it becomes a cause and source of its own changes, a nature. The embryo generated by the seed is alive insofar as its nutritive capacity is complete, which means it has a source of growth and development—but there are other ways of being a source that it needs to develop. So as a source it is not yet complete, and it does not have its nature until its capacities and soul are complete (*GA* 735a13–26, 740a1–24). Until the parts of the organism or the house hold themselves together as *this* organism or house, neither has come to be yet. Neither the house nor the living thing is "beyond" its material parts. Rather, the parts accomplish each of these beings because of their arrangement or form. This is why Aristotle defines soul (using energetic terms) as the form, activity, or *entelecheia* of an organized body insofar as it is in-potency alive (*Soul* II.1 412a20-b10).

Automatic generation provides a strong motive for Aristotle to keep the earlier side of the generative process open, so that automatic processes are able to generate living beings. Automatic generation also makes apparent the role of material processes in generation, whether of artifacts or of living things. This makes it clear how Aristotle's view is compatible with that of Empedocles, but differs in that sources can come to be through organization.

* * *

Generation and teleology matter to ontology because they establish that some things can be sources entirely through the way they are organized. Because they are configurations of material, these structures can come to be. But Aristotle argues that this is what it is to be a *nature*, that is, a proper source of change and rest. It is when such a source-structure has come to be that we say it *is*, properly speaking. Thus, genetic teleology underwrites the claim that being a source is being most of all.

After outlining the scope and issues with teleology, this chapter undertook an analysis of the generation of sources in Aristotle. We started by distinguishing the terms and basic structure of generation. What is generated is the individual *this* (or its attributes), which is an aspectual composite of form and material, and is materially divisible into parts. Genetic processes are discontinuous in the sense that one being is replaced by another; for example, what this liquid here *is* has changed from wine into vinegar. Although genetic processes build up their *telos* part by part, once these parts have coalesced, the concrete, whole being has come to be through coming to be a source. The continuum between what came before and what has come to be, we saw, is constituted starting from the *telos*.

Aristotle, surprisingly, accepts much of Empedocles's view: not only is the nature of material a process of combination, but some materials can combine on their own, since they move themselves, and through the combination of their characteristics they can give rise to living things. But he rejects Empedocles's claim that the individual things thus produced are neither beings nor natures. The pivotal difference is that Aristotle shows that such things can be sources if they are coming to be complete, organized structures. Automatic processes, therefore, do not conflict with the metaphysics of teleology, they are excellent examples of it. This epigenetic theory of structure is a compelling non-essentialist argument against reductivist physics.

The account I have given explains what Aristotle means when he argues that things in the course of coming-to-be do not have their nature. This is best described as a theory of *emergence*, an *emergent teleology*. In previous chapters I have argued that the reason why genetic processes are incomplete is that what is coming-to-be still relies on outside sources, since it is not yet itself a source. In this chapter I argued that generation, as a whole, is a process of composing a structure whose completion is a source, a source that is on the one hand a being-in-potency, and on the other hand a being-at-work. To grasp the originality of Aristotle's account, it will help to situate it in relation to two contexts: contemporary accounts of teleology, and contemporary accounts of emergence.

Gotthelf gives a typology of positions that argue for teleology:[47] Strong Irreducibility holds that material necessity is insufficient to account for the coming-to-be of living organisms, which means that among the material potencies there must be an irreducible potential for form. The Regulative/Pragmatic view holds that material causes are the only causes in things, but that, by contrast, our minds require a teleological account. Proponents of Limited Irreducibility hold that there are two sorts of descriptions: a material description, which exhibits what happens as produced by material necessity, and an assessment of the goodness of something, which depends of necessity on teleology. According to Weak Irreducibility, teleology does not require material explanation to fail, it merely requires a program to be present in the seed that organizes the sequence of material processes to produce the form. Finally, the Intrinsic Cause or Anti-Eliminativist view holds that what is at stake in teleology is not whether organisms are produced by material processes—they are, in this view—but whether the processes are intrinsic and essential or extrinsic and accidental. Thus, this view turns on Aristotle's claim that a seed has an intrinsic efficient cause that brings about the form.

In the view I have put forward, Aristotle aims to show that the *telos* is a real source, not something imported by human thinking. He holds that material necessity gives us an insufficient account of genesis because universal material processes are not specific enough to cause the variety of motions in the world. The concept of *telos* amounts to the appearance of a source or cause of events, which constitutes a level of causality higher than fundamental material processes. This claim has come to be of central importance in current debates over emergence.

We might worry that Aristotle compromises his own case for teleology by claiming that living things can be generated by automatic processes.[48] But in my view, this is a strength, since teleology is not opposed to material flux. Automatic processes can give rise to functionally coherent systems, whose effects have a regularity or organizational specificity that could not reliably be achieved by the automatic processes that generated them. Now, the creations of automatic generation are irregular and tend to be rudimentary because the processes only accidentally converge to produce such a form and source of change. By contrast, a seed is a system that organizes material processes to converge in a way that produces the form and source. But both accident and seed can lead to this form and source, that is, to a *telos*. Aristotle's teleology cannot, therefore, be reduced to a claim that there is a program which is intrinsic to seeds; its argument instead is that the result of any type of generation is a coherent, complete form of activity, a change-organizing complex. Aristotle also does not save teleology from materialism by positing a material element that affects genetic development in a certain way; instead, he secures teleology by showing how composition can lead to the emergence of a source of change, which he calls a *telos* and a being. Therefore, Aristotle's teleology is compatible with a robust role for automatic material processes, and incompatible with a reductivist view of material processes.

A core problem with the views of teleology adumbrated by Gotthelf is that (apart from the Regulative/Pragmatic view) they largely accept the modern claim that causes preexist their effects. They are concerned to show the existence of a form or program in the seed, then work out how it determines the developmental process. But if I am right, Aristotle does not view the genetic process as prospectively determined, but as constituted retrospectively.

Aristotle's teleology is not retrospective in a weak sense, in the way that, to produce an electric car I must work backward from the product to determine which steps are hypothetically required to produce it. In this view of teleology, the product is just the last step in the sequence of production. Of course, the *telos* imposes certain requirements on the process of production, but to say, as Charles does, that the form already contains the genetic program, is a step too far, and needlessly overburdens both the concept of form and telos by tying it to the concept of production.[49] The form or *telos* does not itself need to contain the production routines, because the knowledge of how to take a form and develop a plan for producing it (*poioun*) is *different* than the form or *telos* itself: for artificial beings it is called art (*technē*); for learning geometry it is the teacher's art of teaching, that is, directing students in doing geometry until they can do it themselves; and for natural things it is the work of the outside source of change, that is, the seed, until the embryo becomes such a source of change itself (*PA* I.1 641b29–37). Now, the prediction of the outcome of natural processes ultimately depends on a retrospective theory of the genetic sequence: just as we only know that a particular premature baby has the capacity to survive once it does, we only know that this embryo will likely grow into a human being because we look back on its development with the developed human being in mind. This, I take it, is Aristotle's point in giving such a cautious answer to the question of when a thing can be said to be in potency: a thing is in potency when, in the absence of interference, its *result* (*telos*) comes about, and if it does not come about, it was not in potency (*Met.* IX.7 1048b37–1049a17).

This means that Aristotle's teleology is retrospective in a strong sense. The genetic process is retrospective because the form of activity that comes to be is a source, and being a source is unprecedented in the sequence of genetic development. The *telos* that comes to be is a robust form of activity that is different in kind than the process of production, because, upon completion, it becomes an independent source of motions and changes. Then, upon the arrival of the being, we lay out, retrospectively, a continuum of changes leading up to it. The genetic process is indeterminate, except in retrospect. This does not mean, of course, that such continuities did not exist: they were there, but there were many of them, and it was not certain in advance which ones would describe the genetic pathway. Seen in the right way, this is an astute, epistemically uncontroversial view.[50] But if we pay attention, it explains Aristotle's cautious, scrupulously detailed metaphysics of epigenesis.

Aristotle provides us with one of the earliest accounts of epigenesis, that is, the theory that things are generated in a sequence of different stages.[51] But since emergence is a major problem in contemporary science as well, it will help to ask: what sort of theory of emergence is Aristotle proposing? The current debate is framed in terms of levels of complexity: the fundamental level consists of the basic processes governed by the laws of physics, that is, the behavior of atoms and their parts, while higher levels consist of patterns that emerge from the interaction between these processes, which can be adequately described by different types of laws, for example, the laws of evolution govern subjects that are not basic physical processes, but complex entities. The question is about whether or how these higher-order processes are reducible to the lower-level processes.[52]

Three sorts of emergence have been distinguished: (i) the nominal emergence of group-level properties that do not apply to the parts, for example, how Bessie weighs forty pounds but her heart does not; (ii) weak emergence, in which the behavior of a system is nonlinear or context-dependent and difficult to account for, but nevertheless derivable from more basic processes, as we can see, for example, in the formation of waves or traffic jams; and (iii) strong emergence, in which the higher-level system has some autonomy or is irreducible to constituent processes.

The existence of higher-level systems has been defended recently in several ways, first by the idea that their laws are autonomous in some way from the underlying processes, if the features of the complex system are not derivable from the lower-level phenomena but are explainable by higher-order laws. Second, the higher-level system might be multiply realizable, for example, if the same upper-level features could emerge out of many different lower-level phenomena. Third, the higher level of complexity might alter the lower, in a phenomenon called "downward causation," for example, the way a wave (a higher-order form) destroys a sand castle, affecting the relationships between the grains of sand. Or, fourth, it might be that the *subjects* of laws that govern the lower-level phenomena are different than the subjects described by laws that govern the higher level. For example, Brownian motion is reducible to the lawful activity governing constituent molecules and atoms, but a living species is governed by coherent laws that apply to a higher level subject, such as how well it fits with its ecological context. The two are different sorts of subjects.

The trend today is toward causal fundamentalism, the claim that only the underlying levels are causal. This claim is compatible with weak emergence, but it conflicts with some versions of strong emergence, namely those that argue for downward causation.[53]

The place to look for emergence in Aristotle is in the generation of complete being-in-potency, for example, in how the assembly of materials generates a structure capable of holding the shape of a house. Aristotle clearly treats a being-in-potency (e.g., a building, health, life) as something autonomous, happening of its own accord: it resists destruction, it is multiply realizable and can exist in different materials or in changing materials, and when such a being comes to be, we attribute properties to a different subject than before (e.g., when we say it is the wall that gets damaged, rather than a piece of wood). In this chapter, I have argued, what is decisive for Aristotle is that the emergent form is a source of change (or, in contemporary language, a "causal power").[54] The way he speaks of the form organizing material processes to generate offspring might not imply downward causation (i.e., that the form changes material processes themselves), because form is itself the unity and structure of these material processes, and of their initiation of movement. But for Aristotle wholes *exist*, which means they are aspectually different than their parts. This also means that, insofar as they are parts, the identity of the underlying material parts depends on the whole, as letters change their sounds depending on the whole word (e.g., compare "though" with "thought") (*Met.* VII.17 1041b11–27). And if, as Aristotle appears to hold, it is impossible to conceptualize material except as a part belonging to a whole, then to this extent Aristotle's mereology does allow wholes to modify their parts, though not through downward causation. Since Aristotle's account of causation differs so acutely from the standard view in the current debate, however, it would take a careful adaptation of terms to discover whether there is a separate account of downward causation, and whether it is problematic or not.[55]

CHAPTER 6

Genesis and the Internal Structure of Sources in *Metaphysics* IX.8

Aristotle's claim that change requires being to be multiple in aspect led us to distinguish categorical from dynamic-energetic being, material from form, and potency-like sources from activity (as discussed in chaps. 1–3). Because the analysis of change requires us to distinguish between sources and their accomplishments, we examined the ontology of sources, notably potency (chap. 4) and the teleology of the processes that generate sources (chap. 5). Although we have all along been dealing implicitly with the relationship between potency and activity, Aristotle argues directly that that activity itself is an accomplishment of a different sort than potency. This argument occupies *Metaphysics* IX.8, and this chapter is devoted to analyzing it. The explicit aim of *Metaphysics* IX.8 is to establish the ontological priority of activity over potency. It does so, as I will show, by unpacking the internal teleological structure of genetic processes. The incorporation of teleology into ontology that Aristotle accomplishes in *Metaphysics* IX.8 is one of the most important contributions change makes to ontology.[1]

The teleological structure of generation is what establishes the core contention in *Metaphysics* IX.8 that activity is a source (*archē*), indeed, the governing source of generation and change. This is what establishes the priority of activity. As we saw in the previous chapter, sourcehood is what makes something a being in the primary sense. Similarly, in this chapter, sourcehood is what gives being-at-work its ontological primacy. Potency is a source of generation and change, but activity is a higher kind of completion (*telos*). By presenting activity as the completion of potency, all change is conceived as natural, that is, as an event of becoming actively what a thing already was in potency.

Aristotle extends this analysis of teleology to material and form: he takes the material to be directed at the form the way the capacity for genesis is headed toward its *telos*. Material is addressed as a source that is headed for and then holds onto form, while form is interpreted as the active structure it accomplishes. Thus, categorical being is reworked with dynamic-energetic concepts.

Remarks on This Approach

As I noted in the introduction to this book, the single passage that has been the most influential in scholarship on the relationship between being and change in Aristotle is *Metaphysics* IX.6 1048b18–34, which Burnyeat has nicknamed "the Passage." This text makes a sharp distinction between change and a higher sense of *energeia*, which, it seemed, excluded change from ontology. For example, Kosman, who puts the IX.6 Passage at the heart of his interpretation, views activity as an ontological concept that is independent of and higher than the self-contradictory, suicidal sort of activity that he thinks belongs to change.[2]

But the Passage is perhaps the most corrupt in the corpus, and on both philological and philosophical grounds its location and legitimacy are insecure, and Burnyeat argues that it should be secluded.[3] The chapter this affects the most is *Metaphysics* IX.8, and the conflicts between the two passages have been well-documented.[4] There are readings of the Passage that finesse these conflicts by softening the distinction between *energeia* and *kinēsis*. This approach can also reconcile it with the account of the incompleteness of change that I presented in chapter 3. But because the reading I offer here is based on the argument of IX.8, it does not depend on the removal of the Passage from *Metaphysics* IX, and such a discussion can be set aside.

There are two prevailing views on what *Metaphysics* IX.8 is about, which are determined by views of the subject and purpose of *Metaphysics* IX as a whole. The standard view is that *Metaphysics* IX is ultimately about primary being (*ousia*), a concept that belongs to categorical being. Categorical being is concerned with elements and causes. The underlying structure of categorical objects consists of a material subject and a predicate form (*Met.* VII.1 1028a9–b2, IX.1 1045b28–1046a1). Aristotle's famed hylomorphic account of being consists of the thesis that the pair is unified. After identifying, in *Metaphysics* VII.13–16, fundamental problems that obstruct the possibility of such unity, Aristotle points the way to a solution in *Metaphysics* VIII.6 1045b2–24, namely, to interpret material as potency and form as *energeia*. In this view, *Metaphysics* IX shows that material and potency can solve this problem.[5] Behind this reading is what might be called an Ontology of Substance, which holds that ontology coincides with the account of *ousia*, and that properly speaking, the ontological importance of potency and actuality consists in their relationship to categorical predication. It assumes from the start that priority in being is not based on becoming, because it is based on *ousia*.

The second view is that *Metaphysics* IX is not primarily concerned with *ousiai*, but with sources (*archai*) and/or ends (*telei*). Menn, for example, argues that this examination of sources is not aimed at solving the problem of hylomorphism, but at establishing the primacy of being a source, which paves the way for Aristotle to argue in *Metaphysics* XII that because god is the highest source, he is also the highest being.[6] In this view, however, *Metaphysics* IX can still offer a solution to the problem of hylomorphic ontology. Witt and Charles, for example, argue that the discussion of potency and activity provides a solution through a hierarchical account of being that overlays the categorical sense of substance.[7]

If we put these views together, I think they point in the right direction.[8] The best approach to understanding *Metaphysics* IX, I think, is to take seriously both Aristotle's distinction between elements, causes, and sources in *Physics* I.1 and *Metaphysics* V.1–3, and his distinction between the four senses of being in *Metaphysics* V.7 and VI.1–3. Elements, causes, and sources are different concepts: sources originate changes, generation, being, or knowing (*Met.* V.1). A cause is a categorical object responsible for a being, process, or event (*Met.* V.2). An element is a constituent part (*Met.* V.3).

To review: the four senses of being without qualification are incidental-essential, categorical, dynamic-energetic, and alethic. In this book's introduction, I argued that *ousia* is only the primary sense of categorical being. In contrast to material and form, being-potent and being-at-work are neither properties nor subjects that bear them, but ways of being what something is, that is, coexisting aspects of beings insofar as they function. Potency and *energeia* are names for being, but are also native to the analysis of change and *genesis*: their most authoritative (*malista kurios*) meaning is change (potency, *Met.* IX.1 1045b33; activity, IX.3 1047a30–33),[9] and change can only be defined using this dynamic-energetic sense of being (*Phys.* III.1 200b27–33). Thus, this sense of being is the one appropriate to the discussion of change and its sources. This is true even if there is a kind of source that does not imply change.

In my view, *Metaphysics* IX is not primarily concerned with categorical being, but with being in the sense of potency and *energeia*, that is, insofar as being is an *archē*. It investigates being-potent and being-at-work, which make up the sense of being that allows us properly to investigate sources. As I argued in chapter 4, *Metaphysics* IX would count as ontology even if it never mentioned primary categorical being (*ousia*). The fact that the analysis also draws out some radical implications for our understanding of categorical being and its pivotal concept does not obviously subordinate the energetic sense of being to the categorical, but could just as easily do the opposite. Thus, I take Kosman to be right to argue that Aristotle aims at an account of being as activity, although, as noted, I think this for quite different reasons.[10]

In chapter 4, I argued that the project of *Metaphysics* IX is to develop the analysis of change far enough that it can support a more complete understanding of its key terms (potency and *energeia*). These terms can then illuminate things we do not normally speak of as being in change, namely, the categorical terms "material" and "form."[11] The landmark contribution of *Metaphysics* IX.8 to this task is to show that *energeia* is also an *archē* in an authoritative sense. For Aristotle, the study of change and coming-to-be shows what it is to be a principle, source, or origin.

The Argument of *Metaphysics* IX.8

This chapter offers a commentary on *Metaphysics* IX.8. First it clarifies the way Aristotle uses generation (*genesis*) in the passage on priority in time, and then it divides the argument for priority in being into its parts. The first part argues that the accomplishment (*telos*) is the primary kind of source (*archē*). There I aim to show how this is not an analytic argument, but a synthetic one, made on the basis of the structure of generation. The second part argues that being-at-work (*energeia*) is an accomplishment. There I aim to show that through analyzing the structure of generation Aristotle answers three critical objections to this claim, namely that being-at-work appears to lack its own structure, to be different in kind from the object it accomplishes, and to be external to its accomplishment. The chapter closes by showing how the argument has in fact established that primary being and form are being-at-work using the structure of generation.

Aristotle declares that his aim in *Metaphysics* IX.8 is to show that being-at-work or activity (*energeia*) has priority over potency (*dunamis*), nature (*phusis*), and other similar sources, presumably desire (*orexis*) and choice (*prohairesis*) (*Met.* IX.5 1048a4–14). He argues that being-at-work is prior in four ways: in speech (*Met.* IX.8 1049b12–16), in time (*Met.* IX.8 1049b17–1050a3), in primary being (*ousia*) (*Met.* IX.8 1050a4–b5), and in ontological independence (*Met.* IX.8 1050b6–1051a1).[12]

Of these sorts of priority, the most contentious is the argument that being-at-work is prior in being (*ousia*). This is the most contentious, in part, because its basis is not clear to scholars. The argument does not obviously proceed, for example, by applying a clear, preestablished analysis of priority in primary being.[13] That it does not simply appeal to the concept of *ousia* to decide the case is clear from the fact that the argument actually modifies the concept of *ousia*.

Moreover, Aristotle does not apply a preexisting concept of priority to the case of potency and being-at-work, but makes an immanent argument instead: since potency is paradigmatically a source, his method is to examine the structure of sources.[14] The core claim is that accomplishment (*telos*) is the primary kind of source, and then that being-at-work is an accomplishment. First, there is another kind of source alongside potency-like sources, namely being an accomplishment, and second, *energeia* can in fact be such a source. The basis for the argument, then, is an analysis of the structure of sources. I follow Menn, then, in holding that the subject of *Metaphysics* IX.8 is sources and their accomplishment.[15]

Now, the paradigm Aristotle uses to work out the structure of sources is generation (*genesis*). Aristotle uses generation in two ways in first philosophy: (1) *genesis* names the coming-to-be of any sort of form in underlying material, including *individual being* (*ousia*) (*Phys.* I.7–9, *Met.* VIII.5 1044b21–29). Generation is, then, an important indicator of priority in *ousia*, since it is the process by which non-eternal beings, and their attributes, are constituted. In addition, (2) *genesis* names the coming-to-be of activities (*energeiai*) from potencies, as flute-playing comes from the flute-playing potency (*Met.* IX.8 1050a24–31). It thereby covers all changes whatsoever, and events that do not normally count as changes.

In making this argument Aristotle overshoots his target, establishing not just the claim that being-at-work (*energeia*) is primary in relation to primary being, but also the much stronger claim—the banner claim—that primary being (*ousia*) and form (*eidos*) are at-work (*energeia*) (*Met.* IX.8 1050b2). The extent of this overshoot is significant: it is as though, instead of showing that leaves are more important to plants than roots, he showed that having leaves defines what a plant is.

There are three problems, then, that this chapter aims to address. First, it aims to discern the basis of the argument of *Metaphysics* IX.8. Second, it aims to work out the internal structure of sources, and thereby the meaning of potency and being-at-work. Third, it aims to show how this analysis can plausibly justify the claim that primary being and form are at-work.

Generation is an intuitive basis for the banner claim in the argument of this chapter, because, as we saw in chapter 5, a process only counts as generation if a being (*ousia*) with a form or structure (*eidos*) emerges from it. The source responsible for such an emergence will, thereby, be the source of primary being and form. Because first philosophy seeks the primary sources (*archai*) of being, it makes sense for it to study generation in order to find out what the sources of such things are.[16]

The view I have argued for in this book clarifies the argument of *Metaphysics* IX.8: if change is defined as a positive sort of being, and the dynamic-energetic sense of being is distinguished from the categorical, then there is no longer any motive to separate a change-related sense of potency and activity from a being-related sense. This unified account of dynamic-energetic being is emphatically an account of sources. This makes it clear why Aristotle uses *genesis* in the argument, namely, to reveal the structure of sources in general. By contrast, much existing scholarship on the chapter, presuming a sharp distinction between *energeia* as change and as being, obscures the role of *genesis*, thereby missing what makes the chapter into a single coherent argument, and overlooking both important problems and important claims about the concept of a source.[17]

For example, most scholars hold that *genesis* is not the basis for priority in *Metaphysics* IX.8, but that categorical being (*ousia*) has a structure of priority built into it: it is just by definition, they say, that a man is prior in being to a boy.[18] Since they provide no phenomenal basis for this priority, the ontological structure of teleology appears to be arbitrary. In my view, Aristotle's argument does not require such an appeal to essences: the phenomenon of *genesis* establishes the claim to the priority of being-at-work. To take another example, while I think Broadie's assessment of the stakes of the Location Argument (*Met.* IX.8 1050a23–b2) is correct, I think she does not go far enough.[19] I shall argue that, while she is right that one of the stakes of the chapter is the intelligibility of the natural world, the stakes are, more immediately, to rescue the unlikely claim that activity (*energeia*) is ontologically significant, rather than just a momentary effect of potency.

Priority in Time and *Genesis* (1049b17–1050a4)

The role of priority of sources first becomes clear in the lengthy discussion of priority in time in *Metaphysics* IX.8. To clarify the way Aristotle is approaching *genesis*, it is necessary to examine his lengthy treatment of genetic priority in this section. To sort out the priority of potency and activity in time, Aristotle examines genetic sequence. In mounting his argument, he gives not one but *two* ways of understanding the organization of genetic processes.

In the first, potency precedes activity in time: for example, in time an individual's ability to run, that is, her being a runner, precedes actively running, so potency temporally precedes activity.[20] A capacity to act comes to be before the action; a thing is potentially a particular *this* before it comes to be at-work being *this*. But potency is prior to being-at-work only when the investigation is limited to individual (*tode*) beings, that is, when the analysis of priority is limited to the *Individual Sequence*. The limitation to an individual being excludes the genesis of the being in question, and prevents such a view of priority from being fundamental.

When the restriction to individuals is lifted, however, and we look at a complete being along with its *genesis*, then it is not potency but activity that takes precedence. In this more basic sense of temporal precedence, activity precedes potency:

> Preceding these in time, there are other things that are at work, out of which these particular ones are *generated* . . . some *mover* is always first, and what causes change is already *at work*. (*Met.* IX.8 1049b17–24)[21]

Before this individual was either potential or at work, there was a source of change, which was "the same in form, though not numerically the same" (*Met.* IX.8 1049b18–19).[22] Parents come first, and babies come later. But if the analysis is no longer limited to a particular temporal extent, there is no reason to stop at the parents. Why not continue back to their childhood, to their parents, and on and on? What is it about parents that makes them primary? Even though being a child precedes being a parent, parents are *sources* of children. Their primacy is established through being sources of generation, and the generation of a child, because it brings a new being into the world, is a more fundamental kind of generation than the growth of a child into an adult. Parents are prior in this way insofar as they *actively* generate, not insofar as they are capable of generating.[23]

The temporal order of events is the same in the Individual Sequence, but now, no longer constrained to the temporal limits of an individual life, the intergenerational structure of coming-to-be establishes the fundamentality of *genesis*. We shall call this a *Genetic Priority*, a term Aristotle adds to the last line of the argument: "being-at-work is also in this way prior to potency in *genesis and* time" (*Met.* IX.8 1050a2–3, my trans.). Genetic Priority is not, in fact, the same as temporal priority, but overlies and governs temporal priority.

Three remarks are necessary here: first, activity is prior in time in a more governing way than potency because the framework in which activity is primary encompasses the framework in which potency is primary. The temporal framework of an individual abstracts from the conditions of the individual's emergence, but does not alter them.

Second, the wider view allows individual sources of generation (e.g., parents) to become visible as what they are, namely sources. These sources have been generated, and they are sources of generation: Aristotle does not say a child comes from a man, but that a man comes from a man.[24] This means that Genetic Priority gives us evidence for the structure of priority proper to sources in general, namely, that generated things are sources. In the Individual Sequence, by contrast, things have, in important respects, already come to be.

Third, unlike the Individual Sequence, which accounts for the development of the capacities and activities of *already* existing beings, Genetic Priority accounts for the birth and existence of individual beings themselves. This means that priority in coming-to-be is already priority in being.

Priority in Being: Division of the Argument

Having worked out this distinction between temporal and genetic priority, Aristotle turns to a discussion of priority in being (*ousia*). This argument divides into two sections: the first section, running from 1050a4 to 1050a15, is an argument that being-at-work (*energeia*) is prior to potency because the accomplishment or result (*telos*) is a source in a more governing way than the capacity that is its precondition. The second section, running from 1050a15 to 1050b2, is an argument that being-at-work is indeed a kind of accomplishment. It has a form or structure (*eidos*) (*Met.* IX.8 1050a15–16), this form or structure is determined by the accomplishment (*Met.* IX.8 1050a21–23), and it is in the same location as the accomplishment. With few exceptions, the tendency among scholars is to think that nothing much is at stake in the latter trio of arguments, and they are taken to be fairly self-evident.[25] To remedy this oversight, I shall provide a synopsis of the argument, and then, in the step-by-step analysis, try to clarify the stakes involved in its core claims.

The main thing I aim to establish about the first section of the argument is that in moving from an argument for priority in time to priority in *ousia*, we are not leaving Genetic Priority behind. Viewed as a whole, this first section is quite clearly an analysis of the structure of *genesis*, in the sense indicated by Genetic Priority:

(1) But surely [being-at-work] takes precedence in *ousia* too,
   (a) first because things that are later in *coming into being* take precedence in form and in *ousia*, as a man does over a boy, or a human being over the germinal fluid, since the one already has the form, and the other does not,

(b) and also because everything that *comes into being* goes up to a source and an end,
   i. since that for the sake of which something *is* is a source, and
   ii. *coming into being* is *for the sake of the end*,
(c) but being-at-work is an end, and it is for the enjoyment of this that the potency is taken on. (*Met.* IX.8 1050a4–10)[26]

Step (a) claims that the outcome of *genesis* is a form and *ousia*. Step (b) identifies the accomplishment of such a genetic process as a source (which means that the form and *ousia* in (a) are an *archē* of *genesis*). Step (c) is to argue that potency, likewise, *comes-to-be for the sake of activity*. Therefore being-at-work is prior in *ousia*.

I shall introduce the second section of the argument by examining the reasons why it seems that being-at-work (*energeia*) cannot be an accomplishment (*telos*), and why accomplishment seems to be a bad criterion for establishing its priority. Aristotle answers these concerns in a three-part argument:

(2) Furthermore,
   (a) material is in-potency [*dunamei*] because it comes to [*elthoi*] a form; and
   (b) when it is at-work [*energeiai*], then it is *in* the form. And
   (c) it is similar in other cases, including those in which the accomplishment is change, and that is why teachers display [*apodedōkenai*] a student at work, thinking that they are delivering up the accomplishment, and nature does likewise. (*Met.* IX.8 1050a15–21, my trans.)

(3) For
   (a) the work [*ergon*] is an accomplishment [*telos*], and
   (b) *being at work* [*energeia*] is the work, and
   (c) this is why the name *being at work* is said through the work and
   (d) stretches toward [*sunteinei*] being-complete [*entelecheia*]. (*Met.* IX.8 1050a21–23, my trans.)

(4) [In each case, the activity is at least as much an accomplishment as the potency]
   (a) Whenever only the exercise [*chrēsis*] comes to be [*genesis*], the being-at-work or exercise is just as much an accomplishment as the potency.

(b) And whenever from what is potent both the exercise and a work-object come to be [*genesis*], since the exercise or work-act [*energeia*] of the potency, is *in* the work-object with the *telos*, the *en-erg-eia* is *more* a *telos* more *en-tel-echeia* than the potency. (*Met.* IX.8 1050a23-b2, paraphrased)

From this argument, Aristotle overshoots the conclusion he aimed to establish:

(5) And so
   (a) it is clear that primary being [*ousia*] and form [*eidos*] are being-at-work.
   (b) So as a result of this argument it is obvious that being-at-work takes precedence over potency in primary being. (*Met.* IX.8 1050b2–3)[27]

Each step of the argument examines an aspect of *genesis*. The evidence for claims (1) to (3) is the internal structure of coming-to-be, while claim (4) appeals to its external structure. Because *genesis* is *for* its accomplishment, the accomplishment of genesis is the primary way of being a source. It follows that if *energeia* is an accomplishment, it is therefore a source. The structure of *genesis* thereby anchors Aristotle's claim that sources are ontologically primary.

Accomplishment Is a Source

The Generation Argument (1050a4–6)

The first step of the argument that *telos* is an *archē* relies on the idea that *telos* means an outcome or result. It is based on the argument for epigenesis analyzed in chapter 5.

(a) things that are later in coming into being take precedence in form and in *ousia*, as a man does over a boy, or a human being over the germinal fluid, since the one already has the form, and the other does not. (*Met.* IX.8 1050a4–6)[28]

What comes later is prior because it is the form and being (*ousia*) that results from generation.

Beere argues that Aristotle opposes priority in *genesis* to priority in *ousia* in the phrase "things that are later in coming into being take precedence in form and in *ousia* (as a man does over a boy . . .)" (1050a4–5). This, he claims, means that the argument has moved beyond change to being.[29] But the contrast Aristotle draws here is clearly between precedence in *ousia* and the *Individual Sequence*: in the Individual Sequence, as here, what is prior is the capability of a seed or a child. If Aristotle were referring to Genetic Priority, however, what is prior would be the active adult. In order to make the claim that he leaves *genesis* behind, then, Beere has to overlook the distinction Aristotle has just made between the Individual Sequence and Genetic Priority.[30]

In my argument, this sentence continues the previous discussion of source-based priority. The idea that the mature being (*ousia*) is a source is already on the table, and the discovery of Genetic Priority put it there.[31] In addition, this clause is the first in an argument seven lines long, the rest of which establishes that *energeia* is a source through an analysis of *genesis*. Not only is the active source of generation prior in the sense of coming *before* and *giving rise to* a particular being, but the source of generation is also prior within the development of the individual.

Aristotle usually formulates this claim by saying that what comes later is prior since then it has its nature, as we saw in Aristotle's disagreement with Empedocles (*Met.* V.4 1015a3–12; *Pol.* I.2 1252b34–36; *PA* I.1 640a19–26, 641b23–642a1, II.1 646a25–27; *GA* II.1 734a16–32, II.6, see chap. 5). If Aristotle is indeed making the same argument here in *Met.* IX.8 as he does elsewhere, then the form at the end of a genetic process will be prior in being to earlier phases of *genesis* because it has come to be a nature, that is, a natural source of change and rest.

The Source Argument (1050a6–8)

If the centrality of the concept of *genesis* and *archē* was only implicit in claim (a), it is inescapable in claim (b), which argues that coming-to-be results in a *source*, which is some goal or *telos*:

> (b) everything that comes to be comes up to [*elthoi*] a source [*archē*] and accomplishment [*telos*]. (*Met.* IX.8 1050a6–8, my trans.)

This is a descriptive statement: *genesis* "comes up to" something because things that count as coming-to-be *accomplish* or *yield* something. *Genesis* yields, Aristotle says, something that is a source. To establish this as a general claim, Aristotle offers two premises:

> i. generation [*genesis*] is for the sake of (= goes up to) an accomplishment [*telos*]
> ii. being "what something is for the sake of" is being a source [*archē*] (*Met.* IX.8 1050a6–8)[32]

These premises interpret the "coming up to" that we perceive in a process of generation as its being *for* something, and on this basis they establish that the accomplishment of generation is itself a way of being a source.

It is important to note here that this is not an analytic argument: Aristotle does not claim that to be an accomplishment (*telos*) just means to be a source (*archē*). It is, in addition, not obviously the same thing for something to be *for* something (*heneka*) and for it to have an accomplishment.³³ His argument is, instead, synthetic: it identifies the terms with one another through a proper medium, namely, the process of *genesis*: the accomplishment is a source because they are both *that for the sake of which* or that up to which coming-to-be comes. *Telos* is *archē*, then, because *genesis* has the structure of being *for the sake of something* (*heneka*). It is only because *genesis* is *directed at* something determinate that Aristotle can claim that *that for which* is an accomplishment. The *going toward* that is retrospectively evident in a process of generation is its being-for-the-sake of something.

Crucially, among all changes (alteration, change in size, motion in place, generation), *genesis* is conspicuously *for* something, because from generation a distinct thing *emerges*, the process obviously *yields* something. Of changes that are *for* something, *genesis* is the paradigm. Thus, Aristotle reads the *for*-structure off of *genesis*, and thereby establishes his claim that to be a *telos* is to be an *archē*. This is the case even though, in saying that *genesis* is *for* something, no claim is made about the nature of the *parts* of the process. Generation is not described as having a set morphological pathway or even an inherent character, only that it yields an accomplishment.

On this basis Aristotle introduces a completely new way of being a source: unlike potency-like sources, for being-at-work to be a source is for it to be the final accomplishment sought or aimed at.

We can actually deduce the Generation Argument (a) that preceded it by supplying the implicit premise of argument (b): being a source of *genesis* is, implicitly, being (*ousia*) in the primary sense. Therefore, what completes the genetic process is being in the primary sense. Thus, (a) what comes later in *genesis* is prior in *ousia*, and this is because what comes later is the source of its coming to be. The man into which the boy is growing is that for which he is growing, namely his accomplishment, and thereby the *source* of his being and generation.

The Exercise Argument (1050a9–16)

Now that Aristotle has shown formally how a *telos* can be a source of *genesis*, he has an easy argument at hand, which both confirms the claim about *telos* being a source, and gives him an important argument for the ontological primacy of *energeia* over *dunamis*:

(c) But the *energeia* is an end, and it is for the enjoyment of this that the potency is taken on. (*Met.* IX.8 1050a9–10)[34]

We take up potency in order to exercise it; potency comes to be for activity. This appears to be a very straightforward and, on the face of it, a sufficient argument to establish the primacy of activity over potency. It is so intuitive that it makes the rest of the argument seem pointless: why belabor the details of the relationships between being a source, being for something, and being an accomplishment?

On its own, this argument is not, however, sufficient: it requires the preceding argument to establish the priority and sourcehood of the accomplishment through an analysis of the structure of generation. Coming-to-be (*genesis*) is for the sake of an accomplishment (*telos*). The accomplishment of a process of coming-to-be is a source (*archē*). Being a source is prior in primary being (*ousia*) to the process of coming-to-be of which it is the source. Potency (*dunamis*) comes into being for the sake of being-at-work. Potency's accomplishment is to generate an activity (*energeia*). Therefore, activity is the source of potency. If this argument is successful, saying that potency comes to be *for* activity would be sufficient to establish that activity is prior.

Remarks

To grasp the significance of this argument, and highlight what is left out of it, it will be instructive to step back and look at the philosophical accomplishment of the chapter as a whole. Aristotle announced that his purpose was to show that *energeia* is prior to "every source of change or rest in general" (*Met.* IX.8 1049b7).[35] This category includes nature, potency, choice, and desire, that is, every source that yields an accomplishment. Here he establishes that *energeia* is prior to such sources because it is the source of potency. In what way is it prior? By being a *more governing kind of source*. It is more governing because potency comes to be for it, because the reason we come to have a potency is to use it. The accomplishment of the argument we have just examined, then, is first of all to establish, on the basis of *genesis*, a new, primary way of being a source, *archē*, namely being a *telos*, and second to establish that *energeia* is a *telos* in just this way.

Aristotle has now argued that both potency and its activity are sources. They are not, however, sources in the same way. Being a potency means being the kind of source that sets to work changing an other or being changed by an other when the conditions are right. Potency is what generates the accomplishment (*telos*); it is the potency that makes both the product and the activity come to be; for example, the house-building potency that generates both the house and the activity of building (*Met.* IX.8 1050a30–32). This argument does not establish activity as self-sufficient. In this argument, activity requires potency in order to come to be, and potency persists even while the activity is not there (*Met.* IX.3 1046b29–1047a10).[36]

On the other hand, what the potency is, that is, its being (*ousia*), refers to and is directed toward its activity. But this means the being of the potency depends on its proper activity: it is generated for, and thereby it *is* at all, *for the sake of* the activity.

Potency, then, has two sorts of completion or accomplishment (*telos*): the complete potency (e.g., being a builder), and the accomplishment it sets to work doing (e.g., building). In these respects, potency is neither essentially incomplete, nor is it a state of lacking the activity, as we saw in chapter 4. The fact that potency is *for* activity does not make it inherently incomplete. To the contrary, it is when a potency is complete that its *being-for* is also complete, since it is then that it is the most ready to set to work.[37]

Once we supply Aristotle's pivotal assumption, the conclusion follows. The implicit premise is that sources of *coming-to-be* are prior in being (*ousia*). If this is so, then the accomplishment is prior in being. Therefore, being-at-work is prior to potency in being.

After this argument, the only major premise that Aristotle must establish—and it is not an easy one—is that *energeia* can in fact be a *telos*. This, too, Aristotle works out by examining *genesis*. He must argue that, in each sort of *genesis*, *energeia* is indeed a *telos* (*Met.* IX.8 1050a23–b2).

Activity Is an Accomplishment

The Problem of *Telos*

Having established that potency is *for* the activity, Aristotle appears to have given a complete argument for the priority of being-at-work over potency, since *energeia* is its telic source. Now we face a second question: why, after completing this argument, is Aristotle not finished? He is not even halfway through the argument. What remains to be said, and why does he devote so much work to it?

Most commentators pass over this section in silence, while others examine pieces of it, but do not show how it addresses a single, coherent problem.[38] Broadie is an important exception. She takes up this question in the following way: Aristotle examines the location of activity in transitive and intransitive activities at *Metaphysics* IX.8 1050a23–b2. Transitive activities are those that occur in a further object, for example, a house, or the learning of a student; while intransitive activities do not, for example, theoretical thinking and seeing. Why does it matter, she asks, where the activity (*energeia*) is located?[39] She gives three reasons: first, activity's claim to priority appears problematic because, while activity comes and goes, potency remains. Second, she argues, since transitive activities aim at something else beyond them (i.e., the house), this product, rather than the activity, appears to be the accomplishment. This undermines activity's claim to priority. Third, she says, Aristotle is pushing back on Plato's claim that activity is impermanent and unintelligible in itself, and that it must be directed at a transcendent idea beyond individual beings. Broadie's argument for this point hinges on her claim that form is activity and potency is indeterminate matter. On this supposition, if activity is primary, then we can know the distinctive form of things by examining their activity, but if potency is primary, then because it is indeterminate, she avers, the sources of things in the world will be unknowable.

Broadie is right to raise this concern about the location of *energeia*, and I will extend and add to her argument. But my position differs from hers in several ways. First, while it is true that Aristotle is concerned to show how activity and change are intelligible, his concern does not seem to be centered on the indeterminacy of material. For one, the physicists of Aristotle's time held the position that making sources material makes them *more* intelligible rather than less, and if I am right that for Aristotle potency is evidently independent, then to a certain extent it is also intelligible, especially if it is evident what activity it tends toward (*Met.* IX.5 1048a16–22). The problem Aristotle is concerned with, I aim to show, is not with the intelligibility of underlying processes, but with whether what emerges from them truly count as beings. Broadie's concerns overlap with this problem, but do not raise it. But in this, Aristotle is, as Broadie says, resisting Plato's solution, namely, the argument that changing beings point to an intelligible transcendent being.

Second, Broadie thinks Aristotle's worry about location occupies the passage from *Metaphysics* IX.8 1050a23 to 1050b2, whereas, as I aim to show, the fundamental worry occupies the whole, three-part argument from *Metaphysics* IX.8 1050a15 to 1050b4. As a result of concentrating on only part of the passage, she does not present the problem as sharply as I think it could be presented. I think the worry is not only whether activity is prior, but whether it has a solid claim to being a *telos* at all. Even more critical is the question of whether calling something a *telos* is in fact a legitimate basis for priority.

The problem that motivates this long argument is this: potency appears to make all activity transitive. If this is the case, activity cannot be a *telos*.

If *energeia* is the use or activity *of potency*, it will inherit the structure of potency.[40] Potency is other-directed, which means it has a dispersive, transitive structure: it is the source of change in *another thing* or the same thing *as other*, and this other is where its *telos* is located. Thus, the *telos* of an agent is in the patient: for example, of a builder the *telos* is the change in the buildable things; while the *telos* of a patient seems at first to be in the agent, for example, of buildable things the *telos* is the builder's activity of building.[41]

For this reason, the dispersive structure of potency, that is, its transitive character, is apparent in the word "work" (*ergon*), which has two meanings: a deed or act, for example, the activity of working, and its product, for example, the works of Shakespeare. It forms the root word of being-at-work (*energeia*). Not only is the activity of the worker temporary, it is not ultimately located in the worker, but beyond the worker at the work object. Moreover, the work object appears to be primary, since it is the product and *telos* of working. So the work and its *telos* appear to be different and in different places, and being-at-work is secondary.

From this we can see a reason to doubt that activity can be a *telos* at all. First, activity does not seem to have its own character: on the one hand, it appears merely to be the exercise of potency, so everything determinate about it seems to derive from potency. But to be *telos*, and indeed, to be primary at all, appears to require that something has its own character, that is, that it is in a way something definite. On the other hand, if potency and activity are fundamentally other-directed, we might worry that neither of them has an inherently determinate character. As it stands, then, it seems there is nothing, or nearly nothing, about activity that would justify us calling it a *telos*; it seems false to say that either the capacity to work or the activity of working are accomplishments. Since a *telos* is that at which other things are directed, then both potency and activity are means, and neither is an end in itself.

Furthermore, two things undermine the idea that an accomplishment (*telos*) could indicate primacy. First, Aristotle has established that both potency and activity depend on one another in order to be: potency depends on activity because activity is what it is for, while activity depends on potency because without it, no activity would occur.[42] But activity is temporary: the builder stops and starts building (*Met.* IX.3 1046b29–1047a10). Thus, potency's permanence seems to anchor the ongoing possibility of activity, and thereby override the claim of *telos* to decide which is primary.[43]

Second, since transitive potencies and activities do not seem to coincide with their own accomplishment, they seem to be related to their accomplishment externally or accidentally, rather than through themselves (*kath auto*) or essentially. It is therefore unclear why the accomplishment would decide whether potency or being-at-work is primary: from the fact that both the potency and activity of building give rise to an existing house, it does not obviously follow that activity is prior to potency. Both appear to be equally necessary.

It is possible to present these problems under a single heading. Change comes to an end in other things: the ends of change are always elsewhere than where the source and/or activity of change sets to work. Change is dispersive: a moving thing scatters others like a bowling ball does pins. Dispersion is an interpretation of the structure of change as a whole. The very activity of changing spreads things out in a continuum of place and time, rather than collecting or concentrating them in one whole, so change itself appears to be the very contradiction of *telos*.[44] It seems, then, that, based on the character of potency and activity, neither can give us a genuine accomplishment, because on their own neither one appears to be an end in itself, but each is directed beyond itself. Thus, the attempt to show that change has an accomplishment, and that *energeia* is such an accomplishment, is strewn about. Accomplishments themselves seem more transitory than the changes and the capacities that lead to them.

Aristotle provides three arguments to establish the possibility that activity could be an accomplishment, which we shall go through in the order they occur in the text. First, he needs to show that activity is something, that it has its own character. He will do this by drawing on the way potency extends to the concept of material, and activity to form. This extension shows that both potency and activity are definite, knowable, and articulable. The same is true, he adds, in the case of change. I shall call this the Structure Argument.

Second, Aristotle needs to show that activity has an even more fundamental structure than dispersion. He will show this by arguing that activity arrives at, and converges with, *telos*. In fact, what makes it possible for change to be dispersive in the first place is that change is *for* something, that it is directed. For the outcome of activity could not be in some other thing unless the activity of change *also* and primarily *culminates in something*. Thus, activity is intrinsically related to *telos*. This will remove the worry that being merely the use of potency and therefore being fundamentally other-directed might mean that activity is not the *telos*. I shall call this the Etymological Argument. This sets the table for the claim that activity is *telos*, but does not clinch it, since the transitive activities still appear to be in different locations than their products.

Third, to show that activity can, through itself, be an accomplishment, Aristotle needs to show that it is in the same place as the accomplishment, not apart from and incidental to it. He argues for this by distinguishing between intransitive and transitive activities. Thus, he distinguishes between two senses of *telos*: (i) the fulfillment of a *potency*, for example, the builder's activity of building, or the buildable's activity of being built, and (ii) the product as the fulfillment of *changes* (i.e., of the activity of a being in potency), for example, the house that comes to be. I shall call this the Location Argument.

Crucially, the claims that change is dispersive and that there is a *telos* of change are not mutually contradictory. Change contains asymmetric structures: one of othering or dispersion, and the other of direction and accomplishment.

The Structure Argument (1050a15–16)

Aristotle's task is to establish that being-at-work (*energeia*) can be an accomplishment (*telos*) after all. But he first needs to show that activity is structured. The worry is twofold. On the one hand, insofar as it is the use of potency, being-at-work seems not to have its own form, but to derive whatever structure it has from potency. Similarly, on the other hand, to the extent that it is transitive, its structure could be entirely derivative from what it produces. He shows that activity is structured by specifying how the concept of potency extends to material, and activity extends to form.[45] In the Structure Argument (*Met.* IX.8 1050a15–16), I aim to show, the claim is that the internal structure of the relation between material and form is actually a relation between potency and *energeia*. The defining characteristics of this relation are that material/potency tends toward its counterpart, and that when it is at work, it has the structure of the form. By doing this, Aristotle shows that potency and activity are definite in every sense, specifically including change and being.

Aristotle defines material in terms of potency in several places (*Met.* VIII.1 1042a26–28, VIII.2 1043a15–17, VIII.6 1045b18–19). Describing what is capable of being a house, is, first, to describe the bricks and wood (i.e., the level of material immediately relevant to being a house), rather than its elemental constituents (*Met.* VIII.4 1044a33–b3, IX.7 1049a19–b1). Second, it is to describe this material *exactly insofar as it is capable of being a house*.[46] If you describe a particular whole thing by describing it insofar as it is potent, you are describing material parts as capable of being a particular whole thing. But in these passages, while Aristotle clearly indicates that potency and material are related to one another, he does not describe the relationship between potency and activity, nor does he say explicitly what it is about material that makes it useful to call it potency. The same goes for form. But in the passage that concerns us now, he does just that:

(2) Furthermore,
(a) material is in-potency [*dunamei*] because it comes to [*elthoi*] a form;
(b) and when it is at-work [*energeiai*], then it is *in* the form. (*Met.* IX.8 1050a15–16, my trans.)

This passage describes the relationship between potency and activity very clearly, namely, that material comes to form in the way potency comes to activity. I will examine these claims in order.

(a) This claim expresses the relationship between potency and material. As a source, potency immediately sets to work in an other or is set to work by another when the conditions are right (*Met.* IX.7 1049a5–18). This means that material itself takes on a form when the conditions are right; for example, as metal flakes fit into a certain arrangement when a magnet is present. Material comes to the form the way potency sets to work when the conditions are right. For material to be in potency means, for something natural, that it will be on its own unless something gets in its way, and for something artificial, that it will be if the artificer desires it, as we saw in the section complete potencies in chapter 4 (*Met.* IX.7 1049a5–18). To come to a form, then, is to be in that form unless something gets in the way, that is, to be at work, *energeia*. Thus, this claim characterizes the relationship between potency and activity, and in addition says what it is about material that relates it to the form.

But the argument from *genesis* that we examined earlier in this chapter enriches the description of this structure: potency is on the way to activity because its being is *what* it is for the sake of *generating* activity, so material, too, is *what* it is for the sake of giving rise to a form. Thus trees are cut into planks, making them into materials for building, for example, a house or a table; and the organs of a body come to be what they are for the sake of generating the activity of the living animal.

The word "come to" (*erchomai*) cannot mean that material moves toward form in a literal sense, nor that it changes into form in an ontological sense. For material and form are not the poles that define the continuous magnitude between the opposites involved in change—those poles are form and its privation (*steresis*) (*Phys.* I.7 190b30–191a2). For the same reason, it cannot mean that potency moves toward activity, or is converted into activity. Instead, the word *erchomai* indicates that material is active in its relationship with form, that it tends to generate a form. *Genesis* shows this tendency more clearly than any other phenomenon: a thing's progression from the absence of form F into the organized form F exhibits the tendency, that is, the potency, and potency is, thus, apparent in the way that coming-to-be is *for* its *telos*.

(b) This claim responds to the worry that activity is indeterminate by arguing that activity is itself something distinct, that it has a form. To argue that when the material is active it is *in* the form *just means* that it has come to have a certain active shape. What is the basis for this claim? The preceding argument from *genesis* suggests one, namely, that what *comes to be* is something definite. This is a reasonably intuitive claim: we say *genesis* has occurred when something definite has arisen, that is, something with a distinct form; but if nothing definite has arisen, we do not say that *genesis* has occurred.

The tendency of potency and material to set to work when conditions are right implies that when they are at work they have come to have a definite structure or form. Through this identification of material and form with potency and activity, Aristotle does not just gain a way to indicate the active, source-like aspect of material and form. He also makes it quite clear that activity is structured.

But it was not the case of material and form that led to the worry about indefiniteness; it was the transitive and other-directed character of changes. This is why Aristotle immediately turns back to change:

> (2) Furthermore (a) material is in-potency [*dunamei*] because it comes to [*elthoi*] a form;
> (b) and when it is at-work [*energeiai*], then it is *in* the form.
> (c) And it is similar in other cases, including those in which the accomplishment is change, and that is why teachers display [*apodedōkenai*] a student at work, thinking that they are delivering up the accomplishment, and nature does likewise. (*Met.* IX.8 1050a15–21, my trans.)

Aristotle explicitly marks change as an accomplishment. Change is *not* essentially incomplete, for *change is itself an accomplishment, namely, the accomplishment of potency*.[47] In this case, the student's being-at-work is a change, and *being-at-work is being in a form*. As the *telos* of potency, change has a form, an organization and order. It is because change has a form that it can maintain the organization of material; for example, a body staying the same through continuous change.[48] Applying it here means that changes, not just objects, have structures, patterns, and forms that we can grasp and articulate.

The Etymological Argument (1050a21–23)

The Structure Argument showed that potency and activity are definite, but it did not deal directly with the problem of dispersion. Since potency and activity seem to be other-directed—potency by being a source of change in an other, the activity of potency by being a change in an other, and both by generating a product—they seem always to differ from their *telos*. In his next argument, Aristotle dismantles this problem by showing that the way genetic processes and other changes are oriented, that is, their directedness, actually bolsters activity's claim to being a *telos*. This is a description of how activity extends to *telos*, and thereby to *entelecheia*. I call this the Etymological Argument because it works by connecting the root words that make up *energeia* and *entelecheia*. Although it has the form of an etymological argument, it is clearly philosophical. It is the word "work" (*ergon*) that shows how *energeia* is naturally related to *telos*:

(3) For
    (a) the work [*ergon*] is an accomplishment [*telos*], and
    (b) *being at work* [*energeia*] is the work, and
    (c) this is why the name *being at work* is said through the work and
    (d) stretches toward [*sunteinei*] being-complete [*entelecheia*]. (*Met.* IX.8 1050a21–23, my trans.)

The path joining *energeia* to *telos* is the path from *energeia* to *entelecheia*.[49] To join the two together, Aristotle appeals to the idea that the root word "work" (*ergon*) evidently names an accomplishment. *Ergon* has two basic senses: first, a work-object, possession, or subject matter, and second, an act or deed. An *ergon* is, therefore, naturally related to the idea of a *telos*, because both a work object and an act can be accomplishments, and work objects are clearly outcomes of productive activities. Once this is established, we can substitute "accomplishment" (*telos*) for "work" (*ergon*), yielding the word *en-tel-eia*, which means "completed" or "accomplished." Emphasizing the sense of *ergon* as an act or deed using the concept of holding on (*echein*) gives us *en-tel-ech-eia*, "being-in-the-accomplishment, being-complete, or accomplishing."

The etymology is clear enough, but the argument is more difficult to grasp, for two reasons: "work" could mean either the work-act or the work-object, and to say that being-at-work "stretches toward," "strains toward," "converges with," or "draws tight to" (*sunteinei*) being-complete could mean either that it aims at being-complete, or that being-at-work (*energeia*) and being-complete (*entelecheia*) ultimately mean the same thing.

The clear point of departure is that (a) both the work-object and certain kinds of work-acts are accomplishments, for example, a carpenter's table or a singer's act of singing. Step (b), then, would be the claim that the being-at-work is the work-object (e.g., the activity of a table holding itself together) or the potency at-work (e.g., the activity of building or singing). Steps (a) and (b) set up the claim that being-at-work is a *telos*.

But steps (c) and (d) do not straightforwardly draw this conclusion.[50] They argue instead that the source of the structure of being-at-work is the work that it brings into being.[51] For (c) the claim that being-at-work is named through (*kata*) the work means that the being-at-work takes its name from the work-object that it accomplishes. For the activity to aim at the work is for it to be organized by the work, that is, for its structure to be determined by the work. This is why the building-act takes its name from the building-object that emerges from it, even though the building-act is definitely *not* the same as its object.[52] Thus (d) being-at-work stretches, strains, or extends toward, and draws tight with its accomplishment.

In this reading, the Etymological Argument does not equate being-at-work with being-complete. Instead, the builder's *activity* is what brings the building, that is, the further *telos*, into being; in this case, the being-at-work is the *entelecheia*, that is, that which *accomplishes* the accomplishment. This is what is expressed in the word *sunteinein*.

In sum: I contend that the Etymological Argument addresses an objection to the possibility that being-at-work could be an accomplishment, namely, that since the activity was directed at an *other*, it could not itself be a *telos*. If I am right, the argument shows, by contrast, that because being-at-work stretches toward and brings about a *telos*, it is the intermediate *source* of this *telos*: because building is what creates *a* building, the telic character of the building-object applies to the building-activity as well. Because being-at-work brings the further accomplishment (the product) into being, we call being-at-work an accomplishment (in the sense of accomplish*ing*, i.e., *entelecheia*) as well, and give it a name derived from the whole accomplishment.

The Location Argument (1050a23–b2)

But there is still a crucial problem: the claim that being-at-work is continuous with, and the source of, the *telos* that it accomplishes falls apart if the two are in different locations. If the activity belongs to a different being, then it seems that the relationship between the source and what it generates will be accidental. If so, it seems that whatever is caused by potent beings would be accidental: since the activity would be external to the effects it generates, there would be no per se causes.[53]

The Location Argument solves this problem by marking the location of the accomplishment that belongs to each sort of potency, and shows that in each case being-at-work is alongside its accomplishment, in the same being. At the same time, Aristotle distinguishes the being-at-work of a potency from the product of the work. Thus, the activity of the builder is an accomplishment in a different way than the house is: the activity of the builder is an accomplishment of the capacity to build, whereas the house is the accomplishment of the complete activity of building. But the working is *in* the *thing that is complete*, not apart from it. Thus, Aristotle's distinction between two senses of *telos*—the fulfillment of a potency, and the completed work object—allows him to show that they are located in the same place as the activity (*energeia*), which means the two are related to one another internally, through themselves.

There are two rounds of argument at *Metaphysics* IX.8 1050a23–b2, each of which deals with two cases: where activities are themselves ultimate (*eschaton*), and where activities are productive. In the first round, Aristotle works out the status of "putting to use" (*chrēsis*), and in the second round he locates the activity where the accomplishment is. Instead of quoting directly, I paraphrase here to show the structure of the argument:

(4)
   (a) The potent thing, for example, the seer, the house-building capacity, is responsible for what comes to be, as we saw, but potency relates to the accomplishment it generates in two ways:
   (b) Whenever only the exercise (*chrēsis*) comes to be (*gignomai*), as, for example, in seeing, contemplating, life, and happiness (i.e., natural sources),
      i. The exercise or being-at-work is the last thing, the *telos*.
      ii. Furthermore, the accomplishment of what is potent arises *in* what is potent.
      iii. Therefore, by being active, the potent being is *in* the accomplishment. The *en–erg–eia* is *en–tel–ech–eia*.
      iv. Therefore the being-at-work or exercise is *just as much* an accomplishment (*telos*) as the potency.
   (c) Whenever from what is potent both the exercise and a work-object come to be (*gignomai*), such as building, weaving, and changes in general (i.e., productive potencies),
      i. the change is *in* what is moved, the being-at-work of the builder is *in the thing made* (see also *Phys*. III.3).[54]
      ii. The being-at-work is therefore spatially and temporally together with the work-object that is its accomplishment (*telos*). For example, the house-building occurs *in* the house, and comes to be, and *is at the same time* as the house.
      iii. Therefore, since the exercise or work-act (*energeia*) of the potency is *in* the work-object with the *telos*, the *en–erg–eia*

> is *more* a *telos*, more *entelecheia* than the potency [since the potency to act is *not* in the same being as the *telos*]. (*Met.* IX.8 1050a23-b2)

First, for intransitive activities like singing, seeing, and thinking, since there is no further object generated by the activity of working, it appears that the *telos* is a work in the sense of an act, rather than an object (*Met.* IX.8 1050a23–24).[55] In this case, since the *potency* brings the activity into being, it is *genesis*, in the sense marked out above, that is the basis for its priority. Second, transitive activities are directed beyond themselves at other things. Being-at-work in this case is *genesis*: for example, when building is the activity, it brings into being its *telos*, and is directed toward it. Thus, the basis for the claim that *energeia* aims at *entelecheia* is, again, the structure of *genesis*.

To draw out the import of the argument and its relationship to change, we need to note several things. First, here being-at-work is clearly synonymous with exercise. Second, as noted, *genesis* covers every sort of change. This passage uses *genesis* in two ways: the potency brings into being both the activity of building and the house or any other sort of change. Third, the exercise of the capacity to build (i.e., the activity of building) and the house ultimately exist at the same time, once the house has taken hold of its shape.[56] This bolsters the claim in the Etymological Argument that activity is continuous with its accomplishment. Fourth, potency always has an accomplishment, *telos*, in the same place the *energeia* is. This gives us a very literal use of *entel-. echeia*: the being-at-work is, in fact, *in* the accomplishment, and bound up with it (*sunteinei*).

Fifth, and most importantly, the reasoning seems to be that activity is prior to potency in cases of production because productive activities are located in the *telos* they produce, whereas the productive potency is located in the producer. But the same criterion yields no priority in the intransitive cases. We would expect *energeia* to be more *telos* than potency in every case, and in particular, we might expect intransitive activities like contemplation to be *more teleia* than potency.[57] But Aristotle claims merely that the exercise of intransitive potencies is *at least as much* a *telos* as the potency. This shows that the decisive criterion is not simply *telos*, but, I argue, *archē*.

* * *

I will summarize the argument before turning to the conclusion Aristotle draws from it. Since we only count generation (*genesis*) to have occurred when a definite thing emerges, generation is used as the paradigm of structures that are *for* something. The argument that being-at-work (*energeia*) is prior to potency in being (*ousia*) uses the structure of generation to show that an accomplishment (*telos*) is a source (*archē*) in the most governing way, and then analyzes its structure to show that being-at-work can, in fact, be an accomplishment, that is, a definite structure whose identity derives from and coincides with the product.

The first half of the argument aimed to establish that the accomplishment which results from a genetic process has a privileged status: since the process is *for* something in that something emerges or results from it, the principal source of the process is its accomplishment. Since even the potency is generated for it, the accomplishment must be primary.

The second half of the argument aimed to show that being-at-work has the characteristics required for it to be an accomplishment: it has its own definite structure, this structure derives in each case from the accomplishment, and because it coincides spatially and temporally with the accomplishment, the two can be internally related to each other.

To make these claims, Aristotle throughout uses generation, coming-to-be, as the paradigm for sources. Generation provides the teleological structure of sources in general. It makes it possible to distinguish potency-like sources from *telic* sources, and relates them to each other. Crucially, the claim that an accomplishment has to be a source is based on the fact that things come-to-be *for it*. But the claim of activity (*energeia*) to being an accomplishment and the legitimacy of accomplishment in deciding its priority over potency are also secured through the analysis of the structure of genesis. Without *genesis*, the claim has no basis or content.

From this argument Aristotle draws a stunning conclusion. The stated aim of *Metaphysics* IX.8 was to show that activity is prior to potency in speech, time, *ousia*, and in independent existence. But the argument culminates in a claim (a) that goes well beyond the task of merely establishing the relative priority of activity, to the extent that the original claim (b) is merely tacked onto it:

(5) And so
 (a) it is clear that primary being [*ousia*] and form [*eidos*] are being-at-work [*energeia*].
 (b) So *as a result of this argument* it is obvious that being-at-work takes precedence over potency in *ousia*. (*Met.* IX.8 1050b2–3)[58]

This claim goes far beyond the explicit goals of the chapter: to claim that *energeia* takes precedence in *ousia* does not require saying that *ousia* and *eidos* are themselves essentially kinds or aspects of *energeia*. Aristotle did not signal along the way that he was going to draw this conclusion. Some scholars think that this is because the claim is obvious.[59] If I am right, however, this conclusion is a genuine accomplishment.

This claim is justified by the series of pivotal arguments we have examined: the decisive claim is that (1) being *for* something (*heneka*) has the structure of *genesis*. From this, Aristotle argues that (1b) in anything with a for-structure the accomplishment (*telos*) is the source (*archē*), that (1a) the way a thing is a source determines its primacy in primary being (*ousia*), that (2a–b) the relation of a potency coming up to what it generates is the structure of the relation between material (*hulē*) and form (*eidos*), so that being-at-work (*energeia*) is its own form or structure, that (3) this structure is determined by what it accomplishes, so that both the being-at-work and the work-object are accomplishments, and that (4) activity and its accomplishment coincide with one another.

Thus, through this analysis of *genesis* the argument places *telos* at the heart of ontology. It also clinches the argument against reductive materialism represented by Empedocles and Antiphon because it is being-at-work and not potency that is primary in primary being (*ousia*), individual beings and their forms are prior to material processes.

CONCLUSION

The thinking of being includes the thinking of change. Aristotle's ontology does not just aim at unchanging primary being (*ousia*), it studies all things insofar as they are (*Met.* IV.2 1004b1), including, thereby, the being of change and sources of change. If Aristotle is right, an ontology that includes change must distinguish between aspects of being and between a source and its accomplishment. Ontology therefore includes teleology. Clearing away some of the metaphysical baggage that the concepts of material, form, potency, activity, actuality, and teleology have accumulated leaves us with Aristotle's strong, flexible, and minimal ontology of change.

For change to be at all, Aristotle needed to show that being is multiple in two respects. First, to establish that change is something at all, he needed to distinguish between three ontological aspects of one being: form, privation, and the underlying material (chap. 1). Thus, Aristotle discovers in change (*genesis*) the distinction between incidental and essential being, and the structure of categorical predication. The concepts of material and form are modified by change, for two reasons: first, for something to underlie as material is for it to be the categorical subject of change (chap. 1), and second, material and form must be grasped in and through potency and being-at-work (chap. 6).

But, second, to specify the determinate categorical characteristics of a changing being is precisely not to define what change is. To define change we need a third sense of being that is appropriate to the task, namely dynamic-energetic being. Thus, we must distinguish between incidental and essential properties, categorical objects bearing properties, and dynamic-energetic beings oriented toward activity—three of the senses of being, said simply (*Met.* VI.2 1026a33–b3). Using energetic being to define change does not make change a vague object: on its own terms change is definite because its sources (potencies) can be specified and completed, and because change itself is an active structure or form by being the completion (*telos*) of potency and essentially linked to what it generates.

Aristotle's aspect-theory of being does not subordinate energetic being to categorical being and its concept of *ousia*. This is clear from Aristotle's use of the word "as" (*hē*) to show that material and form make up one cluster of aspects, while being-in-potency and being-at-work compose an essentially different cluster of aspects. Unlike material, a being-in-potency is a concrete particular being considered insofar as it is organized to set to work, while, unlike a form, a being at-work is the same being considered insofar as it is a functioning whole.

To think changing beings is to think them through the concept of sources, so our task was to understand the structure of such sources. One of the core challenges in this book has been to understand how change requires potency, being-at-work, being-complete, and *telos* to be robust and independent sources that make beings what they are, simply and as wholes. Aristotle divides sources into two types: initiating sources such as potency and nature, and telic sources. Initiating sources are beings insofar as they are disposed to act when the conditions are right. Potencies, for example, require others in order to act, and they are therefore able to accomplish opposite things at the same time. Such sources are beings in the proper sense when they are complete. The completion of a potency preserves it as a potency, and reduces or removes its ability to fail. Initiating sources can be beings, then, (i) by being the mere potency for something; this is why a baby who cannot walk and a marathon runner are both the *sort* of being who can run a marathon; (ii) by being the completed potency, for example, a marathon runner; or (iii) by being organized into a natural shape, thereby coming to be an individual being (*ousia*) (chap. 4).

But the other way to be a source is to be a completion (*telos*). An account of sources and their accomplishments must include teleology, that is, the study of how an accomplishment (*telos*) is a source of action. Teleology becomes philosophically important through the being of change and its sources. For an account of the being of sources, the most interesting cases are the following ones. (i) We know change exists because potent beings imply change, since change is the complete being (*entelecheia*) through which they are potent, as, for example, the capacity to build and be built depends on the activity of building (chap. 2). (ii) By completing its potency, something comes to *be*-in-potency; for example, by completing her ability to play the violin, someone becomes a violinist (chap. 4). (iii) Genetic processes are not reducible to underlying material processes: the generation of a being occurs when from these processes a structure emerges that is a source of change. This means that automatic material processes are fully compatible with teleology because change-originating structures can emerge from them (chap. 5). (iv) A completion is a structured activity that potency or change is *for*, so potency is inseparable from its result. Therefore the outcome is the source of organization of both the potency and the genetic process (chap. 6).

CONCLUSION

It is in and through change that we conceive of things as having sources or principles, and it is in and through change that we discover that sources are ontologically primary. This is because it is also in and through change that we think of things as being directed or oriented at all, as accomplishing something, and as being capable of fulfillment.

NOTES

Introduction
1. All Greek will be transliterated, including in quotations.
2. The method of discovery is conspicuous in Aristotle. See Wieland (1975), 135, who writes "The principles stand at the end, not at the beginning of the investigation." See also Halper (1989), xxxiii.
3. Brague (1980), 1–2, argues that since Descartes, it has become commonplace to "define" change as a transition (i.e., a change) in time and space.
4. This book concentrates on single, contiguous arguments in chapters 1, 2, and 6, while chapters 3–5 draw on closely related passages to reconstruct Aristotle's position. Chapter 3 begins with philology, and ends by bringing together passages on the incompleteness of change and potency, while chapter 4 draws out the account of potency across *Metaphysics* IX, and chapter 5 follows Aristotle's engagements with Empedocles.
5. Among those who do such work are Aquinas (1961, 1962, 1963), Brentano (1975), Ross (1924, 1936, 1995), Owens (1978), Charles (1984), M. Frede (1987), Waterlow (Broadie) (1982a), Gill (1989), Witt (1989), Burnyeat (2001), Yu (2003), Lang (2007), Gotthelf (2012), and Kosman (2013).
6. Aristotle describes these terms as related to change most of all (*Met.* IX.1 1045b33–1046a11, 1047a30-b1). For the debate over whether they have a wholly independent ontological sense—which I argue they do not—see "Potency and Activity, Change and Being" in chapter 4.
7. Being in an unqualified sense is many (*Met.* VI.2 1026a33). See especially *Met.* V.7. Other notable uses of the concept: *Phys.* I.2 185a20–32, 185b32–186a3, I.3 186a24–b35, I.9 192a37–38, III.1 200b26–28; *Met.* IV.2 1003a33; *Met.* VII.1 1028a10. Aristotle often simply lists the ways being is said, as at *Met.* IX.1 1045b32.
8. For discussion of the ontological or linguistic meaning of this multiplicity, see Brentano (1975) and Ross in Aristotle (1924), lxxix-xc. Heidegger (1995) and Brogan (2005) address its ontological aspect. Recent discussion of the multiplicity of being has mostly addressed it from the point of view of speech: see Irwin (1981), Shields (1999), Ward (2009), and Brakas (2011).
9. Sachs trans., Aristotle (1999), emphasis added. Each is a sense of its being, simply. This is the case even though each sense of being can itself be divided, with each of these terms depending on a focal sense.
10. In *Met.* V.28 1024b10–18, form, material, and the senses of categorical being exemplify difference in kind; for example, place is not derived from quality, quantity, or *ousia*. It is important to my argument that potency and activity should be added to the list. The four greatest senses of being should be added as well; for example, although the incidental sense of being depends on the essential, categorical sense of being, it can neither be reduced to nor deduced from it.

11. Wieland (1975), 135–36: these systems of principles, he argues, are unitfied only by analogy. Compare Aubenque (2012), 24–28, who claims that Aristotle decides to prioritize ousia, but that his decision is unjustifiable.

12. Ross asserts that the distinction between activity and potency is found within each category, based on *Met.* V.7 1017b2 and IX.10 1051b1. Witt (2003) and Beere (2009) hold this position as well. While it is certainly the case that something can be capable of, or actively be a certain quantity, it does not follow that potency and activity themselves are subdivisions within the categories—a claim that, I contend, would violate Aristotle's assertion that the different senses of being are meant simply or wholly (*haplos*). See "Potency and Activity, Change and Being" in chapter 4.

13. At *Met.* VI.4 1027b35–1028a3, Aristotle argues that incidental being and alethic being concern categorical beings. But this does not indicate that they are reduced to it. By omitting energetic being, Aristotle appears to suggest that through it some nature does come to light apart from categorical being.

14. Sachs trans., Aristotle (1999), translation modified: "thinghood" replaced with "primary being," "complete being-at-work" replaced with "being-complete." Greek added.

15. Chapter 6 argues that the sense of priority governing energetic being consists in being a source. See, for example, the section on the Argument of *Met.* IX.8. The pivotal concept in incidental and essential being is essential being, while truth—particularly the truth of simple beings—is pivotal in alethic being.

16. Heidegger (1995), 10.

17. Ross, in Aristotle (1924), lxxxv. The schemata of the categories are widely regarded as a complete description of the sorts of predication, but also, as Kant (2003), A81/B107 argued, are not systematic. Ross, in Aristotle (1924), says, "Aristotle has no 'deduction of the categories,' no argument to show that the real must fall into just these divisions. He seems to have arrived at the ten categories by simple inspection of reality, aided by a study of verbal distinctions" (lxxxv). It is unclear what "simple inspection of reality" might mean, however. Though several have attempted to deduce the system of the categories, notably Brentano (1975), no one has deduced the four primary senses of being.

18. In *Met.* VII, accepting the Platonic assumptions that the underlying thing is unintelligible material opposed to the intelligible form, Aristotle seeks a way to determine which of the two is truly primary. This project meets with failure, and he starts again in *Met.* VII.17 with a new approach to thinking about the composite.

19. Sachs trans, Aristotle (1995).

20. The word *allo* means something different in any respect, whereas *heteros* means an other in a pair, a correlative other.

21. Thus, in *Phys.* V.1 225a1–b9 Aristotle argues that *genesis* and destruction are not changes (*kinēseis*), because there is no contrary of primary being (*ousia*) and therefore no continuum between something that is and its non-being. Yet, a book later, he treats *genesis* as a continuous process, undermining the objection that made the two incompatible (*Phys.* VI.6 237b10–24; see *Met.* IX.8 1050a7–8).

22. As Helen Lang points out, in Aristotle's use of Greek the verb *kinein*, "to move," never seemed to have had an intransitive middle voice. As Lang (1995), 168, observes, the middle voice transitive of *kinein* is used in comedy for the act of taking someone for your sexual pleasure, and Aristotle's circumlocution at *Phys.* III.1 201a30–35 appears meant to avoid using it in this way. See *Phys.* VIII.5 256a20–22, 35, for possible exceptions.

23. Mourelatos (1970), 117–20.

24. Mourelatos (1970), 116–17.
25. Roark (2011), 64, overlooks this aspect of *genesis* in his category tree for *metabolē*.
26. Unless you count the passages "everything that comes into being goes up [lit. "walks," *badizei*] to a source and an end" (*Met.* IX.8 1050a7–8, Sachs trans., Aristotle 1999) or "material is in potency because it comes to [*elthoi*] a form; and whenever it is at work, then it is *in* that form" (*Met.* IX.8 1050a15–16, my trans.), but neither uses the word *kinēsis*.
27. The core books of the *Metaphysics* work through all three, in succession: Aristotle famously argues in *Met.* VII.17 1041b11–33 that we must leave behind book VII's discussion of elements to start an investigation of causes, and he turns to an examination of sources in *Met.* IX.1–9. The order is the same in the *Physics*: elements in book I, causes in book II, and sources in book III.1–3.
28. Ryle (1954), 102–6; Vendler (1957), 143–60; Hirst (1959), 126–35; and Ackrill (1965), 121–42. Ackrill's formulation of problems with the distinction led to a number of attempts to solve it. See Crombie (1967), 32; Hardie (1968), 305; Mulhern (1968), 237–51; Penner (1970), 393–453; Mamo (1970), 24–34; Hoffman (1976), 89–95; and Pickering (1977), 37–43.
29. Compatibilist readings of the Passage, in which scholars seek to preserve a continuity between *energeia* and *kinēsis*, attempt to secure by other means the relevance of change to the concept of *energeia* and thereby ontology, but risk diminishing or distorting its impact.
30. For example, it conflicts with Aristotle's claim that *energeia* is, in the strictest sense, *kinēsis* (*Met.* IX.3 1047a30–35), and with the claim that all actions (*praxeis*) include motion (*kinēseis*) (*Met.* III.2 996a22–29). Burnyeat (2008), Beere (2009), 227–30, and Menn (n.d.) IIIα2 24–26, point out many other discrepancies between this passage and the surrounding text. But both nevertheless accept a sharp distinction between movement and *energeia*.
31. Burnyeat (2008), 276.
32. Burnyeat (2008) says: "And I am inclined to agree also that the Passage is authentic Aristotle, both in style—Jaeger cites the first-person verb *legō* (1048b35), which is indeed a feature of Aristotle's prose—and in thought. Who else would have such thoughts?" (227). Burnyeat attempts to substantiate the claim that nobody but Aristotle would have thoughts like this. He (2008), 274, cites the tradition among the Aristotelians of disputing the account of pleasure as *genesis* in the *Philebus* (which substitutes *kinēsis* for *genesis*), and posits that a lost text on pleasure by Aristotle both inspired the tradition and contained the passage. This argument, however, indicates just as forcefully that others were writing passages like this, on similar themes, and Theophrastus also uses *legō*. The subject and such claims about style are insufficient to attribute the Passage to Aristotle. Its authenticity, then, comes down to philosophical considerations, and its conflicts with other passages give us reasons to doubt its authenticity.
33. For example, Theophrastus (1993), Fr.307D, makes what looks like the *energeia*-*kinēsis* distinction. See Burnyeat (2008), 275. Burnyeat (2008), 243, conjectures that it was inserted at *Met.* IX.6 to prevent the passage from appearing blasphemous by implying that God, who is *energeia*, could be related to change. Thus, there is a strong motive for inserting it, and there are alternative sources to draw from. I am therefore somewhat inclined to think that the Passage is not by Aristotle. But the argument of this book does not hinge on its authenticity or inauthenticity.

Chapter 1

1. Sachs renders *tēn archēn* in this phrase as "original being," an astute translation in the context of this passage.
2. Those asking this question include Parmenides, Melissus, Empedocles, and Democritus. Charlton trans., Aristotle (1970). Translation modified: changed "things" to "beings," "principles" to "sources," and italicized for emphasis.
3. Compare Bostock (2006), 1–4.
4. Charlton trans., Aristotle (1970).
5. Bostock (2006), 1–2 thinks it is a mistake to use *genesis* to understand being. Charles (2018), 194–97, 203–5 observes that Aristotle assumes the principles of change and of being are the same, at least for natural beings, but emphasizes his failure to find a reason for this assumption.
6. To understand what being (*ousia*, thinghood, substance) is, we must turn to the investigation of what is responsible (*aition*, cause) for beings (*Met.* VII.17 1041a29).
7. Charlton trans., Aristotle (1970). Kelsey (2006) argues that Aristotle here faces the following dilemma: for change to occur, a thing cannot already be the same *kind* of thing that it is coming to be: if something is already an animal, it cannot change into an animal; even if I take one piece of furniture and turn it into another piece, its being furniture is precisely not changed. Therefore, change must relate to what is not. But "kind" in this context means a category or subcategory, that is, a property of a being. I contend, however, that what is at stake for Aristotle is that being has *aspects*, which are not kinds or properties of things at all, but do make such properties possible.
8. Charlton trans., Aristotle (1970).
9. Compare Bodnár (2018), 207, 213.
10. Charlton trans., Aristotle (1970).
11. This sort of evidence is vulnerable, of course, to the charge that in the *Metaphysics* Aristotle is only doing preparatory work, and does not actually do ontology there either. I think this is a mistaken but interesting view.
12. Ross (1924), lxxix.
13. Burnyeat (2001), especially 58–59.
14. Sachs trans., Aristotle (1995).
15. Though it is syntactically more legible to translate *to mē on* as "non-being," the English term suggests both a generality and an entity, so it is better to render it as "*what is not*." But since Aristotle's original difficulty includes the problem of the generality and being of what is not, to preserve or highlight this difficulty I shall also use "non-being."
16. See the discussion of aspects in "The Unruly Number of Being" later in this chapter.
17. This means that epistemology for Aristotle does not break apart into an a priori approach opposed to an experiential one, as Bostock (2006), 6–7, 9, thinks it does. Some of the fault that Bostock finds with Aristotle's argument in *Physics* I.7 is produced through the anachronism of importing the a priori and a posteriori distinction. He admits that this is misleading, but he also has no qualms about claiming that it must be true nonetheless: "For one thing, Aristotle very often seems to take no account of the distinction between an empirical and a conceptual enquiry, and certainly he makes no attempt in this passage to draw the distinction as I suggest. For another, he never in fact states the a priori argument I have just supplied him with. But I think it is helpful to recognize that this argument is at work in his mind, for only so can we explain why he is so confident of his conclusion that in any case of becoming there will be something that persists and some form that it

acquires or loses" (7). The appeal to the idea of an a priori proof or a posteriori evidence is problematic for other reasons as well: the attempt to prove the existence of change a priori would start with a definition and seek to establish the possibility of change, because it is not possible to establish a *reality* through an a priori proof. On the other side, the argument that the existence of change is simply clear without such a definition, a posteriori by examples, would depend on the idea that we just know it when we see it. But this produces Meno's Paradox, namely, that we could not know something unless we already knew it in advance. Aristotle's middle position, that we have a certain kind of knowledge, but it is confused rather than clear, is an effective response.

18. Charlton trans., Aristotle (1970).
19. Charlton trans., Aristotle (1970). Translation modified: "possible" replaced with "potent," "actual" replaced with "at-work."
20. Compare Bodnár (2018), 222–24, who attempts to read the reference to potency and activity as another way of making the very same argument already presented in I.8, but is not fully satisfied with the results of doing so.
21. Graham (1995), 555.
22. Sachs trans., Aristotle (1999).
23. Charlton trans., Aristotle (1970). This is contrary to Ross's (1924), lxxix, assertion that change and potentiality infect being because they are between being and not-being. This is because all change, including coming-to-be, is *from* something that *is* and *to* something that *is*. Aristotle works out the point in further detail: "Since every changing thing changes from something to something, what has changed, when it has first changed, must be in the condition to which it has changed . . . Then since one of the changes is in respect of a contradictory, when something has changed from not-being to being, it has left not-being behind. Therefore it will be in the condition of being, since everything must either be or not be" (*Phys*. V.5 235b8–18; Sachs trans., Aristotle [1995]).
24. Charlton trans., Aristotle (1970).
25. Charlton trans., Aristotle (1970).
26. Mourelatos (1970), 80. Mourelatos reaches this conclusion differently, from an argument that Parmenides is not concerned with the being of particular nonessential attributes, but exclusively with being in the sense of identity.
27. The reason why being and non-being appear symmetrical is that they appear to be one another's opposite. If the opposite of *what is* were *what is not*, we could imagine them negating one another, so that they would both occupy the same ontologically primary level. Being, therefore, would be as simple and general as non-being. Once this parity is considered, the dialectical move beyond it seems to preserve the generality pointed out by non-being: since *there is nothing other than being*, being ultimately has no opposite, and there is *nothing* from which it is to be distinguished; being thus appears all the more emphatically general. But this is a mistake, for the apparent generality of *what is not* would be preserved, even as *what is not* is dismissed: non-being would be the source of the generality that comes to characterize the concept of being, even as, or *because* of its negation. In this view, *the generality of being is the result of the generality of non-being*. Yet this route through non-being in Parmenides (1984), B2, B6, seems not to be the only basis for monism: a nonderivative simplicity of being seems evident in the claim that being is everywhere in contact with being (B8.22–25).
28. Mourelatos seeks to reconcile Parmenides with the diversity of being by claiming that Parmenides's account is in fact an argument concerning the phrase ____ is ____,

where the "is" links a subject with its *essential* predicates, that is, with the predicates that exhaust what it is for the subject to be. For all its insight and scholarly interest, this reading of the text is hard to endorse, since Parmenides nowhere describes such a method of variable use, and nowhere distinguishes the use of the essential "is" from other types—indeed, it would seem to conflict with his argument that "is" is one and homogenous. Kelsey (2006) presents the argument against change as a major problem, though an avoidable one, if coming-to-be consists of things coming to be particular kinds or families of predicates. Mourelatos's (1970), 79, argument that Parmenides is right to exclude predicate families depends on the idea that Parmenides is only concerned with the "is" of identity, and not the "is" that joins subject to accidents. This reading presumes, of course, that Parmenides was working with a theory of being that distinguished between subject and predicate, which appears to have been introduced by Aristotle, likely interpreting the Platonic Socrates.

29. Parmenides's Way of Opinion complicates this view, distinguishing particular things *and* principles of these things. But it is difficult to establish its relationship to the Way of Truth, which denies the existence of multiple particular objects and their generation and passing away, since we do not have Parmenides's whole poem.

30. Anagnostopoulos (2013) claims that the fact that Aristotle takes being to be something in particular shows that his argument merely concerns predication. But it does not follow that Aristotle is limiting the analysis to explanation. As I contend, the fact that being always has a predicate is a necessary ontological claim if the underlying thing and change are to exist: for change to be, being must be definite and have specific properties.

31. Charlton trans., Aristotle (1970).

32. They may be definite for different reasons. It is not clear from these passages how complete this symmetry is.

33. That it is not easy to arrive at these three is clear from the fact that Aristotle accomplishes it by two sets of distinctions, of which, it later becomes clear, one of the terms overlaps. He distinguishes two senses of "what comes to be," namely the white (because it is what emerges) and the rabbit (because it was something else before, and it is what has become white), and two senses of the genitive thing "that of/from which it comes to be," namely the rabbit (because the white is "of" it), and the brown or black (because a thing comes to be white by being taken out of or away from being black). "That which comes to be" has two senses: the form that emerges, and the (underlying) thing that becomes, while "that from which a thing comes to be" also has two senses, namely the underlying thing, and the opposite privation. The opposite privation is more properly called "that from out of which," because it is left behind as a thing comes to be, whereas the underlying thing is precisely what remains.

34. Whether there is form without material is one of the most important questions for first philosophy (*Phys.* II.2 194b13–14).

35. This is why, when Aristotle argues that the underlying thing is different than the form, he says that it is knowable through analogy (*Phys.* I.7 191a8–12), because the particular underlying thing must be sought out starting from the form, led to it (*ana-*) by other distinctions made in speech (*logoi*).

36. Sachs trans., Aristotle (1995). On the activity of material, see chapter 5, especially the section "Automatic Generation."

37. Sachs trans., Aristotle (1995).

38. The Privation Hypothesis, as I call it in Sentesy (2018a), interprets material's apparent formlessness (*Phys.* I.7 191a8–14) as evidence that material is the *opposite* of form. But Aristotle is careful to distinguish formlessness from material (*Phys.* I.7 190b13–15), and the underlying thing from the lack (*Phys.* I.7 191a12–14). The underlying thing, then, is formless *not* because it is the opposite of form (i.e., privation), but because the two are different sorts of being. Moreover, it is easier to notice material as form is added or removed. Proponents of the Privation Hypothesis include Aquinas (1963), III.2.1.285, Waterlow (Broadie) (1982a), 109–10, Kosman (1969, 2013), Heidegger, and Agamben. (See also "Potency and Activity, Change and Being" in chap. 4.)

39. Kelsey (2006).

40. Charlton trans., Aristotle (1970), my emphasis. Translation modified: "by virtue of concurrence" replaced with "incidentally."

41. Compare Bodnár (2018) 211–13.

42. Phenomenologists would argue that taking form to be *that which emerges* is an authentic account of the change of showing-forth proper to phenomena. It is worth suggesting that, by treating form as *that which appears*, Aristotle may be following Parmenides.

43. Charlton trans., Aristotle (1970).

44. Charlton trans., Aristotle (1970). The "under" (*hupo-*) in "underlying" (*hupokeimenon*) suggests that the changing forms are "above" or more visible than the being that changes, and we tend to notice change before we grasp the underlying thing that is changing.

45. The prospect of featureless prime matter is derived from the threefold structure by taking the underlying thing from one analysis (e.g., a man bearing properties) to be a form, searching for what underlies *it* (e.g., his body), and repeating this move until you are forced to say that there is nothing underlying it. There is considerable debate over whether Aristotle believes it to exist or not. Byrne (2018), 120, argues that material "must have properties and causal capacities of its own, independent of that object's formal cause, in order to be able to perform its various functions in the generation, composition, and operation of perceptible objects." See also "Automatic Generation" in chapter 5.

46. Sachs trans. Aristotle (1995).

47. Sachs trans., Aristotle (1999). In the Way of Opinion, Parmenides distinguishes causes into pairs, for example, light and night.

48. Aristotle credits some previous physicists for seeing that there must be an underlying thing, but criticizes them for making it only one (*Phys.* I.9 192a11). Those, such as Timaeus in the Platonic dialogue, who made the underlying thing into a dyad such as great and small, Aristotle says, did not in fact make it into two, presumably because great and small are one in the sense that they mark out a continuum of size. This is why they still fall victim to the other problem that, he says, remains, namely that the great and the small cannot act on each other.

49. Sachs trans., Aristotle (1999).

50. Ross (1995), 69. That privation is not Aristotle's key innovation is also evident from the fact that Aristotle appears to think his predecessors already used it. The idea of a negative opposite is already apparent in the dualists. Aristotle interprets this duality, without argument, as an emerged form and its opposite, that which "is not" any longer after the change. By doing this, he recasts the dualists as describing the process of emergence proper to *genesis*. In this respect, he only needs to show that *sterēsis* genuinely is not when it is considered *as* something definite, that is, as the not-being of that definite thing.

Heidegger might agree with Ross on this point, as his attention to *sterēsis* in the essay on *Physics* B,1 in Heidegger (1998) indicates. There Heidegger argues that *sterēsis* is the trace in Aristotle of a more fundamental account of nature than metaphysics can provide.

51. Charlton trans., Aristotle (1970).

52. What makes it possible, Aristotle says, for something to be both one and many, is being-potent and being-complete (*entelecheia*) (*Phys.* I.2 186a1–4).

53. See "Composite Being" in chapter 2.

54. Charlton trans., Aristotle (1970).

55. It is not important for our purposes here to settle the dispute over whether being something specific means being a certain *kind* or whether it means being an individual thing. See Kelsey (2006) for a discussion of the problem.

56. Ryle (1955), 66; Ross (1958), lxxxiv; and Kosman (2013), 122–50. See also Brentano's discussion of variants of the thesis (with which he disagrees) in Brentano (1975), 49–55.

57. On *logikos* arguments, see Burnyeat (2001), 21: "to proceed 'logically' in this sense is . . . to abstract from the causal principles appropriate to the subject-matter" in such a way that it engages things insofar as we speak or define them, that is, insofar as their elements are separate or abstract in speech.

58. Charlton trans., Aristotle (1970). Aristotle argues in *Phys.* I.2 185a22–33 that because of the differences between quality, quantity, and *ousia*, being must therefore be many, and said of an underlying thing. But the argument relies on us establishing that they are different.

59. See Charlton trans., Aristotle (1970), 70.

60. Furth trans., Aristotle (1985).

61. Being material seems to differ from being an underlying thing, since the latter is a term in a conceptual structure, whereas material is itself something, and initiates movement in its own way. See "Material, Form, and Composite" in chapter 5.

62. Sachs trans., Aristotle (1999).

63. See Kosman (2013), 251–52.

64. Sachs trans., Aristotle (1995). Being-at-work (*energeia*) is grasped first of all as change (*Met.* IX.1 1046a1–4, IX.8 1048b8–10).

65. Edghill trans., in Aristotle (1941). Translation modified: "substance" replaced with "primary being." Bostock argues that Aristotle should hold that the underlying thing is substance (*ousia*) (Bostock 2006, 12–14), noting that Aristotle refrains from drawing that conclusion at *Phys.* I.7 191a19–20.

66. The relationship between change and categorical being in this case is not straightforward. It is complicated by the analysis of *Met.* VII, which adds that being must be knowable, and perhaps also that it must be separate—I say "perhaps" because being separate may be implied in being a *this*. The complication is that from being material first of all, *Met.* VII extends "underlying" to form as well. In doing so, Aristotle attempts to find a way to make form rather than material into the subject of predication. A distinction between material and the underlying thing, if ultimately there is one, may be, as I argued above, that the underlying thing is a position in a formal, structural relationship that is relative to each case, whereas material is not defined as a relative being but as an independent real cause of change. Of course, material can always be addressed as something that *is* relative to form, since it *underlies* form, but in this case it is being addressed insofar as it is a *hupokeimenon*. On material as a source of change, see "Automatic Generation" in chapter 5.

Chapter 2

1. Charlton trans., Aristotle (1970). Translation modified: "possible or as actual" replaced with "potential or as at-work."
2. See Coope (2005), 69–75; Roark (2011), 63–79, 95–119; Harry (2015), 43–47; and Sentesy (2018b), 11–14.
3. *Diēirēmenou* is normally taken to be perfect, "having distinguished. . . ." It is possible to take the phrase to refer back to the first announcement of the distinction between potency and being-complete at 200b28, but it could not refer to the rest of the preamble itself, which is not about the distinction between *entelecheia* and *dunamis*, but about how change is related to, but not exhausted by or defined in terms of the categories. But translating it this way risks leading us to conflate the discussion of categorical being (of relation and the form-privation pair) with the energetic terms. I suggest, then, that Aristotle is using the intensive present perfect *diēirēmenou*, and that he makes the whole clause a genitive absolute modifying the definition itself. This also makes sense of why Aristotle would list kinds of change immediately *following* the definition, namely, because he announced that we ought to distinguish between kinds of change, and he has not already done so.
4. Compare M. Frede (1994), 184.
5. Spengler, Ross observes, points out a parallel passage that supports this reading: "Some things are at-work without potency, such as the first beings, others [are at work] with potency, and others are never beings at work, but are only potencies" (*On Interpretation* 13 23a23–26, Edghill trans. in Aristotle 1941). The last phrase, he observes, could well point out that there is no necessity for a potency to be at work: some potencies will happen, incidentally, never to be at work and yet still be a real potency. Ross rejects this possibility, of a potency that is never at work, by appealing to what he takes to be the "normal doctrine" of potentiality, that is, Aristotle's argument that potencies are directed toward being at work.
6. Compare Beere (2009), Witt (2003), Frey (2015).
7. This suggests that the "modal states" hypothesis, that is, the position of Witt, Beere, and Frey, is false. See below, and Sentesy (2018a), 252–55.
8. Sachs trans., Aristotle (1999).
9. See Sentesy (2018a), 256–58. Aristotle argues that potency must remain even while there is no activity; for example, a violin player remains capable of playing even while she is not playing. This is an argument that potency *exists*. But by the same argument, Aristotle argues that the capacity must remain even while the activity is there. He rules out the possibility that the capacity comes and goes, or takes on different modal states, by arguing that things are either *dunaton* or *adunaton* (*Met.* IX.3 1046b29–1047a29). Then he argues that "[a] if what is lacking a potency is incapable, what is not happening will be incapable of happening; [b] but of what is incapable of happening, it is false for anyone to say either that it is so or that it will be so (since that is what incapable means)" (*Met.* IX.3 1047a12–13, my trans.). In short, if a person lost her capacity to sit, whether this is while she stopped sitting or while she was sitting, then sitting would be impossible for her.
10. Ross (1936), 359.
11. This change is not defined by relation, but that it nevertheless can be articulated in terms of relation eliminates the main objection to the claim that change occurs entirely in and can be fully grasped in each of the categorical senses of being. This means that Waterlow's (Broadie's) (1982b), 111, claim that "the category of relation . . . is chosen to house change" is misleading.

12. Sachs trans., Aristotle (1995). Translation modified: "kinds of being" replaced by "categorical beings."

13. As does Sosa (2010), 3–4, to take one example.

14. The standard translation reads "having divided each kind by being-complete and potential . . ." But it does not make grammatical sense to translate it this way. The word *diaireō*, "distinguish" or "divide," names its criteria by using *kath* and the accusative case, with the object to be divided in the genitive. If Aristotle meant to use the distinction between being-complete and being-potential to make distinctions within the categories, as the modal states hypothesis holds, then he would have said the opposite: *di̯ęrēménou dè katà tòn mèn entelecheía̩ tòn dè dunámei toû hékastou génous*.

15. Some authors (e.g., Beere 2009) read the datives *dunamei* and *energeiai* as naming the ontological sense of these terms, as opposed to their change-related sense. In Sentesy (2018a) I show that Aristotle is not consistent in doing this, and this passage bears out that observation: having distinguished between two datives (*dunamei* and *entelecheiai*), Aristotle uses only one dative in the definition (*dunamei*).

16. Since others, notably Coope (2009), Anagnostopoulos (2010), and Charles (2015), have adequately described the existing scholarly positions on the definition of change, there is no need to review the debate in detail. I group extant approaches to the matter into one of the three aspects of the definition of change: the first addresses the type of potency involved in change, the second specifies the state(s) of being of the potency, and the third marks out what kind of accomplishment change is. The first two can be distinguished by the way they interpret the term "being-in-potency" (*to dunamei on*) in the definition of change, while the last is distinguished by the way it interprets the terms "activity" (*energeia*) and "actuality" (which in chapter 3 I argue is a misleading translation of *entelecheia*). Each makes a claim about the central problem solved by the definition of change. Scholars who take Potency Type to be a key problem typically take the definition to distinguish the capacity for change from the capacity for being. Those whose position turns on the State of Potency problem typically take the definition to identify a special metaphysical state of potency in which it temporarily becomes an actuality. Scholars who instead stake their position on the meaning of the accomplishment have mostly argued that change specifies an activity rather than an actuality.

17. Aristotle describes change as the alteration of the alterable, the generation of the generable (*Phys.* III.1 201a11–18), the carrying of the carryable (*Phys.* III.2 202a8–9). Of the changeable, as changeable, he says, the accomplishment (*entelecheia*) is change (*Phys.* III.1 201a6–7). Different versions of the definition can be found at *Phys.* III.1 201a6–7, 201a10–11 (see also *Met.* XI.9 1065b14–16), 201a25–29, 201b4–6, 201b9–10 (see also *Phys.* III.2 202a2–3); *Phys.* III.2 202a8–9; and *Phys.* III.3 202b25 (see also *Phys.* III.1 201a11–12). The most complete version is at *Phys.* III.3 202b26–27: "[change is the being-complete] of the potentially-active-or-acted-upon *as such*, both simply and in each case" (Sachs trans., Aristotle 1995).

18. See Ross, in Aristotle (1936), 359, 537. For criticism, see Kosman (1969), 41–42; and Anagnostopoulos (2010), 34. It is not necessary to avoid every appearance of circularity or tautology, only the vicious type.

19. Anagnostopoulos (2010), 72–78 (see *Met.* XI.9 1065b14–16; *Phys.* III.1 201b9–10, and III.2 202a2–3). To argue that Aristotle should have used a different word is to adapt the text to the interpretation, and despair of understanding his argument.

20. As Kosman (1969), 42, 55–56, observes, *Met.* XI.1065b16 has *energeia*, but the majority of manuscripts do not. See Blair (1967), 101–17.

21. Charles (2015), 202–3, offers a minimalist account, in which the goal (*telos*) is merely a "success condition," which, depending on the case, could be a state, a being, or a change.

22. The translation of these words into English often requires adding "–able" to the end of a word to make it into an adjective. But this obscures the neutrality of the word by appending the concept of potency. Instead, for example, *oikodomētou* can be rendered as either "what has been built" or "the buildable."

23. Brague (1980), 3–4. Similarly, Anagnostopoulos (2010), 69–73, argues that Aristotle aims merely to certify the scientific respectability of change. Aristotle's own view of the Eleatic impasse in *Phys.* I.8 indicates, however, that the stakes are not merely epistemological, but ontological. It is not enough to say that change can be *known*; Aristotle needs to show that change *is*.

24. Kosman (2013), 52, brings up the Parmenidean impasse, not in reference to the purpose of his definition, but as a reason to think that *entelecheia* in the definition must not mean "process."

25. The most common view is that the change, and thereby the potency, is defined by end-states (as it is in the debate over the *energeia/kinēsis* distinction in *Met.* IX.6 1048b18–35. See particularly Ackrill 1965, Penner 1970, and Pickering 1997). To the extent that the end-state is temporally separated from potency, this view risks presupposing time and/or place in the definition of change. Coope (2005), 5–9, rightly argues that we ought to reject this view, but notes that she does not clearly have a replacement (2009), 288–90, as I attempt to provide here. Difficulties also emerge from defining potency by the stop-conditions of the change, for example, the capacity to walk is defined by the capacity to stop walking. Charles (2010), 183–86, finesses the problem, arguing that the form of the end product determines the form of the changes that produce it, and that there are multiple layers of change to consider (e.g., the act of house-building is guided by the form of the house, but making bricks is not). I shall argue that the potency to change is not derived from the particular *telos*, even though it requires or implies the *telos*.

26. Noting that it amounts to saying that change is the actuality of the capacity to be changing, critics of this view argue that such a distinction makes the definition of change circular. See Kosman (1969), 40–42.

27. For this view, see Ross (1936), Kosman (1969, 2013), Charles (1986), Heinaman (1994), and Beere (2009). The most prevalent view of this kind is Kosman's, in which change is a special state in which potency is itself an actuality. Other adherents of this position include Waterlow (Broadie) (1982b), 93–130; Hussey (1983), 58–62; Coope (2005), 5–9; and Coope (2009). In this reading, change plays a double role, first constituting the change as an actuality, and then constituting the product of the change. Before Kosman, the view appears in Brentano (1975), 44: "While the builder builds, that with which he builds is in a state of potentiality which is constituted by actuality."

28. In Kosman's view, potentialities are not beings on their own; it is only through actuality that potentialities can be. Change is the existence of an actual potentiality, so *it is only in the course of changing that there is actually a potentiality* to become the product (Kosman 2013, 56–57). Moreover, in his account, I lose the ability to become a saxophonist the moment I become one. If all capacity aims at a product, and a capacity cannot be actual at the same time as its product, then the capacity for change must destroy itself in achieving its

own goal. This is an extinction hypothesis; change-potencies are suicidal (Kosman 1984, 127; and Kosman 2013, 67).

29. See Sentesy (2018a).

30. Anagnostopoulos (2010), 45–59; and Charles (2015), 193. Daniel Graham (1988) claims that "the Kosman view erects an ingenious superstructure out of almost no textual evidence, a castle in the sky" (210). In Kosman's account, there must be a capacity either to be or to become an actual capacity (i.e., a change) that precedes the change (i.e., the actual potentiality). If that capacity were to be extinguished when the change exists, then the view would produce a regress, since a thing would need a capacity to have such an actual capacity. See Kosman (2013), 26n26, compare 53–57. He embraces the regress, but calls it odd (2013, 61). If it persists while the change exists, then it is very unclear why this capacity to be a change would be non-suicidal, while the capacity that change *is* when it is actual must be suicidal.

31. On my argument, the key passage (*Phys.* III.1 201b5–13) exhibits no concern at all about the distinction between the actuality of change and the actuality of the product. Aristotle is instead concerned to mark out the subject of change (see Anagnostopoulos 2017), and uses a rough distinction between the product and the process (that once there is a house, at some point building can stop) to argue that there is in fact an *entelecheia* proper to the buildable thing as buildable. See "The Demonstration of Change" below.

32. This forces proponents of the "modal states" hypothesis to make the "ontological" sense of the words radically different in structure than the "change-related" sense. But there is scarcely evidence for this position. See Sentesy (2018a).

33. Upton (1991), 329.

34. Sachs trans., Aristotle (1999).

35. Deslauriers (2007), 43–45. Not all definitions establish both "that" and "what" something is; for example, when we come to know something accidentally, we cannot use this knowledge to say what it is (*Post. An.* II.8 93a27–28). Moreover, if something is simple, or has its cause in itself, definition does not demonstrate that it exists, but we grasp this in another way (*Post. An.* II.9 93b21–25).

36. Wieland (1975) contests the idea that Aristotle used the method of syllogism that he discovered.

37. See Deslauriers (2007), 45–46.

38. Beere (2009) is among those who read this sentence as an assertion that *dunamis* and *entelecheia* are mutually incompatible, that is, that a thing cannot be both at once. The reading in which the two are opposed distorts the Greek in an attempt to support a point that is irrelevant to the immediate argumentative context. To make this reading plausible, Beere inserts dashes both into his translation and the Greek: "Since, in some cases, one thing may be in capacity and in fulfillment F—although not simultaneously, or not in the same respect, but it may, for instance, be in capacity hot and in fulfillment cold—therefore many things will act and be acted on by one another" (173n12). Setting the middle phrase apart aims to make it an appeal to an item of knowledge for which it does not argue, and which contributes nothing to the point of the sentence. Nor is this idea argued for elsewhere—a remarkable omission considering its guaranteed importance to the study of nature and being. But even set apart this way, the passage does not establish incompatibility. If the two were always incompatible, there would be no need to limit it to "some cases," that is, to the ones in which something is potent for something that at the moment it happens not actively to be.

39. Sachs trans., Aristotle (1995). Translation modified: "motion" to "change."

40. Anagnostopoulos (2010), 35. On the role of the "as"-clause in specifying the subject of change, see Anagnostopoulos (2010), 65–67. He reads the clause as having a causal relationship with change, which is right to the extent that a subject is a cause, but wrong to the extent that the discussion of causes is the wrong register of discourse, since causes point us toward discrete categorical beings, when we need to be discussing sources.

41. See Coope (2009), 282.

42. Aristotle's choice of an artifact makes this particularly clear; the distinction is harder to make, but not impossible, for natural beings. For artificial beings, what they are does not include self-movement, so the ability to move and be moved does not of itself lead to change. Such potency, which is a source of change, is incomplete because it does not contain everything necessary for it to change. But since natural beings are sources of change, it follows that what they are includes self-movement, since they are complete and contain everything necessary to change.

43. For such things, the categorical sense of being more clearly takes on the meaning of the energetic sense of being, which we discuss in chapters 5–6. The effect of this collapse is to remove the separation of a thing from itself that constitutes the ontological structure of artifacts.

44. Edghill trans., in Aristotle (1941). Translation modified: "substance" replaced with "primary being."

45. The most reliable manuscripts read *ē gar oikodomēsis energeia tou oikodomētou ē hē oikia*. The subject of the phrase is grammatically ambiguous between *oikodomēsis* and *energeia*. The phrase is normally translated with *energeia* as the subject, omitting *tou oikodomētou*: "for the actuality is either [the act of] building, or [it is] the house." Because the argument identifies *energeia* and *oikodomēsis*, and what decides the case is neither of these terms but the *oikodomēton*, the ambiguity does not compromise the passage. Compare Anagnostopoulos (2010), 54–57. The word "house" (*oikia*) is the root of the words I translate as buildable (*to oikodomēton*) and building (*oikodomēsis*), much as "building" is ambiguous between the activity and its product.

46. If the passage is read with *energeia* as its subject instead of building, the argument would proceed as follows: What is the being-at-work of the buildable thing? The buildable thing is not in its own right a being-at-work, but a being insofar as it is capable of something. Its capability is not for being a house, since when the house is at work, the buildable thing is no longer what is at-work. So the being-at-work of the buildable thing is neither of these: what is it?

47. See Anagnostopoulos (2011), 405–16.

48. Sachs trans., Aristotle (1995). Translation modified: "possible to be" to "admitting of being."

49. See Owen's account of focal meaning in his (1960), 169. On focal meaning and homonymy, see Brakas (2011), Irwin (1981), Shields (1999), and Ward (2009).

50. See Charles (2010), 173–78.

51. See Heidegger (1998).

52. As, for example, Sentesy (2018a) and Anagnostopoulos (2010) have done.

53. Also see Harte (2002), 43–46, 132–33.

54. Joachim, trans. in Aristotle (1941).

55. Sachs trans., Aristotle (1999).

56. Compare Charles (2010), 180n.

Chapter 3

1. Stephen Menn (1994), for example, holds this position. G. A. Blair (2011) defends the same argument. There Blair disagrees with D. W. Graham not about whether Aristotle coined the words, but about how to interpret the act and the results of doing so. Blair argues that Graham takes Aristotle to have coined new words for concepts that are already captured well by existing and related words, making the act of creating a word superfluous. See Graham (1989, 1995), and Beere (2009), 155–61.

2. In the *Topics*, cognates of the word "compose" (*suntithemi*) refer to the grouping of syllables into words. Such grouping was a feature of the process of reading and reading aloud, as well as writing. In the former case, since Greek did not separate words from one another, letters that are visually continuous with one another, for example, "hectorbreakerofhorses," are separated from one another in pronunciation. In the latter case, sounds that run together are separated out into individual letters placed in a spatial sequence.

3. Menn (1994).

4. Anagnostopoulos (2010), 72–78.

5. Beere (2009), 3–5.

6. Gonzalez (2018) maps out the development of these terms in Heidegger's corpus.

7. For example, Graham (1989), 73–80.

8. Kosman (2013), vii–viii. Kosman goes on to say that the customary practice emphasizes change and otherness rather than what he claims is prior, namely being and self-identity. In addition, he argues, it has led to a distortion of these terms into change-concepts, that is, into potentialities and their actualization. There is much to agree with in this condemnation, for example, the claim that "actualization of potentialities" is a distortion of Aristotle's account of change, but I resist Kosman's claim that the terms are not primarily change-words.

9. Anagnostopoulos (2010), section 5.

10. Beere (2009), 4.

11. Graham (1989). He tries to justify reading the interpretation of Aristotle *against* him by saying that we don't know why our sentences are well-formed. To say that we understand what Aristotle meant better than he himself understood it is one thing. It is quite another to say that the traditions inspired by philosophers are more perfect interpreters of their thought than they themselves were. But both of these are extremely dubious principles, and can hardly support the argument that the tradition understands what a key word means better than the one who coined it. Blair (2011), 91, rightly criticizes Graham for this, writing, "if Aristotle coined the word, it would be more plausible to take the word in Aristotle's sense and see if that fit the way he used it better than the traditional meaning, and call the tradition wrong rather than the one who made up the word in the first place."

12. See Sachs in Aristotle (1999), xxxiv–xxxvi.

13. See Wieland (1975) and Sokolowski (1979, 1998).

14. For this sense, see especially the *Nicomachean Ethics* I.10, 12–13.

15. Menn (1994), 78.

16. Blair (2011), 95.

17. See below for the most important of the recent disputes between Blair and Graham. Heidegger's influential reading of *entelecheia* resembles a combination of those of Blair and Graham, namely that *energeia* means being-at-work on the way to completion, whereas *entelecheia* means being-at-an-end or having its end within itself and therefore

being finished or complete. This reading has been strongly contested by Gonzalez (2006). By contrast, Beere's introduction in his (2009) takes *entelecheia* to mean actuality rather unproblematically. Anagnostopoulos (2010), 36–37, holds a similar position.

18. Sachs (2010), §6.
19. Sachs in Aristotle (1999), li–lii.
20. Ross in Aristotle (1924), 2:246.
21. Kosman (2013), 261 n.9.
22. Sachs trans., Aristotle (1999).
23. Sachs trans., Aristotle (1999).
24. Sachs, trans., Aristotle (1999). Translation modified, changing "belongs" to "initiates activity from within [*huparchei*]." Heidegger, problematically, makes *hexis* the cornerstone of his interpretation of potency in Heidegger (1995), 157, compare 161–63, 188. But the second clause is a parallel expression, not the revelation of the basis of the previous expression. Being a source, *archē*, is not secondary to, founded upon, or reducible to the structure of possession, *hexis*. For *huparchei* and *telos* could either be or originate the having that is named in the word *hexis*. See also Menn (1994).
25. Compare Sachs (2010), §2.
26. Blair (1992). Compare, for example, *Met.* IX.3 1047a30 with *Phys.* III.2 202a2–4, and *Phys.* III.1–2 with *Met.* XI.9.
27. Sachs in Aristotle (1999), xl.
28. This is perhaps what Charles (2015), 204–5, intends to articulate by calling changes (*kinēseis*) continuants rather than events. Ross, in Aristotle (1924), following Diels, suggests that Aristotle did not derive *entelecheia exclusively* from an alteration of *endelecheia*: "Hirzel, in *Rhein. Mus.* 1884, 169–208, put forward the view that Aristotle in one of his dialogues ascribed to the soul, as Plato had done, *endelecheia*, continuous change, and that he later invented the word *entelecheia* by a modification of *endelecheia* in order to express the change in his view about the soul. Diels, in *Zeitschr. Für Vergl. Philol.* XLVII. 200–203, successfully controverts this view, and shows that *entelechēs* is a correctly formed equivalent to *to enteles echōn*, 'having perfection,'" (246). It is also worth noting that the sense of "continuous change" is a suggestion of Hirzel and, for example, does not make it into the Liddell and Scott lexicon. Blair suggests that *endelecheia* is a later word that was coined from *entelecheia*, but does not substantiate the assertion.
29. Sachs trans., Aristotle (1995). Translation modified: "motion" replaced with "change."
30. In this I disagree in part with Charles (1984, 10–15), who counts two *energeiai* (he retracts this claim in [2015], 199–201). My argument agrees with Anagnostopoulos (2017, 185–87) that teaching and learning are one in number, but disagrees with his claim that teaching is not essentially a change. It is incidentally true that the teacher does not alter or change *into something else* in exercising her potency, and this is important to the analysis of the relationship between the teacher's potency and her activity. But while the activity that defines teaching does not refer to or presuppose a lack of change in the teacher, it *just is* the assisted learning of the student, and learning is a change. They differ in respect of the subject to which each is referred, but in the primary sense they are the same. Perhaps sensing this problem, Anagnostopoulos (2017, 185) concedes that "the agency, by being one in number with a change, is still a change, but in a weaker sense."
31. Not including *Met.* IX.6 1048b19–35, the passage secluded by Burnyeat (2008).
32. Ross in Aristotle (1936), 439. See also Kosman (2013), 67.

33. See Sentesy (2018a) for an analysis of the thesis that potency and actuality are opposed.

34. See Waterlow (Broadie) (1982a), 131–58, and Coope (2009), 287–88, for an examination of the problem of the incompleteness of change-parts in Aristotle's response to Zeno in *Phys.* VI.6. The impasse they identify is produced by their assumption that change is the incomplete actuality of a potential *for being in some end state*. Since my account does not share this assumption, the criticism does not apply.

35. Ross, trans. Revised by J. O. Urmson; in Aristotle (1984).

36. In this respect, change is unlike the parts of pleasure or sight. The secluded Passage at *Met.* IX.6 1048b19–35 attempts to make a similar argument.

37. Quarantotto (2015) argues that change is complete, and therefore reconciled with being, when viewed "top-down," but not when viewed from the "bottom up."

38. Indeed, in our lived experience, *change is the phenomenon that distinguishes parts from one another*. Before the change of building begins, the builder and what is built appear to be neither of those things because they do not appear in their relation to one another. The man there does not appear to be a builder, and the wood, board, or plank is inert. They only appear as builder and buildable insofar as the change of building grounds their relationship and unfolds this aspect of their being. These two beings are neither together nor separate: they become related and distinguished into different parts of a single change-complex by the change alone. Thus, the change is what makes them parts at all; it is what makes them both one and many at once.

39. If there are complex *entelecheiai* whose changes are complete in their parts (e.g., possibly the circular change of the heavens), then not every complex thing will be incomplete in this way.

40. Anagnostopoulos (2017) draws the correct conclusion that the completeness or incompleteness of an event is decided by the character of the subject rather than by a different telic structure. But his analysis goes awry in analyzing what the subject of change is. I argue, below, that the incompleteness of a change is decided by the character of the source (does the student depend on a teacher's help to think through the math problem?). Anagnostopoulos also counts a subject as incomplete when it lacks certain categorical predicates (being in a certain place, etc.). Confusing the categorical and the dynamic-energetic sense of being, then, leads him to collapse a discussion of the incidental incompleteness of parts into the discussion of the essential incompleteness of change.

41. The tendency to collapse them is a consequence of the fact that *telos*, like *energeia* and *dunamis*, extends from changes, that is, the energetic sense of being, to apply to the categories as well.

42. It is not the potency, but the *change*, that is, the *entelecheia*, which produces the product. See "Etymological Argument" and "Location Argument" in chapter 6.

43. See Sentesy (2018a).

44. Gill (2003) highlights this distinction between activity brought about by a thing and by some other. It does not follow from this distinction, however, that potency's change-related sense is in principle different from its being-related sense (see "Potency and Activity" in chap. 4), since a thing's being, e.g. the being of an eye, may include such other-dependent potencies.

45. Jenkinson trans., in Aristotle (1995).

43. Platt trans., in Aristotle (1995).

47. Platt trans., in Aristotle (1995).

48. See "Etymological Argument" in chapter 6.
49. Moreover, building as a change gets its name from its *telos*: the building itself (see "Etymological Argument" in chap. 6).
50. Beere (2009), 229–30.

Chapter 4
1. Anagnostopoulos (2017), 182–83 also suggests that being in potency and being in activity may not be opposed.
2. Menn (1994), 98. His position draws on Brentano (1975), 44, and Kosman's (1984, 1994, 2013) arguments that change as actuality constitutes certain kinds of potency (on which, see chap. 2, n. 29), while his claim that possibility is the core sense recalls Bonitz (1848).
3. Charlton (1987).
4. Witt (2003), 27–36. She translates *dunamis* as "causal power." The addition of the concept of "cause" to the word "power" indicates that Witt is fusing categorical and energetic terms.
5. Brentano writes: "There is a great difference between what we here mean by the potential [the *dynaton* or *dynamei on*] and what in more recent times is meant by calling something possible in contrast with real, where the necessary is added as a third thing. This is a possibility which completely abstracts from the reality of that which is called possible, and merely claims that something could exist if its existence did not involve a contradiction. It does not exist in things but in the objective concepts and combinations of concepts of the thinking mind; it is a merely rational thing. Aristotle was quite familiar with the concept of possibility so understood, as we can see from *De Interpretatione*, but it bears no relation to what he calls potential being" (Brentano 1975, 27–28). But potency has, in the history of philosophy, often been degraded into bare logical possibility. The idea, for example, that there are possible worlds, and that all of these possible worlds actually exist, is a kind of inverted image of the Megarian thesis: where the Megarians held potency to be only where something is at work, Lewis holds that actuality is wherever there is possibility. The position seems plausible when the concepts of positive potency and *energeia* have shallowed out and almost entirely lost the meaning Aristotle is arguing for, so that potentiality is hardly distinguishable from what is actually the case.
6. People say something is real, according to Aristotle, only if it changes, and they say this, he claims, because *energeia* is change most of all, therefore being actual implies being (*Met.* IX.3 1047a30–b1).
7. M. Frede (1994), 186, 188, 190.
8. Witt (2003), 55.
9. Beere (2009), 167–78. In this reading Beere and Witt echo Ross (1924), cxxxiv: "Potentiality, on the other hand, is a capacity in A of passing into a new state of itself." Witt adds that in using these terms Aristotle introduces a hierarchical, normative conception of being. Witt (2003), 97–109.
10. Sentesy (2018a), 251–55.
11. The claim that there is a second sense of potency and *energeia*, Anagnostopoulos (2011) argues, has "very little textual support" (393). Anagnostopoulos makes his argument in part by showing that Aristotle's programmatic remarks laying out the structure of *Met.* IX refer to kinds of *dunamis* (e.g., matter and *ousia*), rather than to modes of being. He also shows that Aristotle does not meaningfully distinguish the terms "potentiality"

(*dunamei on*) and "actuality" (*energeiai on*) from other uses of the words, as Beere (2009) argued he must. Aristotle appears instead to identify one with the other. See also Sentesy (2018a).

12. Anagnostopoulos (2011), 404.

13. The extension of potency and activity to matter and *ousia* is controversial, Anagnostopoulos says, because it appears to lead to the problem of substantial change: as long as the matter persists, its attributes can change (a wall can become blue without ceasing to be a wall). But whenever there is a change in a substance, the matter does not persist, because it is constituted by the substance (when someone dies, their body is no longer flesh, i.e., the matter of a living being, but earth). Anagnostopoulos (2011), 412–13.

14. Anagnostopoulos (2011), 417.

15. Heidegger's view also changes over time, as Gonzalez (2018) shows.

16. Heidegger (1995), 161. The Megarian argument, Heidegger suggests, is that the being of potency just is its exercise, that is, its actuality. The problem, he argues, is that the Megarians take actuality, that is, presence, too generally. Thus, Aristotle confronts "the decisive question: . . . *How 'is' a capability, thought of not only as potential but rather as actually present, although not being actualized?*" (146), for "the *essence of presence* must be understood *more fully* and *more variously*" (157) than the Megarians had done. Heidegger (1995), 158–62, argues that, in response, Aristotle in *Met.* IX.3 distinguishes between not-acting and being incapable of acting; this variegation in non-being implies a variety of forms of presence. Harboring doubts that Plato and Aristotle truly understood and overcame the Megarian problem, Heidegger (1995), 141, 151–52, 157, argues that Aristotle's decisive move is to ground potency on the structure of "having," *hexis*. It is decisive, he thinks, because *hexis* gives us the kind of presence that distinguishes potency. But Heidegger's solution—the structure of possession—cannot tell us what *potency* is, or the kind of being it has, or in Heidegger's terms, its proper way of being present, just as being god-loved cannot be the definition of piety in the *Euthyphro*. The being of potency can only be grasped by seeking *its being*.

17. It is by grounding his account of potency in the phenomenon of having or possessing that Heidegger is led to read opposition into the distinction between potency and *energeia*: "Here we are dealing entirely with a being that is directly opposed to the *ergon* and its having been produced, namely *dunamis* . . . Aristotle sees the presence of *dunamis* as such in *echein* . . . *Dunamis echein* means that something which is capable is capable in that it '*has*' a capability; it *holds itself in* this capability and *holds itself back* with this capability—and thereby precisely does not enact. This holding itself back now shows itself to us already more clearly as a way of being . . . Here we have to gather all this from the Greek word *echein*." Heidegger (1995), 157, see 161–63, 188.

18. Heidegger (1995), 162. I argued against this view in chapter 2, "The Buildable Thing."

19. Brogan (2005), 121.

20. If potency's being is being actual, and actuality's being is being actual, what distinguishes them? One of them must be actual but in a different way. But what, then, makes the being of potency different than the being of actuality? It must be that the one is potency, and the other is actuality. Thus potency's being must be different than actuality because *it* is different.

21. Sentesy (2018a), 255–56. Heidegger (1995), 162, posits an abrupt reversal of the relationship between potency and its enactment (i.e., at one moment, the capability on

its own holds itself back in opposition to activity, and in the next moment, the capability enacted is fully unified with its activity). For this to find a foothold in the text, Aristotle would have to make a clear and sharp distinction between the two conditions. But he does not make a distinction thus: Heidegger (1995), 157 thinks we have to understand all of this from the fact that Aristotle used the word "having."

22. With the exception of the probably spurious passage in *Phys.* VII. See Olshewsky (2014).

23. Agamben (1999), 180, 182.

24. Agamben (1999) calls the account of self-negation the "mystical Aristotle."

25. Here I disagree sharply with the view that the extended sense of these terms is essentially independent of change (e.g., Kosman 2013, 70).

26. Since Aristotle is already redefining material and form as *dunamis* and *energeia* in *Met.* VIII (material at VIII.1 1042a26–28, material and form at VIII.2 1043a13–26 and 1045b18–22), it seems possible that book VIII was composed after IX, applying this discovery to solve the impasse on which *Met.* VII.13–16 foundered by joining these concepts to the new approach in VII.17. But it is equally possible that Aristotle saw how the concepts could be useful in book VIII, and afterward sought to anchor this claim in IX.

27. This means that Witt's (2003), 61 claim that Aristotle's goal is to "define powers in terms of their activation conditions" gets the priority the wrong way around.

28. Sachs trans., Aristotle (1995).

29. The analogy between the human potency for knowing and the change of fire shows that the ability to know in the highest sense is not supernatural or superior to nature, but instead that in becoming a spontaneously active power, knowing has risen to the dignity of a natural potency.

30. Aristotle reconciles logical potencies, for example, being a doctor, with this picture by pointing out that they act as inalienable conditions of our actions.

31. Charlton trans., Aristotle (1970).

32. Sachs trans., Aristotle (1999).

33. Sachs trans., Aristotle (2004). Translation modified: "perceptive power" replaced by "perceptive potency."

34. It may not ultimately apply to contemplation, however, which might be more like a nature than a potency. For although in a sense the object of thought is ultimately the agent, and is initially something other than the thinking mind (*Soul* III.4 429a13–18), nevertheless the mind becomes its objects, and can think them on its own (*Soul* III.4 429b5–9).

35. Sachs, trans. Aristotle (1999).

36. Natures, by contrast, are not based in patient-potencies, because for them the agent and the patient are one, although see *Phys.* VIII.4–6.

37. See Marmodoro (2007).

38. The *Phys.* III.1 201a19–23 passage concentrates on moved movers, but opens up the possibility of unmoved movers. But these will not move things in the same way, but, for example, the way a final cause is a source of change.

39. One might object that this aspect of potency makes beings depend on other beings, in such a way that its potency would change depending on the things around it, and not due to a change in the being itself; for example, a hot water bottle might be able to heat something, but when nothing nearby is cooler than it, the hot water bottle loses its abil-

ity to heat things. But the objection presupposes the Extinction Hypothesis. Aristotle's position seems to imply instead that a thing's potency for being heated or heating changes neither due to the *immediate* presence or absence of other things, nor due to the current state of the object. Passive potency is instead a permanent, mutual aspect of things; for example, something that can be cooled will always be able to be cooled, because it is a certain kind of body, and there are other bodies of this kind.

40. Sachs trans., Aristotle (1999).

41. This is motivated, in part, by the disputed passage at *Met.* IX.6 1048b18–34 (see Burnyeat 2008), and the lively debate over the claim that *energeia* differs from *kinēsis* because they relate differently to their ends. See especially Ackrill (1965), 121–42. Vendler (1957), 143–60, problematized the distinction by observing that any movement can be described as an *energeia*: instead of saying that someone is walking from A to B, you can, for example, say that someone is going for a walk, which will satisfy the tense test for *energeia*. See also Pickering (1997), 37–43, and the attempt to distinguish achievements from accomplishments in Vendler (1967), 97–121, esp. 103. Graham argues that *energeiai* are states in (1980), 117–30. See also Penner (1970), 393–453. The argument of Hagen (1984), 263–80, attempts to develop that of Penner. Hagen holds that the same activity, say, eating or speaking, could count as *energeia* for one creature and *kinēsis* for another, depending on whether that activity is the creature's *telos* or not (277).

42. Sachs trans., Aristotle (1995). Translation modified. Aristotle uses this to argue that the infinite cannot be actual, but must be potent in a different way.

43. Sachs trans., Aristotle (1999). Translation modified: "independent things" replaced with "primary beings."

44. Sachs trans., Aristotle (1999). Translation modified: "thinghood" replaced with "being."

45. According to M. Frede (1997), here the fact that *energeia* must be real gets extended to potency at *Met.* IX.3 1047a30–b2. But Aristotle seems to have had the reality of *dunamis* in mind far earlier than *Met.* IX.

46. Sachs trans., Aristotle (1999). Greek and material in square brackets added. Translation modified: "comes about" replaced with "comes to be." Note that activity *comes to be*: *genesis* provides the structure of the relation between *dunamis* and *Energeia*.

47. Sachs trans., Aristotle (1999). Greek and material in square brackets added.

48. There is no suggestion in this passage that one sort of potency gets extinguished. See Kosman's analysis of this passage in (2013), 75–78.

49. Brentano (1975), 44.

50. The outside source is traditionally, but misleadingly, named the "efficient cause." This is misleading because in Aristotle's account the outside source is not solely responsible for its outcome; rather, it generates the inside source or sets it to work bringing about the outcome. The contrast can be illustrated as follows: on the one hand, Aristotle helps the geometry student bring about the answer to a problem herself, while on the other hand, a helicopter parent writes down the answer himself. In the first example, the being itself accomplishes the result with the support of the outside source, while in the second, the outside source accomplishes the result.

51. Sachs trans., Aristotle (1999). Translation emended, parentheses added.

52. When the right potencies are together they immediately set to work. Together, their potencies are complete, but only with respect to the whole change. See "Problem of Completeness" in chapter 3.

53. Aristotle takes the heavenly bodies to be in motion by definition, that is, in their being, but they move themselves by nature, rather than being moved by others, so, one might say, they are the paradigmatic natural beings. Yet even eternal things admit of potency. Aristotle's argument that eternal things take precedence over perishable ones says explicitly that eternal things have potencies: for example, "it [the heaven] is not in potency to be moved other than from somewhere to somewhere (and nothing prevents material for this from belonging to it)" (*Met.* IX.8 1050b21–23, Sachs trans., Aristotle 1999). The distinction between eternal and perishable things hinges not on whether a thing is material or potent, but instead on whether or not what it is, its *ousia*, is properly defined as a potential being, as a being-at-work, or as both (*Met.* IX.2 1043a14–25). In terms of what they are, things that are imperishable are not in-potency (*Met.* IX.8 1050b16–18). But they can have other characteristics apart from their being (*ousia*). In particular, imperishable things can be in-potency in particular respects, for example, in kind or place, but *not* insofar as they *are*. In these other respects, they can be potent, but will not be eternal (*Met.* IX.8 1050b8–16). Perishable things, by contrast, grow weary and stop moving for two reasons: (i) because they admit of being-at-work or not (*Met.* IX.8 1050b26–28), and (ii) because their potency is for opposites, for example, hot and cold, up and down. Insofar as they are, they are only at-work, as we saw. But the potency for movement that belongs to eternal things seems to admit of opposites in sense (ii). Aristotle claims that they avoid this problem, however: "Nor do they grow weary in doing this [i.e., revolving], since for them change does not concern the potency for a pair of contradictory things, as it does for destructible things . . . for the cause of this is that the thinghood of destructible things is comprised of material and potency" (*Met.* IX.8 1050b24–28, Sachs trans., Aristotle 1999). The being of eternal moving things is not defined by material, and does not move from opposite to opposite, but in circles. The structure of circular change, the argument goes, is complete at every point: the heavens are always both moving away and toward any position. While the act of building a house is a whole, when you divide it into parts, each part has a different beginning and end than the others, and than the whole house, and because it is thus different in definition, it is different in being. In circular motion, by contrast, each point is the beginning and end of the motion.

54. Charles (2015), 189–90.

55. Unlike other complete potencies, logical potencies are related to their accomplishment in an unusual way, because the same potency is intrinsically capable of producing opposite effects (*Met.* IX.2 1046b4–15). One and the same potency leads to opposite results in this case because speech points out both beings and their absence: perception does not disclose the absence of one's bicycle, only *logos* does that. But this means that knowledge based on *logos* is bi-directional: saying that a column supports a beam is also to say that without the column, the beam will fall. This leads to a problem: while other sources of action set to work immediately in the right conditions, the formulae of logical potencies do not, because no potency can accomplish both opposites at once. So one of them must get chosen. But it is not the logical potency that decides which result to accomplish: "There must therefore be something else that's in charge [*heteron ti to kurion*]; I mean, desire or choice" (*Met.* IX.5 1048a10, my trans.). While the soul is the source of change, it produces both effects *through* the same formula (*Met.* IX.2 1046a20–24). Since a logical potency does not immediately set to work like other sources, in what sense is it truly a source? I think the answer is that the formula (*logos*) constitutes an abstract "causal space" much the way contraries do: knowing that people need iron to live constitutes opposite

possible outcomes, namely having iron or not having it, and a continuum between them, just as hot and cold define a continuum (temperature). So just as the capacity to be hot or cold means that a body must have a temperature, a logical formula defines a condition that determines action, setting out a range of possibilities and requiring one to make a decision about which will be the case. Logical potencies, then, do spontaneously affect what happens, but as conditions rather than as movers. We can call them "conditioning sources."

56. Sachs trans., Aristotle (2004). Translation modified, changing "being-at-work-staying-itself" to "being-complete."

57. Menn makes much of this in a draft of his upcoming monograph *The Aim and the Argument of Aristotle's Metaphysics*.

58. Witt and Beere make a sharp distinction between being-potent and being-in-potency in order to avoid the following problem: if being-in-potency and being-in-actuality alternated, the violinist would cease to be capable in becoming active. If she ceased to be capable, she would be, well, *incapable*. Aristotle makes this point in the following, tortured claim: "What is capable is that which would be in no way incapable if it so happened that the being-at-work of which it is said to have the potency were present. I mean, for instance, that if something is capable of sitting, and admits of sitting, if it so happens that sitting is present to it, it will in no way be incapable of it." (*Met*. IX.3 1046b23–1047a27, Sachs trans., Aristotle 1999). But such a sharp distinction is not borne out by the text. See Anagnostopoulos (2010) and Sentesy (2018a).

59. Since mere potency and complete potency are not stages, but *sorts* of potency, it is misleading to phrase this as a question about what happens when one changes from being merely capable of geometry to being a completely capable geometer.

60. The definition of change in the *Physics* implicitly rejects alteration as the paradigm for change. Alteration comes up in *On the Soul* because it does not presuppose the *Physics*.

61. *Epidosis* has two meanings in the lexicon: intransitively it means "increase," "advance," or "progress," while transitively it means "freely giving over and above," for example, charitable giving.

62. This is an important subject in the literature, and it is taken to distinguish activities from motions or changes (see *NE* X.4 and the disputed passage at *Met*. IX.6 1048b18–34). See the scholarship on the *energeia-kinēsis* distinction, listed above in chapter 1, note 26, and chapter 4, footnote 40.

63. Brentano (1975), 27–28. See chapter 4, note 5.

64. Sachs trans., Aristotle (1999). See Waterlow (Broadie) (1982b), and Witt's (2003) discussion of *Met*. IX.4, and the argument that modality shows that potency and *energeia* must be independent concepts in Sentesy (2018a).

65. See Sentesy (2018a).

66. Waterlow (Broadie) (1982b), 162. Compare Sorabji (1980), Dudley (2012), D. Frede (2014).

Chapter 5

1. See Gotthelf (2013) and Dudley (2012), 176–85, who survey the debate. The apparent opposition between material processes and teleology presupposes modern concepts of mechanism, determinism, and free will that Aristotle does not share.

2. A cause is not the same as a source. By "causally" I mean "in their character as sources of change." There is no other single English word to express this, and the word "archaeologically" has a different meaning in English.

3. Witt (2003), for example, argued that it is through the discussion of potency and actuality that Aristotle introduces teleology, and thereby normativity, into his account of being, while Beere (2007) agrees, but takes form and definition to be already ontologically normative.

4. See Harte (2002), who examines Plato's account of structure with reference to recent analytic mereology. For phenomenological work on parts and wholes, see Merleau-Ponty (2013), Lampert (1989), Sokolowski (1977), and Willard (2003).

5. See Scharle (2008, 2015), Witt (2015), and Bolton (2015).

6. On change as part of what heavenly bodies are, see *Met.* IX.8 1050b16–34, and chapter 4, note 52.

7. On how eternal change accomplishes the being of heavenly things, see Quarantotto (2015). The science that studies the final cause, namely, the good, is natural philosophy, since "final cause" implies change: "this sort of cause [that for the sake of which] is the good, and this belongs among actions and things that are in change, and it moves things first—for that is the sort of thing an end is" (*Met.* XI.1 1059a35–37, Sachs trans., Aristotle 1999). First philosophy seeks the causes and sources not of being insofar as it changes, but of being as being (*Met.* IV.1 1003a30–31), which is the primary reason for examining *genesis* rather than other forms of change, namely, because in it we see sources bring things into being. But insofar as first philosophy is theology concerned with the highest source of change (*Met.* VI.2 1026a18–22, 27–33), physics converges with it.

8. But see Sedley (2007), 194–203. In my argument, natural processes do not require cosmic teleology to be a cause of order. Instead, natural processes are teleological in that, from them, beings emerge.

9. See Witt (2003). See Beere (2009), 309, for an ontological normative concept. See Gotthelf (2013), 71–72, for a discussion of the Regulative/Pragmatic view of teleology, for which teleology is not in things, but in our thinking of them.

10. Prominent in this debate is the question whether teleology originates in the biological, the physical, or the metaphysical works. See Gotthelf (1976, 2013), Cooper (1982), Bradie and Miller (1984), Meyer (1992), Mirus (2004), and Johnson (2005).

11. Teleology is presented as the solution to the problem of hylomorphism, namely, the problem of how material and form genuinely constitute one being. The solution is that form (*eidos*) is precisely the unity, that is, the *telos*, the organization and completeness of material (*Met.* VII.17 1041b11–33, *Met.* VIII.6 1045a21–b26). Hylomorphism is, therefore, inherently teleological. See in particular Yu (1997, 2003), Charles (2010), and Kosman (2013).

12. There appear to be differences, for example, between form considered as the unity of material, form considered as the *telos* or completion of material, and individual form considered as the focal sense of categorical properties, although there are clearly relationships between these determinations of beings. Perhaps the reason why form, rather than material, is the primary and focal sense of categorical being, is that form is the unity of material, in which case *telos* is ontologically decisive. But perhaps the fact that the form unifies material is incidental to the primacy of the form. A solution to this problem calls for an examination of *Cat.* and *Met.* VII and VIII. The question of the role of teleology in thinking the focal senses of being in general is particularly interesting. For example, quantity, quality, place, and secondary substance depend on a *this*: is this due to teleology, or is the convergence of homonyms on a focal meaning another phenomenon? The preceding chapters have suggested an answer: to be a focal being is to be a *telos*. First, as we saw in the demonstration of the existence of change, the focal sense of energetic being is telic in character. Aristotle used being-

in-completion (*entelecheia*) to name the focal sense of being-in-potency: thus, change is itself the completion (*telos*) that gives beings-insofar-as-they-are-potent their meaning as potent. On homonymy and focal sense, see in particular Shields (1999) and Ward (2007, 2009).

13. In this respect, I partly disagree with Lang (2007), 3, 274–75. I agree with Lang's argument that Aristotle is not a proto-mechanist, and has instead a quite different view of nature. But I take issue with her claim that Aristotle's system presupposes the idea that nature produces order. I take the generation of order to be, instead, a phenomenon requiring explanation, making sense of which is the task to which Aristotle devotes significant parts of his corpus.

14. Sachs trans., Aristotle (1995).

15. Byrne (2018), 120–31.

16. We can think the unity of parts and whole, of material and form properly only by interpreting them through the concepts of potency and activity (*Met.* VIII.6 1045b2–24).

17. Sachs trans., Aristotle (1999).

18. Joachim, trans., in Aristotle (1984).

19. Sachs trans., Aristotle (1995). Glosses added.

20. Ogle trans. in Aristotle (1984).

21. As Code (1997), 127, points out, some aspects of Aristotle's reading of Empedocles may not have followed necessarily from what *we* know of Empedocles's position. But we must keep in mind that Aristotle had much more access to Empedocles's thought.

22. Sachs trans., Aristotle (1999). Translation modified: "thinghood" replaced with "being [*ousia*]."

23. See Heinemann (2014).

24. While Aristotle would claim that any structure at all, for example, the properties of the elements, would count as form, he claims that his predecessors lacked the concept of definition and its relation to being (*PA* I.1 642a25–28). This allows him to see their positions as compatible with, rather than as opposed to, his own.

25. Sachs trans., Aristotle (1999).

26. Sachs trans., Aristotle (1999). Translation modified: "thinghood" replaced with *ousia*, "form" translating *eidos*, and "shape" translating *morphē*; my emphasis.

27. Aristotle thinks Empedocles was not consistent in maintaining that individual things are not themselves sources, since he was forced to claim that the cause of some things is its ratio, for example, bones are composed of a certain proportion of elements—a Heraclitean point (*PA* I.1 642a17–24).

28. Sachs trans., Aristotle (1995). Translation modified: "shape" changed to "schema."

29. Aristotle might reasonably infer this to be true for Empedocles. Empedocles thinks that what appear to be individuals do not have natures, *because they are generated* by material processes, that is, by nature. What distinguishes individual things from nature, then, is that the one does not generate, while the other does.

30. The argument works by positioning the terms in the same place in the dynamic structure of coming-to-be, namely, at the *end*.

31. Sachs trans., Aristotle (1999).

32. Part of this argument is, as we saw in chapter 2, that being-in-completion (here, shape or form) is the focal meaning being-in-potency (here, material). But interpreting shape and material as being-in-completion and being-in-potency is one of the things that requires explanation in this chapter.

33. See Allen (2015), 82.

34. Sachs trans., Aristotle (1999). Translation modified: "thinghood" replaced with "*ousia.*"
35. See also Charlton in Aristotle (1970), 91.
36. See also Charlton in Aristotle (1970), 91.
37. In this respect, I disagree with Lennox (1982), 235, who argues that spontaneously generated organisms were not teleological because the agent had a different form than the end product. This argument seems also to assert that for Aristotle a person healed by a doctor was no longer a natural *telos*, and that many living animals and plants were not natural wholes.
38. Thus, the three determinations of nature in *Physics* II.1 are in fact one: (1) nature is a path into itself, a form or arrangement holding itself together (*Phys.* II.1 193b13–19), or (2) nature is what emerges, what comes-to-be (*Phys.* II.1 193b1–3), and (3) nature is "some source and cause of being moved and of coming to rest in that to which it belongs primarily" (*Phys.* II.1 192b22–24, Sachs trans., Aristotle 1995).
39. Compare Wieland (1975b), 150–52.
40. The claim about coming-to-be and nature, then, is also a claim about being (*Met.* VIII.3 1043b23, *Met.* V.4 1015a12–15). In *Met.* VIII.3 1043b23 Aristotle writes: "nature alone is the *ousia* in destructible things," and *Met.* V.4 1015a12–15: "and in an extended sense, every kind of *ousia* in general is directly called a nature for this reason: because nature is some *ousia* . . . [namely] the *ousia* of things that have in themselves a source of change in their own right." Sachs trans., Aristotle (1999), translation modified: "a certain kind of" replaced by "some" (*tis*).
41. There is an ambiguity concerning what "nature" means here. For it seems possible that it could be nature in the sense of a universal, a secondary *ousia*, so that the generation of a particular thing would consist of it heading toward a universal shape. In this view, Witt (1994), 224, says, "Sally's *telos* is the type of species which she will realize, and not the token or individual she will become." But this view cannot be correct, Witt (1994), 225, observes, because universals like genus and species only have being in-potency, while being-at-work, which is the *telos* of generation (*Met.* IX.8 1050a6–10), is never used for universals, but only "for either the individual [composite] or the [particular] form." Therefore, nature means the concrete particular being.
42. Dudley (2012), 172–77.
43. On the apparent contrast between automaticity and teleology, see Allen (2015). See also Bolotin (1997), 31–51.
44. Sachs trans., Aristotle (1999).
45. Sachs trans., Aristotle (1999).
46. Although even if the processes are the same, art will differ from the automatic because it comes from a universal that is the same in kind as the product. See *PA* I.1 640a30–33, and Stavrianeas (2015), 52–54.
47. Gotthelf (2012), 71–74.
48. This may be true even if only rudimentary animals can be so generated. See Stavreanos (2008).
49. Charles (2010), 186–87. This is linked to the claim that a thing's essence is constituted, at least in part, by its production routines.
50. Compare Broadie's (2007), 18–32, criticism of concepts of both forward and backward causation.
51. In particular, Henry (2018) argues that Aristotle does not hold a modern version of epigenesis because natural things cannot make decisions in the course of development.

The thesis that Aristotelian epigenesis turns on the possibility of decision-making has no bearing on the view of teleology I am putting forward here.

52. See, for example, Abbott (2006, 2009), Okrent (2018), Bedau (1997, 2002), Lennox (2014), Henry (2018), and J. Kim (1999, 2006).

53. J. Kim (1999) proposes the exclusion argument, that if the higher level of complexity was causally relevant, it would conflict with the lower-level causal processes, while if they did not conflict, it would be meaningless to call the higher-level processes causally effective, since the lower-level ones would suffice.

54. The term "causal power" conflates causes with sources, and thereby categorical with dynamic-energetic being.

55. See Austin and Marmodoro (2017), and Marmodoro (2017).

Chapter 6

1. Witt (2003), 78–89, 103–14, argues that it is the ontological sense of potency and actuality that brings teleology into ontology.
2. Kosman (2013).
3. Burnyeat (2008).
4. In Burnyeat (2008) and Beere (2009), 221–30.
5. Proponents of this view include H.-K. Kim (2007), Yu (2003), Kosman (1984, 2013), Halper (1989), 200–201, and M. Frede (1994).
6. Menn (n.d.).
7. Witt (1989), (2003), 3–6, 98–103, 112–15; and Charles (2010).
8. The idea that *Met.* IX is just an extension of the discussion of categorical substance is corrected by Witt's claim that the book focuses on an irreducibly different sense of being: not categorical being, but potentiality and actuality. Kosman argues that it shows that even categorical being should be thought as activity, which fills out Menn's claim that the book examines what it is to be a source. Menn's argument that the book focuses on *all* the ways something can be a source (including *energeia*) supplements Witt's focus on *dunameis* and *telei*.
9. Rather than reading the adjective *kurios* as meaning "authoritative," Anagnostopoulos (2010) reads it as meaning "vernacular," with the implication that it is less philosophically important. This is within the semantic range of the word, and although Aristotle speaks of a further sense of the word that is more "useful for what we now want" (*Met.* IX.1 1045b34–35, Sachs trans., Aristotle 1999), I see no principled reason to diminish the philosophical importance of the change-related sense of potency. More directly to the point, we saw in chapter 4 that, as Aristotle elaborates it, the change-related sense of potency is certainly not a vernacular, common-sense view, but it has important implications for ontology.
10. Kosman (1984, 1994, 2013).
11. In outlining the plan of the book, Aristotle says explicitly that he will first discuss potency and *energeia* in their primary sense, namely as change (*kata kinēsin*). This will help us understand how potency and *energeia* extend to things that are not spoken of in reference to change (*Met.* IX.1 1045b31–1046a3). Aristotle's interest in extending these senses includes *ousia* and the material-form structure of categorical beings (see Anagnostopoulos 2011). But such an interest does not establish that this is his main purpose.
12. See Panayides (1999).
13. Aristotle's general list of kinds of priority varies from text to text, but they can be divided into two types: those ordered by an *archē* (*Met.* V.11 1018b9–29, *Cat.* 12 14a26–b8),

and asymmetrical dependence (Plato's Criterion) (*Met.* V.11 1019a2–5, XIII.2 1077b1–12; *Cat.* 12 14b10–23; *Phys.* VIII.7 260b17–19). Scholars worry that the general criteria for priority to which Aristotle refers do not provide an adequate basis for his claims to priority in *Met.* IX.8. Witt (1994, 1998) claims, in response, that the priority of *energeia* is established because potency depends for its existence on the existence of *energeia*, but not vice versa, that is, Plato's Criterion (*Met.* V.11 1019a2–5). Menn (n.d.), IIIα3, 11, and Beere (2009), 289, hold that this criterion is not successful. Broadie (2010), 201, argues that Plato's Criterion cannot be found in *Met.* IX.8, and that the attempt to assimilate IX.8 to it should be abandoned. Peramatzis (2011) defends a reading of priority that he thinks can assign ontological primacy to *energeia* in cases of potency-*energeia* relations. Panayides (1999) notes that in *Physics* VIII.7 261a12–20 Aristotle distinguishes between priority in *ousia* and priority due to independent existence, and shows that this distinction obtains in *Met.* IX.8.

14. In *Met.* V.11 1019a4–8, Aristotle says that in a way all things are said to precede or follow according to the order determined by potency and being-complete. Parts are prior in potency since they continue once the whole has been dismantled, but wholes are prior in being-complete (*entelecheia*), since the whole has some independence; for example, it can remain though the parts change, and it guides the assembly of the parts.

15. See Menn (n.d.).

16. Studying sources in this way does not amount to doing physics: first philosophy studies all things, including change and changing things, not insofar as they change, but insofar as they are. Moreover, being a source is being in the primary sense, and being a source of change and generation is the primary way of being a source (*Met.* I.3 983a25–27, *Met.* IV.2 1003b16–19, *Met.* XII.8 1073a23–b2). Menn (n.d.) argues that the purpose of *Met.* IX is to prepare the concept of *archē* to play its role in the culmination of the *Metaphysics* in the account of god in *Met.* XII.

17. See Makin in Aristotle (2006b), 195. M. Frede (1994), 184–86, argues that even when claims in this passage appear to be about the change of things, they are actually made about an ontological sense of potentiality and actuality. Charles (2010), 189–90, makes a similar move, introducing a distinction between the potential to become and the potential to be, and finesses the problems this introduces by saying that in some cases the one implies the other. He argues that though the distinction is not explicit in the text, it is implied. My position is that the two are not metaphysical alternatives, since nothing prevents a potency for change from being part of what defines a being, that is, part of its essence. The distinction is, instead, between a potency conceived as a source, and the derivative concept of a potency for a categorical being (e.g. primary being, quality, quantity, etc.). As we shall see below, Menn and Beere each attempt to base priority in the passage on ontological concepts of priority that could apply to material and form: Beere (2009), 302–12, introduces a concept of ontological norms that he argues is required, though not mentioned, in the text; and Menn (n.d.), IIIα3 19–37, maintains a distinction between *energeia* as actuality and change, even while arguing that the subject of IX.8 is not *energeia* in the sense of *ousia*, but in the sense of a source, *archē*, which evidently can be a source of change.

18. See, for example, Makin in Aristotle (2006b), 195, and Beere (2009), chap. 8.

19. Broadie (2010).

20. For example, "there must be something burnable before being burned and something that can set it on fire before setting it on fire" (*Phys.* VIII.1 251a15–16, Sachs trans.,

Aristotle 1995). Add to this that actively being the case implies the capacity to be the case, while potency continues even when the activity is not there, and the case for the priority of potency over *energeia* looks extremely strong. See *Met.* IX.3 1046b2–1047a10 and XII.6 1071b24–1072a18. See Menn (n.d.) IIIα1 9–11. In his argument, the physicists and Platonists hold that if the cosmos came to be, potency must come first or have ontological primacy.

21. Sachs trans., Aristotle (1999). Translation modified: "were generated" to "are generated," my emphasis.

22. Sachs trans., Aristotle (1999).

23. Moreover, Aristotle adds, activity generates dispositional potencies: to be a builder, that is, to be-in-potency, one must first build (*Met.* IX.8 1049b29).

24. Note also that because the phenomena are structured by genetic priority, both the being that generates and the being that is generated already appear to be mature adults or skilled agents. This is clear from the way Aristotle describes the case: once he has established that the center of a genetic analysis is not the seed or the child, but the mature being who can and actively does generate, he does not say that a child comes to be from an adult, but that a man comes to be from a man. Even the being that is generated is, ultimately and properly, the one who can generate, that is, the source of being.

25. Broadie (2010) and Charles (2010) are the notable exceptions.

26. Sachs trans., Aristotle (1999). Translation modified: "thinghood" replaced with "*ousia*," parentheses removed, emphasis added. Sachs has translated *hustera* correctly as "later," since it refers to the individual genetic sequence, rather than to genetic priority simply.

27. Sachs trans., Aristotle (1999). Translation modified: "thinghood" replaced with "primary being."

28. Sachs trans., Aristotle (1999). Translation modified: "thinghood" replaced with "*ousia*," parentheses removed. In the phrase *ēdē echei to eidos*, *echei* is used as a being-replacing word.

29. Beere (2009), 304–12.

30. Even Beere's (2009) 304–12 claim that the basis for substantial priority is a constitutive normative non-reciprocity between stages of generation (i.e., that "man" constitutes the being of the boy in a way that "boy" does not constitute the being of the man) turns out to depend on *genesis*, because being *from* something ultimately depends on what the structure of *genesis* is (thus, the relevant ways of being *from* something in *Met.* V.24 depend on the structure of *genesis* in *Met.* IX.8).

31. Compare *Physics* I.5 188b26–28, where the source-like character of form is explicit: "the sources must come neither from one another nor from anything else, and everything else must come from them" (my trans.).

32. Argument reversed and paraphrased. See Ross in Aristotle (1924), 262.

33. I can aim to run a whole marathon, but if I am out of shape, I can try instead to run as much of a marathon as I can. If being *for the sake of* something is going to mean being for an accomplishment (*telos*), we need to specify what it is an accomplishment of. In this case, the accomplishment is the activity or use of a potency. In this example, in both cases, I am completing or exercising my being a marathon runner, or my incomplete ability to run.

34. Sachs trans., Aristotle (1999). Translation modified: "being-at-work" replaced with *energeia*.

35. Sachs trans., Aristotle (1999). Translation modified: "motion" replaced with "change."

36. If there are kinds of activity that have no corresponding potency, then the claim is limited to the sort of activity that does involve potency.

37. In this respect, I disagree with Panayides's (1999) interpretation of the argument. He claims that the growing boy is potent because he is intrinsically lacking his end, whereas the end is by definition complete. My claim is that the boy is not yet fully in-potency, that is, his potency is not complete until he has grown. Thus, potency's lacking its activity is not the relevant sort of incompleteness.

38. Makin in Aristotle (2006b), 197–204, takes the worries to be (1) how to include the case of material potency in the argument for priority, and (2) how to relate the capacity to its exercise teleologically (a problem that I take Aristotle to have solved in the first half of the argument for priority in *ousia*). Beere (2009), 310–13, similarly, presents the purpose of the passage to be chasing down individual cases to show that the capacity is *for* the *energeia*. Witt (2003), 88–89, takes this passage to clear up the difference between potency for activity and potency for the hylomorphic product of the activity. By contrast, I take the extension of potency and *energeia* to material and form and of *energeia* to *entelecheia* to depend on the way that the product is evidently a *telos* to show that *energeia* is in fact *telos*.

39. Broadie (2010).

40. The relationship between activity and use is prominent: "living and acting are a using [*chrēsis*] and a being-at-work" (*EE* II.1 1219b1–2, my trans.). See *Protrepticus* B79, B80. See also Beere (2009), 161–66, and Menn (1994). On *energeia*'s inheritance of the structure of potency, recall the impasses that Aristotle faces in *Physics* III.3.

41. A further worry, not addressed in this *Met.* IX.8 passage, but featuring decisively in the argument for the primacy of eternal beings (*Met.* IX.8 1050b6–1051a2), is whether potency in fact has a single accomplishment, since only part of what something is capable of being can actively be at a time. Aristotle could respond to this by saying that this is not the case for natural or dispositional completed potencies.

42. In the first half of this *Met.* IX.8 passage, Aristotle argued that the way potency is a source is secondary to activity, since it comes to be only for the activity. Thus, it appears that both activity and potency depend on one another in different ways in order for them to come to be. The argument so far concerning priority in primary being (*ousia*) appears to have drawn potency and activity to a stalemate concerning Plato's Criterion.

43. Potency appears to have a better claim to primacy because of its permanence: the parts of some things are more primary in being, at least in the sense that they remain when the whole is destroyed (*Met.* V.11 1019a8–15, VII.15 1040a22–24). Moreover, since potency is the *source* of change, while *energeia is* change, potency remains while *energeia* comes and goes (*Met.* IX.3 1046b29–1047a10). See Menn (n.d.).

44. This is one of the strongest arguments Plato has against the being of change (e.g., Plato, *Timaeus* 38b). But in fact the criticism only applies to the quantity of change, for example, the space or distance it covers, and not to the change itself, which is itself a source of unity: "what is called continuous is that of which the change is one in its own right" (*Met.* V.6 1016a4–5, my trans.). See Plato's *Theaetetus* 153a–c.

45. Aristotle announced that potency and activity could be extended to material and *ousia* in *Met.* IX.6 1048a32–b9, but there he described the extension through examples, and characterizes the relationship between the change-related terms and the material-*ousia* related terms as analogous. Since in the *Rhetoric*, being analogous (*analogon*) means being the same (*homoios*), Anagnostopoulos (2010), 416–24, argues that between the two senses of the terms there is a single shared relation between potency and activity, i.e., that

the terms apply in the same way to both cases. Pointing out the identity of the relation between potency and activity, and other uses of the words, Anagnostopoulos claims that the dative case (being in-potency, *dunamei*, and being-in-work, *energeiai*) and the nominative case (potency, *dunamis*, and being-at-work, *energeia*) are interchangeable, that is, the dative case offers no special "ontological" sense of the terms.

46. Note that, *contra* Panayides, material is not related to form as a lack (*steresis*) is related to form, as Aristotle explicitly warns: "For we say that material and lack are different things, and of these the one is a non-being incidentally, namely the material, while the lack is so in its own right, and the one, the material, is almost, and in a certain respect is, an *ousia*, which the other is not at all" (*Phys.* I.9 192a3, Sachs trans., Aristotle 1995).

47. Only the parts of changes are incomplete. The whole change is complete (*NE* X.4 1174a13–b23).

48. As Socrates suggests, drawing on Heraclitus: "Doesn't the condition of bodies get destroyed by quiet and idleness, but get preserved for the most part by exercises and motion?" (*Theaetetus* 153b, Benardete trans., Plato 1984).

49. Aristotle coined both the terms *energeia* and *entelecheia* to have this philosophical relationship, which is one reason why translating them less literally (e.g., rendering both as "actuality," or one or the other as "reality," "activity," etc.) prevents the words from functioning as resources for understanding the concepts.

50. There is a difference between saying that (b) being-at-work *is* the work and saying that (c) being-at-*work* is named through or by the work, since the latter could be a different thing. This conflict could be resolved by claiming that being-at-work only means the work-act, and that claim (b) is about priority instead of identity, that is, being-at-work is the work *more* than the work-object. The problem with this is that it conflicts with another of Aristotle's positions, namely that the transcendent work-object takes priority over the act of production.

51. At first, it seems that the argument could amount to the claim that *energeia* means being-*in*-the-*telos*: (c) the claim that being-at-work is named through the work could draw both on the root *ergon* and also on the *en*-prefix. In this reading, the *en*- prefix of *en-erg-eia* would mean "in," recalling the claim that being-in-*energeia* is being *in* the form (*hotan de ge energeiai ēi, tote en tōi eidei estin*) from the Structure Argument. Thus, being *en-erg-eia* would mean being-*in*-the-work in the sense of being *in* an accomplished form, whether the work/*telos* is a table or a song. This makes step (d) a strong claim, that being-in-work *just is* being-in-the-*telos*. For example, the activity of the builder is *in* the work-object or form, the activity of a runner has the form "running," that is, the movement of running is its *entelecheia*, and the activity of thinking is *in* the form "thinking." This is quite a literal interpretation of *energeia*. What is at-work is *in* the *telos*. This leads directly to the Location Argument, which we shall turn to in a moment. But there are two worries with this reading. First, it seems to define *energeia* as something static, whereas Aristotle uses it in the surrounding passages as a synonym for the activity of use (*chrēsis*). The solution is to make both being-in and the work into activities, for example, because a living animal and a table both are actively being what they are. But we might hold back from reading the passage this way for a more serious reason: because there is a conflict between saying that the *ergon* is the *telos* (*Met.* IX.8 1050a21) or that *energeia* is the *telos* of potency (*Met.* IX.8 1050a9–10) and saying that *energeia* means being *in* the *telos* (*Met.* IX.8 1050a15–16), since the latter seems to make the *telos* something else than the *energeia*. The problem is that, however literal a rendering it is of *energeia*, being-in-the-work-*telos* seems to

substitute the *relation between* potency and *energeia*, or between material and form, for the definition of *energeia* itself. This problem is particularly acute, since what is at stake is *telos*. Saying that this is what *energeia* itself is produces an infinite regress. To finesse this problem by restricting the Etymological Argument to cases in which *energeia* has a further product means to resort to an ad hoc solution, and it is thin on textual support.

52. At the time, activities of production would have been recognizably related to their products. This is far less clear in an industrialized manufacturing process, especially with the advent of modular parts. But the claim does not depend on this.

53. For a compatible but different solution to this problem, see Kelsey's (2003) argument that for a change to be by nature just means that the change is happening to a being that is its proper subject.

54. See also *Phys*. III.3 202b6–8.

55. It is misguided to read Aristotle as giving an account of activities like singing, seeing, and thinking as producing separate objects. But it seems possible to allow a work-act to play the role of a work-object in the sense that it has a definite form. Taking them this way makes such activities implicitly transitive, that is, intentional: singing will stretch out toward the song, thinking toward its object, seeing toward what is visible. But Aristotle reverses the direction of this relationship: he takes thinking and seeing to be affected by their objects, rather than extending toward them: even though the knower can put her knowing to work on her own, for her to be capable of thought or perception is for her to actively allow herself to be affected (*Soul* II.4 429a14–18, b6–9).

56. Some scholars are vexed by the claim that house-building comes to be and is at the same time as the house, since it conflicts with their view that the potency for building is extinguished when the house comes to be. Kosman (1969, 2013) requires potencies for change, like building, to annihilate themselves by completing themselves. The problem is not removed by saying that something of the *telos* has already come into being along the way (*Met*. IX.8 1049b35–1050a2), because what has come to be already is not the complete thing; for example, when the foundation of the house has come to be, but the house has not yet (see *Phys*. VI.6 237b10–24, and the section of chapter 5 on the continuity and discontinuity of *Genesis*). To solve the apparent conflict, Charles (2010), 184.n., 189–90, argues that *genesis* constitutes two potencies at once: one for becoming a house, the other for being a house, noting that the claim in this context "may mean no more than that the house building occurs in the same place as the house." This appears to be straightforwardly correct. For her part, Broadie (2010), 208, argues that *energeia* has two senses: the ongoing activity of building that occurs for the sake of the house, and the thing's perfect aspect of *having-been-completed*, that is, the *entelecheia*, and that the latter coincides with the house.

57. Broadie (2010) appears to treat the intransitive activities as obviously prior to their potencies, whereas the productive activities are the ones that are problematic.

58. Sachs trans., Aristotle (1999). Translation modified: italics added, "thinghood" replaced with "primary being."

59. For example, Beere (2009), 311, 313, makes this conclusion an unstated premise in an earlier argument, suggesting that Aristotle failed to mention it there because it was too obvious. Makin in Aristotle (2006b) does not mention the conclusion in his commentary, presumably for the same reason. Ross in Aristotle (1924) says that it follows from the whole argument for priority in *ousia*, noting in particular what I have called the Structure Argument.

BIBLIOGRAPHY

Primary Texts

Aristotle. 1924. *Metaphysics: A Revised Text with Introduction and Commentary.* Edited by W. D. Ross. Oxford: Oxford University Press.

———. 1929. *Physics.* Translated by P. H. Wicksteed and F. M. Cornford. Cambridge, Mass.: Harvard University Press.

———. 1933. *Metaphysics.* Translated by H. Tredennick. Cambridge, Mass.: Harvard University Press.

———. 1936. *Physics: A Revised Text with Introduction and Commentary.* Edited with introduction and commentary by W. D. Ross. Oxford: Oxford University Press.

———. 1938. *The Categories.* Translated by H. P. Cook. Cambridge, Mass.: Harvard University Press.

———. 1941. *The Basic Works of Aristotle.* Edited by Richard McKeon. New York: Random House.

———. 1949. *Categoriae et Liber de Interpretatione.* Edited by L. Minio-Paluello. Oxford: E. Typographeo Clarendoniano.

———. 1970. *Physics Book I and II.* Translated by William Charlton. Oxford: Oxford University Press.

———. 1976. *Metaphysics Books M and N.* Translated and edited by Julia Annas. Oxford: Clarendon.

———. 1978. *De motu animalium.* Translation, commentary, and interpretive essays by Martha Nussbaum. Princeton, N.J.: Princeton University Press.

———. 1984. *The Complete Works of Aristotle—The Revised Oxford Translation.* 4th printing. Edited by Jonathan Barnes. Princeton, N.J.: Princeton University Press.

———. 1985. *Metaphysics: Books Zeta, Eta, Theta, Iota (VII-X).* Translation and notes by Montgomery Furth. Indianapolis, Ind.: Hackett.

———. 1993a. *Physics Books III and IV.* Translated by E. Hussey. Oxford: Oxford University Press.

———. 1993b. *Metaphysics Book Γ, Δ, and E.* Translated by Christopher Kirwan. 2nd ed. Oxford: Clarendon.

———. 1995. *Physics: A Guided Study.* Translated by Joe Sachs. New Brunswick, N.J.: Rutgers University Press.

———. 1996. *Physics.* Translated by R. Waterfield. Oxford: Oxford University Press.

———. 1999. *Metaphysics.* Translated by Joe Sachs. Santa Fe, N.M.: Green Lion.

———. 2002. *Nicomachean Ethics.* Translation, glossary, and introduction by Joe Sachs. Cambridge: Hackett.

———. 2004. *On the Soul and On Memory and Recollection.* Translated by Joe Sachs. Santa Fe, N.M.: Green Lion.

———. 2006a. *Poetics.* Translated by Joe Sachs. Newburyport, Mass.: Focus.

———. 2006b. *Metaphysics Book Θ.* Translated by Stephen Makin. Oxford: Oxford University Press.

---. 2018. *Metaphysics Book Iota*. Translation, introduction, and commentary by Laura M. Castelli. Oxford: Clarendon.
Graham, D. W., ed. 2010. *The Texts of Early Greek Philosophers, Part 1*. Cambridge: Cambridge University Press.
Kirk, G. S., J. E. Raven, and M. Schofield, eds. 1984. *The Presocratic Philosophers: A Critical History with a Selection of Texts*. 2nd ed. Cambridge: Cambridge University Press.
Plato. 1984. *The Being of the Beautiful: Plato's Theaetetus, Sophist, and Statesman*. Translated by Seth Benardete. Chicago: University of Chicago Press.
---. 1996. *Sophist: The Professor of Wisdom*. Translation, introduction, and glossary by Eva Brann, Peter Kalkavage, and Eric Salem. Newburyport, Mass.: Focus.
---. 1997. *Complete Works*. Edited by John M. Cooper. Indianapolis, Ind.: Hackett.
---. 2004. *Theaetetus*. Translated by Joe Sachs. Newburyport, Mass.: Focus.
Theophrastus. 1993. *Theophrastus of Eresus: Sources for His Life, Writings, Thought and Influence*. 2 vols. Edited by W. W. Fortenbaugh, D. Gutas, P. M. Huby, and R. W. Sharples. Leiden: Brill.

Secondary Sources

Abbott, R. 2006. "Emergence Explained: Abstractions: Getting Epiphenomena to Do Real Work." *Complexity* 12, no. 1: 13–26.
---. 2009. "The Reductionist Blind Spot." *Complexity* 14, no. 5: 10–22.
Ackrill, J. L. 1965. "Aristotle's Distinction between *Energeia* and *Kinēsis*." In *New Essays on Plato and Aristotle*, edited by R. Bambrough, 121–41. New York: Routledge.
---. 1997. *Essays on Plato and Aristotle*. Oxford: Oxford University Press.
Agamben, G. 1999. *Potentialities: Collected Essays in Philosophy*. Stanford, Calif.: Stanford University Press.
Allen, J. 2015. "Aristotle on Chance as an Accidental Cause." In *Aristotle's Physics: A Critical Guide*, edited by Mariska Leunissen, 66–87. Cambridge: Cambridge University Press.
Anagnostopoulos, A. 2010. "Change in Aristotle's *Physics* 3." *Oxford Studies in Ancient Philosophy* 39: 33–79.
---. 2011. "Senses of *Dunamis* and the Structure of Aristotle's *Metaphysics* Θ." *Phronesis* 56, no. 4: 388–425.
---. 2013. "Aristotle's Parmenidean Dilemma." *Archiv für Geschichte der Philosophie* 95, no. 3: 245–74.
---. 2017. "Change, Agency and the Incomplete in Aristotle" *Phronesis* 62, no. 2: 170–209.
Annas, J. 1975. "Aristotle, Number, and Time." *Philosophical Quarterly* 25, no. 99: 97–113.
Aquinas, T. 1961. *Commentary on the Metaphysics of Aristotle*. Translated by J. P. Rowan. Chicago: Henry Regnery.
---. 1963. *Commentary on Aristotle's Physics*. Translated by R. J. Blackwell et al. New Haven, Conn.: Yale University Press.
---. 1970. *Commentary on the Posterior Analytics of Aristotle*. Translated by F. R. Larcher. Albany, N.Y.: Magi Books.

Aubenque, P. 2012. "Relativity or Aporicity of Ontology? From Quine to Aristotle." In *The Furniture of the World: Essays in Ontology and Metaphysics*, edited by F. M. Quesada and E. Sosa, 19–31. Amsterdam: Rodopi.
Augros, M. 1994. "Aristotle on the Unity of a Number." *Philosophia Perennis* 1, no. 2: 67–94.
Austin, C. J., and A. Marmodoro. 2017. "Structural Powers and the Homeodynamic Unity of Organisms." In *Neo-Aristotelian Perspectives on Contemporary Science*, edited by William M. R. Simpson, Robert C. Koons, and Nicholas J. Teh, 167–82. New York: Routledge.
Austin, J. L. 1979. "Ἀγαθόν and Εὐδαιμονία in the Ethics of Aristotle." In Austin, *Philosophical Papers*, edited by J. O. Urmson and G. J. Warnock, 1–31. 3rd ed. Oxford: Oxford University Press.
Backman, J. 2006. "Divine and Mortal Motivation: On the Movement of Life in Aristotle and Heidegger." *Continental Philosophy Review* 38: 241–61.
Badiou, A. 2005. *Being and Event*. Translated by Oliver Feltham. New York: Continuum.
Barnes, J. 1982. *The Presocratic Philosophers*. New York: Routledge.
———. ed. 1995. *The Cambridge Companion to Aristotle*. Cambridge: Cambridge University Press.
———. 2001. *Early Greek Philosophy*. 2nd ed. New York: Penguin Classics.
Bedau, M. 1997. "Weak Emergence." *Philosophical Perspectives* 11: 375–99.
———. 2002. "Downward Causation and the Autonomy of Weak Emergence." *Principia* 6, no. 1: 5–50.
Beere, J. 2006. "Potentiality and the Matter of Composite Substance." *Phronesis* 51, no. 4: 303–29.
———. 2009. *Doing and Being: An Interpretation of Aristotle's Metaphysics Theta*. Oxford: Oxford University Press.
Berti, E. 2001. "Multiplicity and Unity of Being in Aristotle." *Proceedings of the Aristotelian Society* 101: 185–207.
———. 2015. "The Relevance of Aristotle's Philosophy Today." *Journal of Philosophical Research* 40 (supplement): 113–21.
Blair, G. A. 1967. "The Meaning of 'Energeia' and 'Entelecheia' in Aristotle." *International Philosophical Quarterly* 7, no. 1: 101–17.
———. 1992. *Energeia and Entelecheia: "Act" in Aristotle*. Ottawa, Can.: University of Ottawa Press.
———. 1995. "Unfortunately, It Is a Bit More Complex: Reflections on Ἐνέργεια." *Ancient Philosophy* 15: 92–93.
———. 2011. "Aristotle on Ἐντελέχεια: A Reply to Daniel Graham." *American Journal of Philology* 114, no. 1: 91–97.
Bodnár, István. 2018. "*Physics* I.8" in *Aristotle's* Physics *Book I: A Systematic Exploration*. Edited by Diana Quarantotto. Cambridge: Cambridge University Press. 206–25.
Bolotin, D. 1997. *An Approach to Aristotle's "Physics": With Particular Attention to the Role of His Manner of Writing*. Albany, N.Y.: SUNY Press.
Bolton, R. 1991. "Aristotle's Method in Natural Science: *Physics* I." In *Aristotle's Physics: A Collection of Essays*, edited by Lindsay Judson, 1–29. Oxford: Oxford University Press.
———. 2015. "The Origins of Aristotle's Natural Teleology in *Physics* II." In *Aristotle's* Physics: *A Critical Guide*, edited by Mariska Leunissen, 121–43. Cambridge: Cambridge University Press.
Bostock, D. 1980. "Aristotle's Account of Time." *Phronesis* 25, no. 2: 148–69.

———. 2006. *Space, Time, Matter, and Form: Essays on Aristotle's "Physics."* Oxford: Oxford University Press.
Bowin, J. 2010. "Aristotle on the Unity of Change: Five Reductio Arguments in *Physics* viii 8." *Ancient Philosophy* 30: 319–45.
———. 2011. "Aristotle on Various Types of Alteration in 'De Anima' II 5." *Phronesis* 56, no. 2: 138–61.
———. 2012. "Aristotle on 'First Transitions' in De Anima II 5." *Apeiron* 45, no. 3. 262–82.
Brague, R. 1980. "Aristotle's Definition of Motion and Its Ontological Implications." *Graduate Faculty Philosophy Journal* 13, no. 2: 1–22.
Brakas, J. (George). 2011. "Aristotle's 'Is Said in Many Ways' and Its Relationship to His Homonyms." *Journal of the History of Philosophy* 49, no. 2: 135–59.
Brambaugh, R. 1978. "The Unity of Aristotle's Metaphysics." *Midwestern Journal of Philosophy* 6: 1–12.
Brennan, S. O. 1961. "The Meaning of 'Nature' in the Aristotelian Philosophy of Nature." *Thomist: A Speculative Quarterly Review* 24, no. 2: 383–401.
Brentano, F. 1975. *On the Several Senses of Being in Aristotle*. Translated by Rolf George. Berkeley: University of California Press.
Broadie, S. 2007. *Aristotle and Beyond: Essays on Metaphysics and Ethics*. Cambridge: Cambridge University Press.
———. 2010. "Where Is the Activity? (An Aristotelian Worry about the Telic Status of *Energeia*)." In *Being, Nature, and Life in Aristotle*, edited by J. G. Lennox and R. Bolton, 198–211. Cambridge: Cambridge University Press.
Brogan, W. 2005. *Heidegger and Aristotle: The Twofoldness of Being*. Albany: State University of New York Press.
Bruell, C. 2013. "Aristotle on Theory and Practice." In *Political Philosophy Cross-Examined*, edited by T. L. Pangle and J. H. Lomax, 17–28. New York: Palgrave Macmillan.
Buchheim, T. 2001. "The Functions of the Concept of *Physis* in Aristotle's Metaphysics." *Oxford Studies in Ancient Philosophy* 20 (Summer): 201–34.
Burnyeat, M. 1984. *Notes on Books Eta and Theta of Aristotle's Metaphysics*. Oxford: University of Oxford Faculty of Philosophy.
———. 2001. *A Map of Metaphysics Zeta*. Pittsburgh, Pa.: Mathesis.
———. 2008. "*Kinêsis* vs. *Energeia*: A Much-Read Passage in (but Not of) Aristotle's Metaphysics." *Oxford Studies in Ancient Philosophy* 34: 219–92.
Byrne, C. 2018. *Aristotle's Science of Matter and Motion*. Toronto, Can.: University of Toronto Press.
Carli, S. 2008. "Commentary on Lang." *Proceedings of the Boston Area Colloquium in Ancient Philosophy* 24, no. 1: 218–27.
Charles, D. 1984. *Aristotle's Philosophy of Action*. Ithaca, N.Y.: Cornell University Press.
———. 2010. "Actuality and Potentiality in Metaphysics Θ.7-8: Some Issues concerning Actuality and Potentiality." In *Being, Nature, and Life in Aristotle: Essays in Honor of Allan Gotthelf*, ed. James Lennox and R. Bolton, 168–97. Cambridge: Cambridge University Press.
———. 2015. "Aristotle's Processes." In *Aristotle's Physics: A Critical Guide*, edited by Mariska Leunissen, 186–205. Cambridge: Cambridge University Press.
Charlton, W. 1987. "Aristotelian Powers." *Phronesis* 32, no. 3: 277–89.
———. 1989. "Aristotle on the Uses of Actuality." *Proceedings of the Boston Area Colloquium in Ancient Philosophy* 5: 1–22.

Chen, C.-H. 1956. "Different Meanings of the Term *Energeia* in the Philosophy of Aristotle." *Philosophy and Phenomenological Research* 17, no. 1: 56–65.
———. 1957. "Aristotle's Concept of Primary Substance in Books Z and H of the *Metaphysics*." *Phronesis* 2, no. 1: 46–59.
———. 1975. "Aristotle's Analysis of Change and Plato's Theory of Transcendent Ideas." *Phronesis* 20, no. 2: 129–45.
Cleary, J. J. 1985. "On the Terminology of 'Abstraction' in Aristotle." *Phronesis* 30, no. 1: 13–45.
Code, A. 1988. *Aristotle on the Many Senses of Priority*. Carbondale: Southern Illinois University Press.
———. 1997. "The Priority of Final Causes over Efficient Causes in Aristotle's PA." In *Aristotelische Biologie: Intentionen, Methoden, Ergebnisse*, edited by Wolfgang Kullman and Sobine Föllinger, 127–43. Stuttgart: Franz Steiner Verlag.
———. 2003. "Changes, Powers and Potentialities in Aristotle." In *Desire, Identity, and Existence: Essays in Honor of T.M. Penner*, edited by Naomi Reshotko, 253–71. Kelowna, Can.: Academic Printing & Publishing.
Cohen, S. 1994. "Aristotle on Elemental Motion." *Phronesis* 39, no. 2: 150–59.
———. 1996. *Aristotle on Nature and Incomplete Substance*. Cambridge: Cambridge University Press.
Coope, U. 2001. "Why Does Aristotle Say That There Is No Time without Change?" *Proceedings of the Aristotelian Society* 101: 359–67.
———. 2005. *Time for Aristotle: Physics IV.10–14*. Oxford: Oxford University Press.
———. 2009. "Change and Its Relation to Actuality and Potentiality." In *A Companion to Aristotle*, edited by Georgios Anagnostopoulos, 277–91. Malden, Mass.: Blackwell.
———. 2012. "Aristotle's Physics VII.3. 246a10–246b3." In *Reading Aristotle Physics VII.3: What Is Alteration?*, edited by Stefano Maso, Carlo Natali, and Gerhard Seel, 57–72. Las Vegas, Nev.: Parmenides.
———. 2015. "Self-Motion as Other-Motion in Aristotle's *Physics*." In *Aristotle's Physics: A Critical Guide*, edited by Mariska Leunissen, 245–64. Cambridge: Cambridge University Press.
Crombie, I. M. 1967. Review of *New Essays on Plato and Aristotle*. *Classical Review* n.s. 17: 32.
De Groot, J. 2008. "*Dunamis* and the Science of Mechanics: Aristotle on Animal Motion." *Journal of the History of Philosophy* 46, no. 1: 43–67.
De La Mettrie, J. O. 1912. *Man a Machine*. Translated by Gertrude Carman Bussey, revised by M. W. Calkins, M. Carret, and George Santayana. Chicago: Open Court.
Decker, J. E. 2015. "Everliving Fire: The Synaptic Motion of Life in Heraclitus." *Epoché* 19, no. 2: 173–80.
Demos, R. 1944. "The Structure of Substance according to Aristotle." *Philosophy and Phenomenological Research* 5, no. 2: 255–68.
Dudley, J. 2012. *Aristotle's Concept of Chance: Accidents, Cause, Necessity, and Determinism*. Albany: SUNY Press.
Falcon, A. 1997. "Aristotle's Theory of Division." *Bulletin of the Institute of Classical Studies* 41: 127–46.
———. 2005. *Aristotle and the Science of Nature*. Cambridge: Cambridge University Press.
Ferejohn, M. 1994. "Matter, Definition and Generation in Aristotle's *Metaphysics*." *Proceedings of the Boston Area Colloquium in Ancient Philosophy* 10, no.1. 35–65.

———. 1980. "Aristotle on Focal Meaning and the Unity of Science." *Learning* 25, no. 2: 117–28.
Fraassen, B. Van. 1980. "A Re-Examination of Aristotle's Philosophy of Science." *Dialogue* 19: 20–45.
Frede, D. 2014. "Accidental Causes in Aristotle." *Synthese* 92, no. 1: 39–62.
Frede, M. 1987. *Essays in Ancient Philosophy*. Minneapolis: University of Minnesota Press.
———. 1994. "Aristotle's Notion of Potentiality in *Metaphysics* Theta." In *Unity, Identity, and Explanation in Aristotle's Metaphysics*, edited by T. Scaltsas, D. Charles, and M. L. Gill, 173–93. Oxford: Oxford University Press.
Freeland, C. 1986. "Aristotle on Possibilities and Capacities." *Ancient Philosophy* 6: 69–89.
Furth, M. 1987. "Aristotle on the Unity of Form." *Proceedings of the Boston Area Colloquium in Ancient Philosophy* 2, no. 1. 131–67.
Gelber, J. 2010. "Form and Inheritance in Aristotle's Embryology." *Oxford Studies in Ancient Philosophy* 39: 183–212.
Gershenson, D. E., and D. A. Greenberg. 1961. "Melissus of Samos in a New Light: Aristotle's 'Physics' 186a10–16." *Phronesis* 5, no. 1: 1–9.
Gill, M. L. 1980. "Aristotle's Theory of Causal Action in 'Physics' III 3." *Phronesis* 25, no. 1: 129–47.
———. 1989. *Aristotle on Substance: The Paradox of Unity*. Princeton, N.J.: Princeton University Press.
———. 2003. "Aristotle's Distinction between Change and Activity." In *Process Theories*, edited by J. Seibt, 3–22. Dordrecht: Springer.
———. 2005. "Aristotle's Metaphysics Reconsidered." *Journal of the History of Philosophy* 43, no. 3: 223–41.
Gonzalez, F. 2006. "Whose Metaphysics of Presence? Heidegger's Interpretation of *Energeia* and *Dunamis* in Aristotle." *Southern Journal of Philosophy* 44, no. 4: 533–68.
———. 2018. "Δύναμις and *Dasein*, Ἐνέργεια and *Ereignis*: Heidegger's (Re)Turn to Aristotle." *Research in Phenomenology* 48: 409–32.
Gorman, M. 2006. "Independence and Substance." *International Philosophical Quarterly* 46, no. 2: 147–59.
Gotthelf, A. 1976. "Aristotle's Conception of Final Causality." *Review of Metaphysics* 30, no. 2: 226–54.
———. 2013. *Teleology, First Principles, and Scientific Method in Aristotle's Biology*. Oxford: Oxford University Press.
Graham, D. W. 1980. "States and Performances: Aristotle's Test." *Philosophical Quarterly* 30: 117–30.
———. 1987. *Aristotle's Two Systems*. Oxford: Oxford University Press.
———. 1988. "Aristotle's Definition of Motion." *Ancient Philosophy* 8: 209–15.
———. 1989. "The Etymology of *Entelecheia*." *American Journal of Philology* 110: 73–80.
———. 1995. "The Development of Aristotle's Concept of Actuality: Comments on a Reconstruction by Stephen Menn." *Ancient Philosophy* 15: 551–64.
———. 1996. "The Metaphysics of Motion: Natural Motion in *Physics* II and *Physics* VIII." In *Aristotle's Philosophical Development*, edited by William Wians, 171–92. Lanham, Md.: Rowman and Littlefield.
Greene, M. 1965. "Aristotle's Circular Movement as a Logos Doctrine." *Review of Metaphysics* 19, no. 1: 115–32.

Gulley, J. 2017. "Mixture, Powers, and Reality in Empedocles and Aristotle." Ph.D. diss., Purdue University.
Guthrie, W. K. C. 1981. *Aristotle: An Encounter*. Cambridge: Cambridge University Press.
Hagen, C. 1984. "The ἘΝΕΡΓΕΙΑ-ΚΙΝΗΣΙΣ Distinction and Aristotle's Conception of ΠΡΑΙΞΙΣ." *Journal of the History of Philosophy* 3, no. 22: 263–80.
Halper, E. 1984a. "Aristotle on Knowledge of Nature." *Review of Metaphysics* 37, no. 4: 811–35.
———. 1984b. "*Metaphysics* Z 12 and H 6: The Unity of Form and Composite." *Ancient Philosophy* 4: 146–59.
———. 1989. *One and Many in Aristotle's Metaphysics the Central Books*. Ohio State University Press.
———. 2005. *One and Many in Aristotle's Metaphysics: The Central Books*. Columbus, Ohio: Parmenides.
Hardie, W. F. R. 1968. *Aristotle's Ethical Theory*. Oxford: Oxford University Press.
Harry, C. 2015. *Chronos in Aristotle's Physics: On the Nature of Time*. Dordrecht: Springer.
Harte, V. 2002. *Plato on Parts and Wholes: The Metaphysics of Structure*. Oxford: Oxford University Press.
Havelock, E. A. 1986. "The Alphabetic Mind: A Gift of Greece to the Modern World." *Oral Tradition* 1, no. 1: 134–50.
Heidegger, M. 1969. *Identity and Difference*. Translated by Joan Stambaugh. New York: Harper and Row.
———. 1972. *On Time and Being*. Translated by Joan Stambaugh. New York: Harper and Row.
———. 1976. *What Is Called Thinking?* Translated by Fred D. Wieck and John Glenn Gray, introduction by John Glenn Gray. New York: Harper Collins.
———. 1981. "A Recollection (1957)." In *Heidegger: The Man and the Thinker*, translated by H. Seigfried, edited by Thomas Sheehan, 21–23. Chicago: Precedent.
———. 1995. *Aristotle's Metaphysics Θ 1–3: On the Essence and Actuality of Force*. Translated by Walter Brogan and Peter Warnek. Bloomington: Indiana University Press.
———. 1998. "On the Essence and Concept of Φύσις in Aristotle's *Physics* B,1." In *Pathmarks*, translated by Thomas Sheehan and William McNeill, 183–230. Cambridge: Cambridge University Press.
———. 1999. *Contributions to Philosophy (From Enowning)*. Translated by Parvis Emad and Kenneth Maly. Bloomington: Indiana University Press.
———. 2000. *Introduction to Metaphysics*. Translated by Gregory Fried and Richard Polt. New Haven, Conn.: Yale University Press.
———. 2001. *Phenomenological Interpretations of Aristotle: Initiation into Phenomenological Research*. Translated by Richard Rojcewicz. Bloomington: Indiana University Press.
Heinaman, R. 1994. "Is Aristotle's Definition of Change Circular?" *Apeiron* 27, no. 1: 25–38.
———. 1995. "Activity and Change in Aristotle." *Oxford Studies in Ancient Philosophy* 13: 187–216.
———. 1998. "Alteration and Aristotle's Activity—Change Distinction." *Oxford Studies in Ancient Philosophy* 16: 227–57.
———. 2007. "Actuality, Potentiality and 'De Anima II.5.'" *Phronesis* 52, no. 2: 139–87.

Heinemann, G. 2014. "Is Regularity according to Empedocles Imposed upon or Inherent in Things?" Presentation to the International Association for Presocratic Studies, Thessaloniki, Greece.

Henry, D. 2006. "Aristotle on the Mechanism of Inheritance." *Journal of the History of Biology* 39, no. 3: 425–55.

———. 2015. "Substantial Generation in *Physics* I.5–7." In *Aristotle's Physics: A Critical Guide*, edited by Mariska Leunissen, 144–61. Cambridge: Cambridge University Press.

———. 2018. "Aristotle on Epigenesis." In *Aristotle's Generation of Animals: A Critical Guide*, edited by A. Falcon and D. Lefebvre, 89–107. Cambridge: Cambridge University Press.

Heraclitus. 1979. *The Art and Thought of Heraclitus: A New Arrangement and Translation of the Fragments*. Translated by Charles Kahn. Cambridge: Cambridge University Press.

Hintikka, J. 1959. "Aristotle and the Ambiguity of Ambiguity." *Inquiry* 2, nos. 1–4: 137–51.

———. 1999. "On Aristotle's Notion of Existence." *Review of Metaphysics* 52, no. 4: 779–805.

———. 2007. "It All Depends On What 'Is' Is: A Brief History (and Theory) of Being." In *On Language: Analytic, Continental, and Historical Contributions*, edited by Jon Burmeister and Mark Sentesy, 51–64. Newcastle, Eng.: Cambridge Scholars.

Hirst, R. J. 1959. *The Problem of Perception*. London: George Allen and Unwin.

Hoffman, W. M. 1976. "Aristotle's Logic of Verb Tenses." *Journal of Critical Analysis* 6: 89–95.

Irwin, T. 1981. "Aristotle on Homonymy." *Review of Metaphysics* 34, no. 3: 523–44.

Johnson, M. R. 2005. *Aristotle on Teleology*. Oxford: Oxford University Press.

Jones, B. 1974. "Aristotle's Introduction of Matter." *Philosophical Review* 83, no. 4: 474–500.

Judson, L., ed. 1991. *Aristotle's Physics: A Collection of Essays*. Oxford: Oxford University Press.

Kahn, C. 2003. *The Verb "Be" in Ancient Greek*. Indianapolis, Ind.: Hackett.

———. 2009. *Essays on Being*. Oxford: Oxford University Press.

Kant, I. 2003. *Critique of Pure Reason*. Translated by Norman Kemp Smith. New York: Palgrave Macmillan.

Katz, E. C., and R. Polansky. 2006. "The Bad Is Last but Does Not Last: Aristotle's *Metaphysics* Θ 9." *Oxford Studies in Ancient Philosophy* 31: 233–42.

Kelsey, S. 2003. "Aristotle's Definition of Nature." *Oxford Studies in Ancient Philosophy* 25: 59–87.

———. 2006. "Aristotle *Physics* I 8." *Phronesis* 51, no. 4: 330–61.

———. 2008. "The Place of I 7 in the Argument of Physics I." *Phronesis* 53, no. 2: 180–208.

———. 2015. "Aristotle on Interpreting Nature." In *Aristotle's Physics: A Critical Guide*, edited by Mariska Leunissen, 31–45. Cambridge: Cambridge University Press.

Kenny, A. 1963. *Action, Emotion and Will*. New York: Routledge.

Kim, H.-K. 2007. "*Metaphysics* H 6 and the Problem of Unity." *Journal of the History of Philosophy* 46, no. 1: 25–42.

Kim, J. 1999. "Making Sense of Emergence." *Philosophical Studies* 95: 3–36

———. 2006. "Emergence: Core Ideas and Issues." *Synthese* 151: 547–59.
Knuuttila, S. 1993. *Modalities in Medieval Philosophy.* New York: Routledge.
Kosman, A. 1969. "Aristotle's Definition of Motion." *Phronesis* 14, no. 1: 40–62.
———. 1984. "Substance, Being, and *Energeia.*" *Oxford Studies in Ancient Philosophy* 2: 121–49.
———. 1994. "The Activity of Being in Aristotle's Metaphysics." In *Unity, Identity, and Explanation in Aristotle's Metaphysics*, edited by T. Scaltsas, D. Charles, and M. L. Gill, 195–213. Oxford: Clarendon.
———. 2013. *The Activity of Being: An Essay on Aristotle's Ontology.* Cambridge, Mass.: Harvard University Press.
Kung, J. 1978. "Metaphysics 8.4: Can Be but Will Not Be." *Apeiron* 12, no. 1: 32–36.
Lang, H. S. 1995. "Aristotle's *Physics* IV, 8: A Vexed Argument in the History of Ideas." *Journal of the History of Ideas* 56, no. 3: 353–76.
———. 1995. "Review of Simplicius, On Aristotle's Physics 7, and Philoponus, On Aristotle's Physics 5–8 with Simplicius, On Aristotle on the Void." *Review of Metaphysics* 49, no. 1: 167–70.
———. 2000. "Review: Graham, D.W. *Aristotle: Physics Book VIII.*" *Ancient Philosophy* 20, no. 1: 224–28.
———. 2007. *The Order of Nature in Aristotle's Physics: Place and the Elements.* Cambridge: Cambridge University Press.
———. 2008. "Body, Natural Things, and the Science of Nature." *Proceedings of the Boston Area Colloquium in Ancient Philosophy* 24, no. 1: 197–217.
———. 2012. "Aristotelian Physics: Teleological Procedure in Aristotle, Thomas, and Buridan." *Review of Metaphysics* 42, no. 3: 569–91.
———. 2014. "Why Fire Goes Up: An Elementary Problem in Aristotle's 'Physics.'" *Review of Metaphysics* 38, no. 1: 69–106.
Lennox, J. G. 1982. "Teleology, Chance, and Aristotle's Theory of Spontaneous Generation." *Journal of the History of Philosophy* 20, no. 3: 219–238.
———. 2014. "Aristotle on the Emergence of Material Complexity: *Meteorology* IV and Aristotle's Biology." *HOPOS: The Journal of the International Society for the History of Philosophy of Science* 4, no. 2: 272–305.
———. 2015. "How to Study Natural Bodies: Aristotle's μέθοδος." In *Aristotle's Physics: A Critical Guide*, edited by Mariska Leunissen, 10–30. Cambridge: Cambridge University Press.
Liddell, H., R. Scott, H. S. Jones, and R. McKenzie. 2011. *The Online Liddell-Scott-Jones Greek-English Lexicon.* Irvine: University of California Press.
Lloyd, A. C. 1970. "Aristotle's Principle of Individuation." *Mind* 79, no. 316: 519–29.
Makin, S. 1996. "Megarian Possibilities." *Philosophical Studies* 83: 253–76.
———. 2007. "About Time for Aristotle." *Philosophical Quarterly* 57, no. 227: 280–93.
Mamo, P. S. 1970. "*Energeia* and *Kinesis* in Metaphysics Θ.6." *Apeiron* 4, no. 2: 24–34.
Marmodoro, A. 2007. "The Union of Cause and Effect in Aristotle: Physics III 3." *Oxford Studies in Ancient Philosophy* 32: 205–32.
———. 2017. "Power Mereology: Structural Powers versus Substantial Powers." In *Philosophical and Scientific Perspectives on Downward Causation*, edited by Michelle Paoletti and Francesco Orilia, 110–27. New York: Routledge.
Marx, W. 1977. *Introduction to Aristotle's Theory of Being as Being.* The Hague: Martinus Nijhoff.

Menn, S. 1994. "The Origins of Aristotle's Concept of Ἐνέργεια: Ἐνέργεια and Δύναμις." *Ancient Philosophy* 14: 73–114.
———. 1995. "The Editors of the Metaphysics." *Phronesis* 40, no. 2: 202–8.
———. n.d. "The Aim and Argument of Aristotle's Metaphysics." https://www.philosophie.hu-berlin.de/de/lehrbereiche/antike/mitarbeiter/menn/contents.
Meyer, S. S. 1992. "Aristotle, Teleology, and Reduction." *Philosophical Review* 101, no. 4: 791–825.
Moravcsik, J. 1991. "What Makes Reality Intelligible? Reflections on Aristotle's Theory of *Aitia*." In *Aristotle's Physics: A Collection of Essays*, edited by Lindsay Judson, 31–47. Oxford: Oxford University Press.
Morison, B. 2002. *On Location: Aristotle's Concept of Place*. Oxford: Oxford University Press.
Morrison, D. 1993. "The Place of Unity in Aristotle's Metaphysical Project." *Proceedings of the Boston Area Colloquium in Ancient Philosophy* 9, no. 1: 131–67.
Mulhern, M. M. 1968. "Types of Process according to Aristotle." *Monist* 52: 237–51.
Noble, C. I. 2013. "Topsy-Turvy World: Circular Motion, Contrariety, and Aristotle's Unwinding Spheres." *Apeiron* 46, no. 4: 391–418.
Nussbaum, M. 1983. "The 'Common Explanation' of Animal Motion." In *Zweifelhaftes im Corpus Aristotelicum*, edited by Paul Moraux and Jürgen Wiesner, 116–56. Berlin: De Gruyter.
———. 1984. "Aristotelian Dualism: Reply to Howard Robinson." *Oxford Studies in Ancient Philosophy* 2: 197–207.
Okrent, M. 2018. *Nature and Normativity: Biology, Teleology, and Meaning*. New York: Routledge.
Olshewsky, T. 2014. "The Bastard Book of Aristotle's *Physics*." *Classical Quarterly* 64, no. 1: 58–74.
Owen, G. E. L. 1960. "Logic and Metaphysics in Some Earlier Works of Aristotle." In *Aristotle and Plato in the Mid-Fourth Century: Papers of the Symposium Aristotelicum Held at Oxford in August, 1957*, edited by I. Düring and G. E. L. Owen, 162–90. Göteborg: Elanders Boktryckeri Aktiebolag.
———. 1965. "Aristotle on the Snares of Ontology." In *New Essays on Plato and Aristotle*, edited by Renford Bambrough, 69–95. New York: Humanities.
———. 1986. *Logic, Science and Dialectic*. Edited by Martha Nussbaum. Ithaca, N.Y.: Cornell University Press.
Owens, J. 1978. *The Doctrine of Being in the Aristotelian Metaphysics*. Toronto: Pontifical Institute of Mediaeval Studies.
———. 1988. "The Self in Aristotle." *Review of Metaphysics* 41, no. 4: 707–22.
Page, C. 1985. "Predicating Forms of Matter in Aristotle's Metaphysics." *Review of Metaphysics* 39, no. 1: 57–82.
Panayides, C. 1999. "Aristotle on the Priority of Actuality in Substance." *Ancient Philosophy* 19: 327–44.
Parmenides of Elea. *Fragments*. Translated by David Gallop. Toronto, Can.: University of Toronto Press.
Pearson, G. 2005. "Aristotle on Being-as-Truth." *Oxford Studies in Ancient Philosophy* 27: 201–31.
Penner, T. 1970. "Verbs and the Identity of Actions—A Philosophical Exercise in the Interpretation of Aristotle." In *Ryle: A Collection of Critical Essays*, edited by Oscar Wood and George Pitcher, 393–453. New York: Anchor Books.

Peramatzis, M. 2011. *Priority in Aristotle's Metaphysics*. Oxford: Oxford University Press.
Pickering, F. R. 1978. "Aristotle on Zeno and the Now." *Phronesis* 23, no. 3: 253–57.
———. 1997. "Aristotle on Walking." *Archiv für Geschichte Philosophie* 59: 37–43.
Polansky, R. 1983a. "Aristotle's Treatment of Ousia in *Metaphysics* V, 8." *Southern Journal of Philosophy* 21, no. 1: 57–66.
———. 1983b. "*Energeia* in Aristotle's Metaphysics IX." *Ancient Philosophy* 3: 160–70.
———. 2007. *Aristotle's "De Anima": A Critical Commentary*. Cambridge: Cambridge University Press.
Politis, V. 2004. *Aristotle and the Metaphysics*. New York: Routledge.
Quarantotto, D. 2015. "A Dynamic Ontology: On How Aristotle Arrived at the Conclusion That Eternal Change Accomplishes *Ousia*." In *Aristotle's Physics: A Critical Guide*, edited by Mariska Leunissen, 162–85. Cambridge: Cambridge University Press.
———. ed. 2018. *Aristotle's* Physics *Book I: A Systematic Exploration*. Cambridge: Cambridge University Press.
Rangos, S. 2015. "First Philosophy, Truth, and the History of Being in Aristotle's *Metaphysics*." In *The Bloomsbury Companion to Aristotle*, edited by Claudia Baracchi, 173–88. London: Bloomsbury.
Roark, T. 2009. "Review of *Time for Aristotle: Physics IV.10–14*, by Ursula Coope." *Mind* 118 (April): 459–63.
———. 2011. *Aristotle on Time*. Cambridge: Cambridge University Press.
Rorty, A. O. 2012. "Aristotle on the Metaphysical Status of 'Pathe.'" *Review of Metaphysics* 37, no. 3: 521–46.
Ross, W. D. 1995. *Aristotle*. New York: Routledge.
Ryle, G. 1954. *Dilemmas*. Cambridge: Cambridge University Press.
———. 1955. "Categories." In *Logic and Language*, edited by A. G. Flew, 66. Oxford: Blackwell.
Sachs, J. 2010. "Aristotle: Motion and Its Place in Nature." Internet Encyclopedia of Philosophy. http://www.iep.utm.edu/a/aris-mot.htm.
Sallis, J. 2016. *The Figure of Nature: On Greek Origins*. Bloomington: Indiana University Press.
Scharle, M. 2008. "Elemental Teleology in Aristotle's *Physics* ii.8." *Oxford Studies in Ancient Philosophy* 34: 147–83.
———. 2015. "Man from Man but Not Bed from Bed: Nature, Art and Chance in *Physics* II." In *Aristotle's Physics: A Critical Guide*, edited by Mariska Leunissen, 88–106. Cambridge: Cambridge University Press.
Sedley, D. 2007. *Creationism and Its Critics in Antiquity*. Berkeley: University of California Press.
Sentesy, M. 2018a. "Are Potency and Actuality Compatible in Aristotle?" *Epoché* 22, no. 2: 239–70.
———. 2018b. "The Now and the Relation between Motion and Time in Aristotle: A Systematic Reconstruction." *Apeiron* 51, no. 3: 1–45.
Sheehan, T. 1975. "Heidegger, Aristotle and Phenomenology." *Philosophy Today* 19, no. 2: 87–94.
Shields, C. 1999. *Order in Multiplicity: Homonymy in the Philosophy of Aristotle*. Oxford: Oxford University Press.
Shoemaker, S. S. 1969. "Time without Change." *Journal of Philosophy* 66: 363–81.

Sokolowski, R. 1977. "The Logic of Parts and Wholes in Husserl's *Investigations.*" In *Readings on Edmund Husserl's Logical Investigations*, edited by J. N. Mohanty, 94–111. The Hague: Martinus Nijhoff.

———. 1979. "Making Distinctions." *Review of Metaphysics* 32, no. 4: 639–76.

———. 1998. "The Method of Philosophy: Making Distinctions." *Review of Metaphysics* 51, no. 3: 515–33.

Sorabji, R. 1969. "Aristotle and Oxford Philosophy." *American Philosophical Quarterly* 6, no. 2: 127–35.

———. 1980. *Necessity, Cause, and Blame: Perspectives on Aristotle's Theory.* Ithaca, N.Y.: Cornell University Press.

———. 1983. *Time, Creation, and the Continuum: Theories in Antiquity and the Early Middle Ages.* Ithaca, N.Y.: Cornell University Press.

Sosa, J. E. 2010. "A Short Notice on Robert Heinaman's Account of Aristotle's Definition of κίνησις in *Physica* III." *Journal of Ancient Philosophy* 4, no. 2: 4–8.

Stavrianeas, S. 2008. "Spontaneous Generation in Aristotle's Biology." *Rhizai: A Journal for Ancient Philosophy and Science* 2: 303–38.

———. 2015. "Nature as a Principle of Change." In *Aristotle's Physics: A Critical Guide*, edited by Mariska Leunissen, 46–65. Cambridge: Cambridge University Press.

Suárez, F. 2004. *A Commentary on Aristotle's Metaphysics, or "A Most Ample Index to the Metaphysics of Aristotle."* Translated by J. P. Doyle. Milwaukee, Wis.: Marquette University Press.

Taylor, A. E. 1925. "Review of Ross *Metaphysics.*" *Mind*, n.s. 34, no. 135: 351–61.

Thorp, J. 1982. "Aristotle on Being and Truth." *De Philosophia* 3: 1–9.

Torrijos-Castrillejo, D. 2017. "Propuestas de Franz Brentano para una correcta interpretación de Aristóteles." *Pensamiento* 73: 21–44.

Vendler, Z. 1957. "Verbs and Times." *Philosophical Review* 60: 143–60.

———. 1967. *Linguistics in Philosophy.* New York: Cornell University Press.

Vigo, A. 2014. "First Philosophy." In *The Bloomsbury Companion to Aristotle*, edited by Claudia Baracchi, 147–72. London: Bloomsbury.

Von Leyden, W. 1964. "Time, Number, and Eternity in Plato and Aristotle." *Philosophical Quarterly* 14, no. 54 (January): 35–52.

Waterlow (Broadie), S. 1982a. *Nature, Change, and Agency in Aristotle's Physics.* Oxford: Oxford University Press.

———. 1982b. *Passage and Possibility: A Study of Aristotle's Modal Concepts.* Oxford: Oxford University Press.

Ward, J. 2009. "Aristotelian Homonymy." *Philosophy Compass* 4, no. 3: 575–85.

Wieland, W. 1975. "Aristotle's Physics and the Problem of Inquiry into Principles." In *Articles on Aristotle I: Science*, edited by Jonathan Barnes, Malcolm Schofield, and Richard Sorabji, 127–40. London: Duckworth.

———. 1975b. "The Problem of Teleology." In *Articles on Aristotle I: Science*, edited by Jonathan Barnes, Malcolm Schofield, and Richard Sorabji, 127–40. London: Duckworth.

Winslow, R. 2014. "Aristotelian Definition: On the Discovery of *Archai.*" In *The Bloomsbury Companion to Aristotle*, edited by Claudia Baracchi, 41–56. London: Bloomsbury.

Witt, C. 1989. "Hylomorphism in Aristotle." *Apeiron* 22, no. 4: 141–58.

———. 1990. "Charlton on the Uses of Actuality." *Proceedings of the Boston Area Colloquium in Ancient Philosophy* 5, no. 1: 23–26.
———. 1994. "The Priority of Actuality in Aristotle." In *Unity, Identity, and Explanation in Aristotle's Metaphysics*, edited by T. Scaltsas, D. Charles, and M. L. Gill, 215–28. Oxford: Oxford University Press.
———. 1995. "Powers and Possibilities: Aristotle vs. the Megarians." *Proceedings of the Boston Area Colloquium in Ancient Philosophy* 11, no. 1: 249–73.
———. 1998. "Teleology in Aristotelian Metaphysics." In *Method in Ancient Philosophy*, edited by Jyl Gentzler, 253–69. Oxford: Oxford University Press.
———. 2003. *Ways of Being: Potentiality and Actuality in Aristotle's Metaphysics*. Ithaca, N.Y.: Cornell University Press.
———. 2015. "In Defense of the Craft Analogy: Artifacts and Natural Teleology." In *Aristotle's Physics: A Critical Guide*, edited by Mariska Leunissen, 107–20. Cambridge: Cambridge University Press.
Wolfe, C. J. 2012. "Plato's and Aristotle's Answers to the Parmenides Problem." *Review of Metaphysics* 65, no. 4: 747–64.
Yu, J. 1997. "Two Conceptions of Hylomorphism in *Metaphysics* ZHΘ." *Oxford Studies in Ancient Philosophy* 15: 119–45.
———. 2003. *The Structure of Being in Aristotle's Metaphysics*. Dordrecht: Kluwer Academic.

INDEX

accomplishment: 39, 40, 76, 102–5, 104, 125, 143; activity and, 149, 154, 157; agent-patient relationship and, 102, 150; as form of material, 111; automatic processes and, 130; being-at-work and, 138, 142, 143, 146, 150–52, 156, 160, 194n51; change and, 76; defined, 111; *echein* and, 70; *energeia* and, 79, 139, 148, 151, 155; *entelecheia* and, 62, 69, 73, 78–79; epigenesis and, 111, 144; excellence and, 69; form and, 130, 187n12; generation or *genesis* and, 8, 111, 112, 128, 144–47; hylomorphism and, 111; nature and, 121, 124; ontological significance of, 160; potency or *dunamis* and, 62, 93, 94, 131, 156, 175n25, 185–86n55, 186n59, 193n41; priority of, 148, 150–51; source or *archē* and, 8, 70, 92, 109, 123, 129, 138, 139, 144–47, 158–60; spontaneous generation and, 189n37; teleology and, 109–11; work and, 155. *See also entelecheia*; teleology
activity: 58–59, 66–68; accomplishment or *telos* and, 79, 138, 139, 142–44, 148–52, 155–60, 194n51; actuality and, 64–65; *arche* and, 138; being of potency and, 102, 148; buildable thing and, 58; categorical being and, 42, 54; different senses of in Aristotle's work, 73, 87; *dunamis* and, 50, 83, 84, 183n26; emergence and, 132; energetic being and, 12, 86; *energon* and, 67; being-complete or *entelecheia* and, 7, 59, 71, 72, 141, 155, 156, 178–79n17; work or *ergon* and, 67, 155–56; etymology of, 66–67, 150, 194n49; form and, 136, 139, 152–54; generation or *genesis* and,

129, 139, 141, 145, 157; Genetic Priority and, 141; incompleteness and, 79; change, movement, or *kinēsis* and, 15, 46–47, 63, 136, 139, 167n25, 167n30, 184n41; meaning of, 194–95n51; ontological meaning of, 83, 140, 147; primary being or *ousia* and, 123, 139, 143, 159; potency and, 8, 9, 42, 43, 53, 79–82, 86–89, 95, 102, 106, 135, 140, 140–42, 148, 152, 173n3, 181–82n11; priority of, 138–39, 147–49, 159, 191–92n20, 191n13; source and, 138, 147–48; as source of potency, 147; translation of, 64–66, 67–68, 71–72; usage in Aristotle's time, 63; work object and, 194n50
actuality: activity and, 64–65; *dunamis* and, 84; potency and, 42, 47–48, 83, 136–37, 182n20; potentiality and, 74; presence and, 83; subject of change and, 6. *See also entelecheia*; *energeia*
Agamben, Giorgio, 83, 85–86, 96, 183n24
agency, 90, 102
agent-patient relationship, 89, 90
alethic being, 166n13
allo, 166n20
alloiōsis. *See* alteration
alteration, 12, 103, 104
Anagnostopoulos, Andreas: on activity and actuality, 64–65; on being in potency and being in activity, 181n1; on *dunamis* and *energeia*, 84; on potency and activity, 182n13; on potency and actuality, 83; on the predication of being, 170n30; on the reality of potency, 86; on the second sense of potency and *energeia*, 181–82n11; on the subject of change, 180n40

211

Antiphon, 122
Any Opposite Principle, 93, 95, 104, 106
a posteriori, 168–69n17
a priori, 168–69n17
archē. *See* source
art, 130
"as" clause: being-in-potency and, 52; definition of change and, 50–52, 54, 55; buildable thing or *oikodomēton* and, 57; subject of change and, 177n40
automatic processes, 109, 120, 124–30, 189n37

Beere, Jonathan: on activity and actuality, 68; on activity and potency, 166n12; on *dunamis* and *entelecheia*, 176n38; on *energeia*, 193n38; on *energeia* and *entelecheia*, 65; on *genesis*, 192n30; on modality, 84, 102; on ontological norms, 191n17; on ontological priority, 144, 145; on Plato's Criterion, 190–91n13; on potency, 186n58, 187n3; on potency and activity, 85; on potentiality and actuality, 181–82n11
being: aspect and, 24, 168n7; coming-to-be and, 19; determinacy of, 26; four senses of, 11, 137; generality of, 25; generation and, 144; *logos* and, 20; as multiple in aspect, 32; non-being and, 169n27; priority in, 142; simplicity and, 24–25; source and, 8, 18; specificity and, 24–25. *See also* energetic being; incidental being; *ousia*
being-at-work. *See* activity
being-complete: 7, 103, 141, 68–71; accomplishment or *telos* and, 62, 69, 73, 78–79, 158; activity or *energeia* and, 59, 71, 72, 155–56, 178–79n17; categorical being and, 42, 62; change and, 7, 48, 55–56, 63, 76; coining of, 194n49; *echein* and, 69; energetic being and, 12; etymology of, 66–67, 69; *ousia* and, 123; potency or *dunamis* and, 12, 39, 42–43, 46–47, 49, 50, 55, 56, 61–62, 83, 100–102, 172n50, 176n38, 191n14; prefix of, 69; teleology and, 70; translation of, 46–47, 64–66, 68–69, 71–72; usage in Aristotle's time, 63; uses of, 79
being-in-potency, 102, 103, 129. *See* potency
Binary Principle, 94, 95, 96, 106
Blair, George Alfred, 67, 178n1, 179n28
Bodnár, István, 169n20
Bostock, David, 168n17, 172n65
Brague, Rémi, 165n3
Brentano, Franz, 83, 98, 166n17, 181n5
Broadie, Sarah: on the category of relation, 173n11; on *energeia*, 195n56; on the Location Argument, 140; on modality, 106; on Plato's Criterion, 190–91n13; on *telos*, 148–49
Brogan, Walter, 85
building, 57–61, 72–79, 83, 89–93, 98, 102–4, 115, 127–28, 148, 150–52, 156–58, 177nn45–46, 180n38. *See also* activity; buildable thing
buildable thing, 55–61, 152, 175n22, 177nn45–46, 180n38. *See also* building; potency
Burnyeat, Myles, 15, 136, 167n32
Byrne, Christopher, 113

capacity. *See* potency
categorical being: 6, 136, activity and, 84; alethic being and, 166n13; change and, 36, 42, 44, 52, 87; completeness and, 76; definition of change and, 42, 44, 45; dynamic-energetic sense of being and, 39, 40, 45–46, 136; energetic being and, 41–42, 53, 61–62, 87, 138, 177n43; form and, 187n12; incidental being and, 166n13; individual being and, 9; manifoldness of, 11; material and, 86; multiplicity of being and, 34; *ousia* and, 86, 137; potency and, 54, 76, 84; predication and, 172n66; priority of, 140; self-coincidence of,

51, 55; subject-predicate relation and, 42; teleology and, 111; as underlying material, 53
cause, 14, 49, 137, 186n2
change: accomplishment and, 151, 154; activity and, 151, 174n16; actuality and, 174n16; being-at-work and, 172n64; being-in-potency and, 174n16; categorical being and, 36, 44, 46, 87, 172n66, 173n11; as complete, 74; complete being and, 74, 76; as composite, 23–24, 31, 80; defined, 12–13, 46–47; dispersion and, 151; distinction between form and underlying material and, 35–36; dynamic-energetic sense of being and, 161; *energeia* and, 136151, 167n29; *entelecheia* and, 56, 63; existence of, 55–57; *genesis* and, 158; heavenly bodies and, 187n7; incompleteness of, 7, 74, 77, 180n40; manifoldness of being and, 5, 18, 33, 36, 39; nature and, 124; ontological import of, 87; parts of, 74, 76; place and, 175n25; potency and, 47, 77, 154; as self-contradictory, 6; source and, 8, 40, 137; study of nature and, 20; subject and, 12; *telos* and, 76, 151, 154; time and, 41, 175n25; underlying material and, 73, 170n30; ways of being and, 5. *See also* alteration; coming-to-be; *kinēsis*; *metabolē*
Charles, David: on *energeia*, 179n30; on form, 130; on *genesis*, 195n56; on ontological sense of potential, 191n17; on potency and activity, 137; on *telos*, 175n21
Code, Alan, 188n21
coming-to-be: 13, 127–28, 139; accomplishment or *telos* and, 8, 111–12, 143, 146–47; activity or *energeia* and, 129, 139, 140–41, 145, 157; the ancients and, 36; being and, 19, 144; change and, 13, 19, 166n25; composite being and, 26–27, 30, 114; composite particulars and, 114;

emergence and, 171–72n50; form and, 27; Genetic Priority and, 142; in Empedocles, 119; individual being and, 120, 139; monism and, 24; nature and, 145, 189n40; ontology and, 128, 168n5; number of being and, 32; Parmenides and, 19; pleasure and, 167n32; potency and, 129, 153, 157; primary being or *ousia* and, 141, 144, 146, 166n21; privation and, 27; senses of, 170n33; source or *archē* and, 8, 20, 122, 139, 145, 159; teleology and, 135; transitivity of, 146, 158; underlying material and, 27, 139, 170n33. *See also* epigenesis
complete activity. See *entelecheia*
complete being. See *entelecheia*
completion. *See* accomplishment; *telos*
composite being, 26–27, 29. *See also* material
conditioning sources, 186n55
contemplation, 183n34

definition, 49; of change, 46–48; 176n35; *diaireō*, 174n14; *diēirēmenou*, 173n3
demonstrative syllogism: cause and, 49; definition and, 49
dependent properties, 42
Diels, Hermann, 179n28
dualism, 171–72n50
Dudley, John, 126
dunamis. *See* potency
dynamic-energetic sense of being, 12, 39, 40, 45; activity and, 9, 86; categorical being and, 6, 41–42, 53, 61–62, 87, 138, 177n43; completeness and, 76; concreteness of, 54; potency and, 9, 86; properties and, 54; source and, 11, 166n15. *See also* energetic being

echein, 69, 70
efficient cause, 184n50
eidos, 159
emergence, 131–32, 171–72n50

Empedocles: on the being of change, 33; on individuals, 117–22, 128, 188n27, 188n29; knowledge of views of, 188n21; on nature as a source, 125–26; as representative of reductive materialism, 110
energeia. See activity
energetic being. *See* dynamic-energetic sense of being
energon, 67. See also *energeia*
entelecheia. See being-complete; *see also* accomplishment
epidosis, 186n61
epigenesis, 109, 111, 131, 144, 189–90n51
epistemology, 168n17
ergon. See work
essential properties, 42
Etymological Argument, 151, 154–56, 158, 195n51
experience, 22
Extinction Hypothesis, 59, 61, 91, 183–84n39

final cause, 187n7
first actuality. *See* potency
first potency. *See* potency
form: activity and, 154; alteration and, 103; being-at-work and, 139; categorical being and, 187n12; change and, 35, 36; coming-to-be and, 27; *energeia* and, 136; material, 172n66; material and, 35, 123, 153, 154, 160; nature and, 121; negation and, 32; predication and, 172n66; prime matter and, 113; privation and, 37, 103; shape and, 123; as source, 117; teleology and, 135–36; *telos* and, 111, 130, 187n12; underlying material and, 28, 34, 35
Frede, Michael, 83–86, 184n45, 191n17

generation. *See* coming-to-be; *see also* epigenesis
genesis. See coming-to-be
Genetic Priority: activity and, 141; *genesis* and, 142; the Individual Sequence

and, 145; *ousia* and, 142; source and, 142, 145; temporal priority and, 141
Gill, Mary Louise, 180n44
Gotthelf, Allan, 130
Graham, Daniel, 65, 176n30, 178n1, 178n11, 184n41

Hagen, Charles, 184n41
heavenly bodies, 185n53, 187n7
Heidegger, Martin: on *entelecheia*, 64; on *hexis*, 179n24; on the Megarian argument, 182n16; on the multiplicity of being, 11; on potency, 83, 85, 96; on potency and enactment, 182n21; on privation, 172n50
Henry, Devin, 189–90n51
heteros, 166n20
hexis, 179n24
huparchei, 179n24
hupokeimenon, 172n66
hylomorphism, 136–37, 187n11

incidental being 9, 28, 30–32, 34, 101, 104, 161, 165n10, 166n115, 187n12; *genesis* and 116, 122; continuity between opposites as 115–16. *See also* automatic processes
incompleteness, 7, 74, 77, 79
individual being: *genesis* and, 120, 139; nature and, 119; source and, 128; as source of change, 118, 121, 121–22
Individual Sequence, 141, 142, 144, 145

Kant, Immanuel, 166n17
Kelsey, Sean, 169n28
kinēsis, defined, 12–13, 46–47; 15, 167n30, 184n41. *See also* change
knowledge, 22
Kosman, Aryeh: on activity, 136; on actuality, 68; on capacity, 176n30; on *energeia* and *entelecheia*, 64–65; on *entelecheia*, 175n24; on potencies for change, 195n56; on potentialities, 175n28; on the prefix of *entelecheia*, 69; on priority, 178n8

Lang, Helen, 166n22, 188n13
Lennox, James, 189n37
living beings, 99
Location Argument, 140, 151, 156–58
logical potency, 185–86n55
logos, 20

Makin, Stephen, 193n38, 195n59
material: accomplishment or *telos* and, 111; primary being or *ousia* and, 36, 86, 122; as source of change, 120 (*see also* automatic processes), 117; as underlying change, 36; activity or *energeia* and, 60; categorical being and, 86; change and, 35, 36; coming-to-be or *genesis* and, 27, 139, 170n33; completion and, 127; composite being and, 29; defined, 113; duality of, 30–31; form and, 28, 34–37, 53, 123, 127, 153–54, 160, 172n66; nature and, 53, 122, 127; negation and, 32; organisms and, 127; part-whole relationships and, 132–33; potency and, 41, 52–53, 136, 152–53; predication and, 9, 36, 172n66; prime matter and, 171n45; privation and, 27–28, 30, 37, 171n38; teleology and, 135–36
material processes, 127, 186n1. *See also* automatic processes; material
Mourelatos, Alexander, 169–70n28, 169n26
Menn, Stephen: on *energeia*, 191n17; on hylomorphism, 137; on modality, 181n2; on Plato's Criterion, 190–91n13; on potency and activity, 85; on sources and their accomplishment, 139
Meno's Paradox, 169n17
metabolē, 12, 167n25. *See also* change
metaphysics, 3
modality, 105–6
movement, 63
multiplicity of being: categorical being and, 34; change and, 33, 36, 39; four senses of, 8–10; non-being and, 6; ontology and, 33–34; ontology of change and, 5; Parmenides and, 34; sources and, 31

nature: agent-patient relationship and, 183n36; ambiguity in meaning of, 189n41; change and, 124; coming-to-be and, 189n40; form and, 121; *genesis* and, 145; individual being and, 119; material and, 122, 127; order and, 188n13; *ousia* and, 119–20, 121; particulars and, 121; *phusis* 98, 124; potency and, 90; source and, 124; *telos* and, 121, 124
negation, 103–4
non-being, 25, 26, 32, 169n27

oikodomēsis. *See* building
oikodomēton. *See* buildable thing
ontology: etymology of, 3; generation and, 128; history of, 3; metaphysics and, 3; multiplicity of being and, 5, 33–34; physics and, 19–20; potency and, 81; source and, 14; of Substance, 136; teleology and, 5, 110, 128, 161
operation, 39
ousia. *See* primary being; *see also* being

Panayides, Christos Y., 193n37, 193n46
Parmenides: on change, 17, 19, 24, 32; on how many being is , 24, 34; on predication, 170n28; Way of Opinion and, 170n29, 171n47; Way of Truth and, 170n29
particulars, 113, 114, 121
Peramatzis, Michail, 190–91n13
phusis. *See* nature
physics, discipline of, 191n16
Plato, 149, 179n28, 193n44; Plato's Criterion, 190–91n13, 193n42
poiēsis, 98
possibility, 105
potency: 9, 85, 86, 103–4, 173n9; being-complete or *entelecheia* and, 46–47, 49, 50, 55–56, 61–62, 77, 83, 176n38; categorical being and, 42, 54, 62, 76; change and, 77, 90;

potency, *continued*
  change-related sense of, 190n9;
  defined, 90–95; definition of change
  and, 48; different senses of in
  Aristotle's work, 87; *energeia* and,
  50, 83–87, 95, 152, 158, 181–82n11,
  183n26; energetic being and, 12, 86;
  eternal things and, 185n53; finitude
  of, 94; first actuality and, 100; first
  potency and, 100; form and, 53;
  genesis and, 153, 157; incompleteness
  and, 7, 77, 90; independent being
  of, 96–97; living beings and, 99;
  material and, 136, 152–53; modality
  and, 105–6; nature and, 90; ontology
  and, 81, 83, 147; *phusis* and, 98;
  poiēsis and, 98; possibility and,
  105, 181n5; potentiality and, 74,
  86; presence and, 83, 85; primary
  being or *ousia* and, 53, 96; priority
  of, 149, 191–92n20, 193n42; reality
  of, 83, 184n45; second actuality
  and, 100–101; second potency and,
  100; source and, 87–92, 95, 99,
  147–48, 193n42; subject of change
  and, 6–7, 62; *telos* and, 78, 131,
  158, 175n25; the "as" clause and,
  52; the Extinction Hypothesis and,
  183–84n39; transitivity of, 51, 150;
  translation of, 181n4; underlying
  material and, 41, 52–53
Potency Type, 174n16
potentiality. *See* potency
predication, 36, 172n66. *See also*
  categorical being
presence, 83, 85
presence and, 83
primary being: activity or *energeia* and,
  123, 139, 143, 159; as composite
  of form and matter, 113–14;
  categorical being and, 10, 86, 93,
  136–37; *entelecheia* and, 123; eternal
  things and, 185n53; coming-to-be
  or *genesis* and, 141–46, 166n21;
  Genetic Priority and, 142; material
  and, 36, 86; nature or *phusis* and,
  119–21, 124; potency and, 53, 96;
  primacy of, 10; source and, 124, 160;
  the Individual Sequence and, 144,
  145; underlying material and, 122
prime matter, 113; underlying material
  and, 171n45. *See also* material;
  underlying material
prime mover, 111
privation: alteration and, 103; coming-
  to-be and, 27; form and, 37,
  103; as innovation of Aristotle's,
  171–72n50; non-being and, 32;
  underlying material and, 27–28, 30,
  171n38
Privation Hypothesis, 171n38
Product Puzzle, 59; definition of change
  and, 47

Quarantotto, Diana, 187n7

relation, 44
Ross, W. D., 166n12, 166n17, 169n23,
  195n59

Sachs, Joe, 67, 68, 71
second actuality. *See* potency
second potency. *See* potency
shape, 123, 127
Singularity Principle, 94, 95, 104, 106
Socrates, 194n48
source: accomplishment and, 8, 92,
  109, 138, 139, 145, 159, 160; as
  fundamental in ontology, 62;
  as ontologically primary, 144;
  being and, 18; cause and, 186n2;
  change and, 137; completion and,
  161; defined, 14, 88; *dunamis* as,
  62; efficient cause and, 184n50;
  emergence and, 132; *energeia*
  and, 138; energetic being and, 12,
  166n15; form and, 117; generation
  and, 8, 20, 122, 128, 139, 145, 159;
  Genetic Priority and, 142; *hexis* and,
  179n24; individual being and, 121–
  22, 128; matter and, 117; nature and,
  124; physics and, 191n16; potency
  and, 87–92, 95, 99, 161, 193n42;
  primary being and, 124, 160;

priority of, 190–91n13; teleology and, 109; *telos* and, 70, 123, 129, 144–147, 158
spontaneous generation. *See* automatic processes
State of Potency problem, 174n16
sterēsis. *See* privation
Structure Argument, 151, 152–54, 194n51, 195n59
subject of change, 6, 62. *See also* buildable thing

teleology: defined, 110; accomplishment and, 109; automatic processes and, 129; categorical being and, 111; as descriptive concept, 111; *entelecheia* and, 70; epigenesis and, 109, 131; form and, 135–36; generation and, 135; *genesis* and, 111; genetic process and, 125; hylomorphism and, 187n11; material and, 135–36; material processes and, 186n1; ontology and, 5, 110, 128, 161; reducibility and, 129; as retrospective, 130–31; Scholastic understanding of, 70; source and, 109; *telos* and, 110
telos: defined, 111; activity and, 149, 154, 157; agent-patient relationship and, 150; *archē* and, 123, 144, 146, 147, 158; art and, 130; automatic processes and, 130; being-at-work and, 150, 156, 194n51; change and, 76; completeness and, 125; *echein* and, 70; *energeia* and, 79, 148, 155; *entelecheia* and, 69, 73, 78–79;

epigenesis and, 111, 144; excellence and, 69; form and, 130, 187n12; as form of material, 111; *genesis* and, 111, 112, 146–47; genetic process and, 128; hylomorphism and, 111; nature and, 121, 124; ontological significance of, 160; potency and, 131, 175n25; source and, 70, 129, 145; spontaneous generation and, 189n37; teleology and, 110. *See also* accomplishment; teleology
Theophrastus, 167n32, 167n33
theory of forms, 35
Timaeus, 171n48
time, 41, 175n25

underlying material. *See* material
underlying thing. *See* material
unmoved movers, 40–41, 183n38

Vendler, Zeno, 184n41

Way of Opinion, 170n29
Way of Truth, 170n29
Wieland, Wolfgang, 165n2, 166n11, 176n36
Witt, Charlotte: on activation conditions, 183n29; on hierarchical conception of being, 181n9; on modality, 84, 102; on Plato's Criterion, 190–91n13; on potency, 186n58, 187n3, 193n38; on potency and activity, 85, 110, 137; on the priority of *energeia*, 191n13; on the translation of *dunamis*, 181n4
work, 67, 150, 155. *See also energeia*

www.ingramcontent.com/pod-product-compliance
Lightning Source LLC
Chambersburg PA
CBHW032034290426
44110CB00012B/798